Essential Readings

ON Motivation

Edited by Jacquelynn A. Malloy, Barbara A. Marinak, and Linda B. Gambrell

INTERNATIONAL
Reading Association
800 BARKSDALE ROAD, PO BOX 8139
NEWARK, DE 19714-8139, USA
www.reading.org

Executive Editor, Books   Corinne M. Mooney
Developmental Editor   Charlene M. Nichols
Developmental Editor   Tori Mello Bachman
Developmental Editor   Stacey L. Reid
Editorial Production Manager   Shannon T. Fortner
Design and Composition Manager   Anette Schuetz

Project Editor   Christina M. Terranova

Cover   Design, Linda Steere

Library of Congress Cataloging-in-Publication Data

Essential readings on motivation / edited by Jacquelynn A. Malloy, Barbara A. Marinak, and Linda B. Gambrell.
    p. cm.
  Includes bibliographical references.
  ISBN 978-0-87207-810-9
  1. Reading. 2. Motivation in education. I. Malloy, Jacquelynn A., 1957- II. Marinak, Barbara A., 1957- III. Gambrell, Linda B.
  LB1573.E83 2010
  372.42--dc22
                                                                                    2009049025

Contents

Section Three: Creating Contexts for Motivation and Engagement   137

About the Editors

Jacquelynn A. Malloy is an assistant professor in elementary education and literacy in the Graduate School of Education at George Mason University in Fairfax, Virginia, USA, where she teaches literacy methods, differentiation, assessment, and research methods. As a university facilitator at two elementary schools in Prince William County, Virginia, Jackie supervises yearlong interns and collaborates with teachers and school administrators. She has been a featured International Reading Association convention speaker, and she has published on the contributions of peer-group discussion to reading comprehension and critical thinking and on motivation in the literacy classroom. Her research interests include developing instructional methods for peer-group discussions to improve comprehension and engagement and supporting students' online reading comprehension skills and strategies.

Barbara A. Marinak is an assistant professor of education and graduate program coordinator for literacy education in the School of Behavioral Sciences and Education, Penn State University at Harrisburg, Middletown, Pennsylvania, USA. She teaches graduate courses in the psychology of reading, reading diagnosis, and literacy leadership, and she directs the summer reading program. Barb holds a PhD in curriculum and instruction with a concentration in literacy from the University of Maryland, College Park, USA. Prior to joining the faculty at Penn State Harrisburg, she spent more than two decades in public education, working as a reading supervisor, elementary curriculum supervisor, and acting superintendent. She has consulted to the Pennsylvania Department of Education on a number of projects, including coauthoring the Pennsylvania System of School Assessment Reading Instructional Handbook and coediting the Pennsylvania Literacy Framework, and she was recently appointed to the International Reading Association's Commission on Response to Intervention. Her research interests include the observation of reading and writing, reading engagement, intervention practices, and the use of informational text.

Linda B. Gambrell is Distinguished Professor of Education in the Eugene T. Moore School of Education at Clemson University, South Carolina, USA, where she teaches graduate and undergraduate literacy courses. She began her career as an elementary classroom teacher and reading specialist in Prince George's County, Maryland, USA. From 1992 to 1997, she was a principal investigator at the National Reading Research Center at the University of Maryland, College Park, USA, where she directed the Literacy Motivation Project. Linda has served as an elected member of the board of directors and president of the three leading professional organizations for reading—the International Reading Association, National Reading Conference, and College Reading Association. Her major research areas are comprehension and cognitive processing, literacy motivation, and the role of discussion in teaching and learning. Her research has been published in numerous books and scholarly journals.

Introduction
We Hope You Dance: Creating a Community of Literate Souls

Jacquelynn A. Malloy, Barbara A. Marinak, and Linda B. Gambrell

The profession of teaching literacy requires as much art as it does skill. Knowledge of the reading and writing processes, sound instructional methods, and ways to assess and differentiate learning are essential components of effective literacy instruction. But just as important is "the dance."

The dance occurs in the space between what is taught and what is learned. It is the carefully choreographed back-and-forth negotiation of knowledge that occurs in powerfully effective classrooms. You can feel it when you enter the room, hear it in the way students and teachers relate to one another, and see it in the work that is created. Everyone in the classroom is engaged in a dance of seeking and sharing knowledge—they are occupied and involved, inclusive and responsive. You feel, as you enter, that you're witnessing a community of literate souls.

The dance is something that we look for in classrooms because we know that motivation "makes the difference between learning that is superficial and shallow and learning that is deep and internalized" (Gambrell, 1996, p. 15). Teachers who create motivating contexts for learning are expert at noticing who is involved and engaged and who is disconnected. Which students are always participating, and which students contribute variably or not at all? Cultivating an eye for the well-connected, motivated, and engaged classroom is the first step in creating one. Then comes the craft of choreographing just the right combination of moves that bring the dance to life in the classroom, as each group of students brings different needs and talents. Neither too fast nor too slow, neither too tame nor too wild, the dance embraces the "just right-ness" of a learning community.

Although we do not standardize or test it, motivation deserves our attention for its contribution to learning. It is what moves our students to participate fully in our instruction, to sustain effort and use strategies, even when the work is challenging. In fact, well-motivated students seek challenge, take risks, and make use of the knowledge teachers provide—particularly if it is interesting and useful, and if students perceive their own growing competence (Eggen & Kauchak, 1997; Wigfield, 1997). In this volume, we present powerful research and insight to inspire you to motivate and engage students in ways that let reading and writing resonate in the community of your classroom.

Although the study of literacy motivation is only a few decades old, our understanding of an individual's motivation to read, and of what constitutes engaging classroom instruction and contexts, is growing. The most recent research and theorizing on motivation moves beyond consideration of individual-level impetus to create a situational interest in learning that, in turn, supports the development of individual motivation (Guthrie et al., 2006; McCombs, 2003; Nolen, 2007; Ryan & Deci, 2000). Therefore, in this volume we focus on the student, the instruction, and the context of classrooms with the realization that although teachers cannot control every aspect of these three elements, it is quite possible to influence many of them. We begin by operationally defining the constructs of *motivation* and *engagement* as they apply to the individual student and move on to examine the types of instruction and classroom contexts that support and encourage the development of a community of literate souls.

Motivating the Student

Motivation refers to the likelihood of choosing one activity over another, as well as the persistence and effort exerted when participating in the chosen activity. Students make choices in their free time or at home, such as whether to read a book or play a video game. In schools, where choices are more limited, students may be required (externally motivated) to participate, but they may withhold persistence and effort for some tasks if they are not internally motivated to engage in the activity. Students who fully participate in literacy tasks do so because they *choose* to participate and are *willing* to extend the effort required, even when the work is challenging.

Some students may be frustrated in their attempts to read and write and may actively avoid participating in reading activities. Motivations can be spoken of generally, as in when you observe students in your classroom who often or always choose to participate in literacy tasks, or those who perennially avoid these tasks. We refer to the former as "motivated readers" and to the latter as "unmotivated readers"; however, each of these types of students may respond to certain classroom activities with more or less zeal, depending upon the nature of the task.

Engagement with text occurs when students are motivated to participate and strategic in their reading. Engaged students choose to participate in reading tasks and persist in their attempts to make meaning, using learned strategies that are appropriate to the text. Wigfield (1997, included as the first article of this volume) refers to this as the *engagement perspective* and proposes it

as a framework for research and instructional practices. Readers who make use of strategies to understand text for relevant and authentic reasons are on the path to become "highly engaged, self-determining readers who are architects of their own learning" (Alvermann & Guthrie, 1993, p. 2).

Foundations of Motivation and Engagement

Numerous theories have been proposed to explain why we choose to do some things and to not do others. Much of what we know about reading motivation extends from the scholarly literature in psychology and from research on achievement motivation or motivation to learn. Behaviorist researchers such as Skinner (1953) and Watson (1913) thought that our choices were based on what happened in the environment—that is, if the response to our behavior was pleasant, we were likely to choose to engage in the same behavior again. Other researchers, with a more humanistic view of personal agency, believe that we choose to participate in certain activities based on our internally designed needs or goals (e.g., Ames, 1992; Dweck & Elliot, 1983) and our self-concepts (Bandura, 1986, 1995; Eccles, 1983).

Learning and Performance Goals

Research designed to understand why students choose to learn has settled on two broad categories of goals (Ames, 1992; Dweck, 1986). The first category contains learning (or mastery) goals, as when a student wants to improve or master a skill such as reading, long division, or archery. The second orientation involves performance (or ability) goals, which are focused on how well students feel they perform in relation to others. Students who present a learning goal orientation to reading want to become better readers because they enjoy the activity or because they value the knowledge or entertainment that reading offers. Students who participate in reading activities with a performance goal orientation do so because they want to compare favorably to other readers, or because they want to earn a high grade or the praise or recognition of a valued other. Although students' goals for learning may vary across content areas and may even differ according to the nature of the task presented, researchers contend that students develop a particular stance toward activities such as reading with either a learning orientation or a performance orientation, and that this orientation may influence their engagement in learning tasks (Ames, 1992; Dweck & Elliot, 1983).

As performance-oriented students are mainly interested in how well they read when compared with their peers, they may be less willing to take risks in the classroom and may actively seek to avoid failure. These students view challenging tasks as potentially threatening to their ability status or feelings of success; they are the students who often forget what they were taught once the test is completed and the grade has been posted. On the other hand, students with a learning goal orientation are not concerned with how their reading compares with others but engage in reading activities because they are personally interested in a topic or because they seek to become better readers. These are the students who welcome challenge, take risks, and make use of strategies to get the most out of the reading activity (Eggen & Kauchak, 1997, p. 361).

Intrinsic and Extrinsic Motivation

Intrinsic motivation can be described as self-generated interest in an activity that brings pleasure that is inherent in engaging the activity itself (Deci & Ryan, 1985; Lepper & Hodell, 1989; Ryan & Deci, 2000). Students may be intrinsically motivated to read because they find the text's topic interesting or because they have a desire to achieve a reading-related goal, such as being an author. On the other hand, extrinsic motivations are externally oriented and can include tangible rewards (stickers, coupons for pizza, and so on) or intangible rewards, such as teacher praise or parental attention. Although students may be sufficiently motivated for either intrinsic or extrinsic reasons to participate in learning tasks, there is some discussion in the literature

regarding which of these is preferable in education. The Marinak and Gambrell (2008) article included as the fifth selection in this volume offers a review of past research as well as new findings that shed light on how our classroom incentives may affect student engagement.

Self-Efficacy for Reading

Students may also choose to participate in one learning activity over another on the basis of how well they expect to do, or their *expectancy*. According to Eccles (1983), perceptions of expectancy are influenced by the students' sense of competence in completing a specific task successfully. Her work is based on Bandura's (1977, 1982) ideas of self-efficacy, which he describes as students' perceived success in a domain-specific activity. In short, we tend to engage more readily in activities where we feel we are competent than in tasks where we perceive we are lacking in skill.

In exploring the importance of self-concept in learning, studies by Marsh and Craven (1997) and Marsh, Byrne, and Yeung (1999) drew ties between academic self-concept and achievement. In earlier work with 141 U.S. elementary and junior high students (Gottfried, 1985) and more recent research with 385 French Canadian students (Guay, Marsh, & Boivin, 2003), researchers found continuing evidence to support a reciprocal-effects model, wherein achievement affected self-concept and self-concept had an effect on achievement. These studies are fundamental to our understanding of how students' performance can affect perceived efficacy and therefore future performance.

With regard to reading, a review of studies related to self-concept (Chapman & Tunmer, 2003) found that students' self-concepts develop in response to their early experiences with reading—whether these are perceived as being pleasant and eventually successful or uncomfortable and difficult. Students who experience early and repeated difficulties with reading may develop a self-concept as a "bad reader," which then colors their expectancy for engaging in other reading tasks. They may participate, but without a positive expectancy for success they may not persist in the task or give much effort (Linnenbrink & Pintrich, 2003; Wigfield, Guthrie, Tonks, & Perencevich, 2004). It is easy to see how this situation could become self-perpetuating if left unnoticed or unchecked by a concerned educator.

In writing about improving the self-efficacy of struggling readers, Margolis and McCabe (2006) recommend tasks and materials designed to promote success with moderate effort on the part of the student. The authors also describe methods for preteaching or scaffolding essential content and emphasize the importance of continually assessing for progress.

Development of Reading Motivation

When considering how students' motivation to read changes throughout the school years, Eccles and her colleagues (1993) report findings to suggest that older elementary children value reading less and have decreasingly positive beliefs regarding their abilities when compared with younger children. In a cross-cultural study, Mazzoni et al. (1996) found that while reading motivation increased for first graders during the school year, motivation for second graders did not. This finding was consistent for the same grade children in the United States and in Finland, even though Finnish children enter the first grade one year later than do U.S. children. It appears from these results that the initial effort of learning to read is more motivating than continued reading growth. In related research, Oldfather and McLaughlin (1993) posit that motivation declines in later grades as a result of changes in school and classroom environments. Middle schools and high schools tend to be larger and less personal, and they permit fewer opportunities for student choice and personal or authentic literacy activities. These results have strong implications for instruction in the upper grades.

In a survey of 18,185 U.S. students, researchers McKenna, Kear, and Ellsworth (1995) sought to determine the developmental course of reading attitudes (both recreational and academic) for students in first through sixth grades using the Elementary Reading Attitudes Survey (McKenna & Kear, 1990). The principle findings indicate that reading attitudes are most positive in the first grade but decline as students progress to the sixth grade. Negative attitudes toward recreational reading were more prevalent and rapidly declining for low-ability readers, and this ability gap in attitudes increased with age. As regards attitudes for in-school reading, however, the negative trend occurs despite ability. In short, able readers maintain positive attitudes toward reading outside of school whereas high- and low-ability readers alike exhibit increased negative attitudes toward in-school reading. Low-ability readers develop sharply increased negative attitudes toward reading in both school and recreational settings as the elementary years progress. In general, girls possess more positive reading attitudes than boys in all settings. Although the gender gap increases with age for recreational reading, it remains constant in the academic setting and does not appear to be related to ability.

McKenna and his colleagues (1995) further conclude from this research that something was going very awry in terms of reading instruction, given the evidence of this five-year trend of decreasing attitudes in the elementary grades. Subsequent research on the types of tasks and contexts that support engaged and purposeful reading, as well as the classroom contexts that involve students of various ability levels and interests, have helped to identify some of the important factors that have the potential to remedy this alarming trend.

Crafting Instruction

Research on instructional methods and practices that increase motivation has resulted in the emergence of three important themes: *choice*, *access*, and *social interactions*. Students are more likely to participate in reading tasks where they have some choice in terms of the reading material, the response to the reading, or the product required. Turner and Paris's (1995) research on open versus closed tasks, included as the sixth article in this volume, presents evidence that opportunities to choose materials and design tasks are prevalent in engaging classrooms. Allowing students to choose their own texts for independent reading increases the likelihood of reading with greater interest and persistence (Gambrell, 1996; Samblis, 2006; Schiefele, 1991; Swartz & Hendricks, 2000).

Students also respond with greater evidence of motivation when they have access to sufficient and varied reading materials, whether print based or online, narrative or expository. A print-rich classroom supports varied reading interests by offering high-quality literature in a variety of genres to support wide reading (Allington & McGill-Franzen, 1993; Edmunds & Bauserman, 2006; Gambrell, 1996). Similarly, classrooms that support social interactions about books are associated with increases in students' intrinsic motivation, learning, and thinking skills (Almasi, 1995; Almasi, O'Flahavan, & Arya 2001; Edmunds & Bauserman, 2006; Gambrell et al., in press; Guthrie et al., 1998; Guthrie & Cox, 2001; Malloy & Gambrell, 2009).

Creating Contexts

Integrating these identified motivating factors—choice, access, and social interactions—to create engaging classroom instruction has the potential for creating situational interest in activities that can be transferred into a more stable, continuing motivation to participate in reading tasks (Guthrie, Hoa, Wigfield, Tonks, & Perencevich, 2006; Hidi, Bernforff, & Ainley, 2002; Nolen, 2007; Renninger & Hidi, 2002; Ryan & Deci, 2000). When motivating instruction is provided that supports students in becoming strategic and skillful readers, opportunities to develop positive self-concepts for reading increase. Research on the synergistic qualities of creating engaging classroom contexts is emerging and shows promise for changing the way teachers and students learn together using texts in their classrooms.

Most notably, Guthrie and his colleagues conducted research on the effects of Concept-Oriented Reading Instruction (CORI) to explore the features of classroom contexts related to long-term reading engagement in upper elementary students. The CORI program introduced by

Guthrie et al. (1996, included as abridged form as the ninth article in this collection) was designed to merge reading strategy instruction and content material, such as science or social studies, in order to produce a combined positive effect on both reading comprehension and motivation. Their results (Guthrie et al., 1996, 2006; Guthrie & Cox, 2001) suggest that strategic instruction that uses text-to-self connections, interesting trade books, student choice in reading, and small-group collaborations resulted in significantly higher measures of motivation for fifth-grade students, based on the Motivation for Reading Questionnaire (Wigfield & Guthrie, 1997).

Other research focused on creating authentic reasons to participate in reading and writing tasks. Gambrell et al. (in press) sought to determine whether having personally relevant reasons for engaging in a literacy task would increase motivation and engagement in the activity. Students read books and discussed them with their peers in order to prepare to exchange ideas about the shared texts with an adult pen pal. Findings indicate that having a personal reason for interacting about texts—one that's not evaluated or graded by the teacher—resulted in increased value and self-concept for reading based on the Literacy Motivation Survey over the course of the school year, especially for boys. Having an adult who was interested in their thoughts and ideas about a text and who would not judge or grade their interactions may have provided a sufficient social impetus for students to put forth the effort and persistence required to think and write about the text in the pen pal exchanges.

Nolen's (2007) longitudinal study with first through third graders explored motivations for reading and writing and how these were related to classroom contexts. Based on observations and interviews involving 67 students, the general findings indicate that social context is an important factor in the developing motivations of young students. Students are motivated to attain mastery of reading and writing processes early on, but once attained, motivation to continue working on these skills (such as fluency or decoding) drops off unless the task is of particular interest to the student in his or her social context. Social interactions were successful in maintaining interest of students in literacy tasks, as was the use of texts that were familiar or were based on favorite topics.

In general, and as Nolen's (2007) research supports, the importance of reading and writing abilities evolves as part of the social context of the classroom. In some classrooms, social status can be achieved through attaining reading excellence, and struggling students may feel marginalized when, for example, they are kept inside during recess to complete difficult or unfinished literacy tasks. The way in which social ease is distributed in classrooms often revolves around ability, which leaves struggling readers and writers at the fringes of the classroom with declining self-concepts, which in turn hinders their attempts to improve skills or learn new strategies. These findings highlight the importance of structuring the classroom environment in ways that provide social and situational support for the engaged and inclusive participation of all readers.

Promoting Community

The concept of a "community of learners," as explored by Brown and her colleagues (Brown, 1992; Brown et al., 1993; Brown & Campione, 1994; Campione, Shapiro, & Brown, 1995), suggests that reading, writing, speaking, and listening can become essential tools for coconstructed learning. Their research was conducted prior to the current era of data-driven accountability and mandated instruction in our schools, so the teachers in the experimental classrooms were supported in covering few topics, but doing so in an in-depth manner. Students worked in groups to follow lines of inquiry that were student generated while the teacher facilitated learning by teaching appropriate strategies and securing resources. The Guthrie et al. (1996, 1998, 2006) CORI research is based on similar principles, and students in these studies were found to work with increased engagement and conceptual learning.

The idea that teachers and students can learn more by joining forces to construct meaning is important to creating contexts for student engagement and learning (Pressley, El-Dinary, Marks, Brown, & Stein, 1992; Pressley & Woloshyn, 1995). Some researchers refer to this joint collaboration as "distributed authority," wherein all members of the class take equal responsibility for understanding a text or learning a concept (Meichenbaum & Biemiller, 1998; Wells & Chang-Wells, 1992). In these inclusive classroom structures, all students contribute and all students benefit—a welcome situation for struggling readers. When the class is engaged and involved in learning more about a topic, the contributions of all members become important, whatever those contributions might be. Literacy tasks that are highly engaging to students can also be opened sufficiently to allow each student's individual talents and interests to be put into play to add to the learning of all.

Even in our current curricular climate, which seems to promote teaching a "mile-wide and inch-deep" (Brophy, 2008, p. 137), teachers can develop communities of learning in their classrooms by presenting literacy instruction that is tightly integrated with content areas. Well-planned integrated or thematic units maximize the amount of time available for learning concepts and big ideas and can therefore integrate motivational factors such as choice, access, and social interaction across multiple lines of inquiry. Providing choice in selecting topics, tasks, or culminating products allows for optimum interest development and learning that is relevant to students backgrounds and futures. The teacher-as-facilitator can then provide access to quality materials for learning according to interests and needs and can teach the strategies that are essential to learning the concepts important for the grade level. Classroom communities designed to optimize learning and engagement make use of social interactions for students to discuss, write, draw, and present about what they are learning. With the broad range of interests and modalities that can be included in such a community, there is a place and a way for each student to contribute to the combined knowledge base, using a variety of texts at a range of reading levels.

Although it might seem difficult to rethink the ways we teach in a standards-based environment, we should consider the potential for increasing the learning and engagement of all students when the classroom is focused on learning collaboratively rather then competitively—when the students become adept at negotiating meaning instead of accepting it "whole piece" from the teacher. The classroom that learns by collaborating on relevant issues for authentic purposes has the potential to reach students where they are and to take them where they want to be. It prepares them for a real world where reading and writing are essential tools for learning and for pleasure. We hope this volume inspires you to get there—we hope you dance!

Using This Volume

This book is divided into three main sections: *foundations* of motivation and engagement, *crafting instruction* for motivation and engagement, and *creating contexts* for motivation and engagement. The articles included in each section were selected to provide you with both information and inspiration and were chosen to represent general and special education viewpoints, to address elementary and secondary learners, and to include teacher, researcher, and student voices. Following each article is a set of engagement activities that we hope guides you in pursuing each topic in more depth with your colleagues in a community of practice, as well as in applying new ideas to your classrooms. We encourage you to join with others in these activities and to seek out and discuss the suggestions for further reading that accompany the activities.

References

Allington R.L., & McGill-Franzen, A. (1993, October 13). What are they to read? Not all children, Mr. Riley, have easy access to books. *Education Week*, p. 26.

Almasi, J.F. (1995). The nature of fourth graders' sociocognitive conflicts in peer-led and teacher-led discussions of literature. *Reading Research Quarterly, 30*(3), 314–351.

Almasi, J.F., O'Flahavan, J.F., & Arya, P. (2001). A comparative analysis of student and teacher development in more and less proficient discussions of literature. *Reading Research Quarterly, 36*(2), 96–120.

Alvermann, D.E., & Guthrie, J.T. (1993). *Themes and directions of the National Reading Research Center* (Perspectives in Reading Research, Vol. 1). Athens, GA: National Reading Research Center.

Ames, C.A. (1992). Classrooms: Goals, structures, and student motivation. *Journal of Educational Psychology, 84*(3), 261–271.

Bandura, A. (1977). Self-efficacy: Toward a unifying theory of behavioral change. *Psychological Review, 84*(2), 191–215.

Bandura, A. (1982). Self-efficacy mechanism in human agency. *American Psychologist, 37*(2), 122–147.

Bandura, A. (1986). *Social foundations of thought and action: A social cognitive theory*. Englewood Cliffs, NJ: Prentice Hall.

Bandura, A. (1995). Exercise of personal and collective efficacy in changing societies. In A. Bandura (Ed.), *Self-efficacy in changing societies* (pp. 1–45). New York: Cambridge University Press.

Brophy, J. (2008). Developing students' appreciation for what is taught in school. *Educational Psychologist, 43*(3), 132–141.

Brown, A.L. (1992). Design experiments: Theoretical and methodological challenges in creating complex interventions in classroom settings. *Journal of the Learning Sciences, 2*(2), 141–178.

Brown, A.L., Ash, D., Rutherford, M., Nakagawa, K., Gordon, A., & Campione, J.C. (1993). Distributed expertise in the classroom. In G. Salomon (Ed.), *Distributed cognitions: Psychological and educational considerations* (pp. 188–228). New York: Cambridge University Press.

Brown, A.L., & Campione, J.C. (1994). Guided discovery in a community of learners. In K. McGilly (Ed.), *Classroom lessons: Integrating cognitive theory and classroom practice* (pp. 229–270). Cambridge, MA: MIT Press/Bradford.

Campione, J.C., Shapiro, A.M., & Brown, A.L. (1995). Forms of transfer in a community of learners: Flexible learning and understanding. In A. McKeough, J.L. Lupart, & A. Marini (Eds.), *Teaching for transfer: Fostering generalization in learning* (pp. 35–68). Hillsdale, NJ: Erlbaum.

Chapman, J.W., & Tunmer, W.E. (2003). Reading difficulties, reading-related self-perceptions, and strategies for overcoming negative self-beliefs. *Reading and Writing Quarterly, 19*(1), 5–24.

Deci, E.L., & Ryan, R.M. (1985). *Intrinsic motivation and self-determination in human behavior*. New York: Plenum.

Dweck, C.S. (1986). Motivational processes affecting learning. *American Psychologist, 41*(10), 1040–1048.

Dweck, C.S., & Elliot, E.S. (1983). Achievement motivation. In E.M. Hetherington (Ed.), *Handbook of child psychology: Socialization, personality, and social development* (Vol. 4, pp. 643–681). New York: Wiley.

Eccles, J. (1983). Expectancies, values, and academic behaviors. In. J.T. Spence (Ed.), *Achievement and achievement motives: Psychological and sociological approaches* (pp. 75–114). San Francisco: W.H. Freeman.

Eccles, J., Wigfield, A., Harold, R.D., & Blumenfeld, P. (1993). Age and gender differences in children's self- and task perceptions during elementary school. *Child Development, 64*(3), 830–847.

Edmunds, K.M., & Bauserman, K.L. (2006). What teachers can learn about reading motivation through conversations with children. *The Reading Teacher, 59*(5), 414–424.

Eggen, P.D., & Kauchak, D.P. (1997). *Educational psychology: Windows on classrooms* (3rd ed.). Upper Saddle River, NJ: Prentice Hall.

Gambrell, L.B. (1996). Creating classroom cultures that foster reading motivation. *The Reading Teacher, 50*(1), 14–25.

Gambrell, L.B., Hughes, E., Calvert, W., Malloy, J.A., & Igo, B. (in press). The role of authentic tasks in elementary students' literacy motivation and critical thinking. *The Elementary School Journal.*

Gottfried, A.E. (1985). Academic intrinsic motivation in elementary and junior high school students. *Journal of Educational Psychology, 77*(6), 631–645.

Guay, F., Marsh, H.W., & Boivin, M. (2003). Academic self-concept and academic achievement: Developmental perspectives on their causal ordering. *Journal of Educational Psychology, 95*(1), 124–136.

Guthrie, J.T., & Cox, K.E. (2001). Classroom conditions for motivation and engagement in reading. *Educational Psychology Review, 13*(3), 283–302.

Guthrie, J.T., Cox, K.E., Anderson, E., Harris, K., Mazzoni, S., & Rach, L. (1998). Principles of integrated instruction for engagement in reading. *Educational Psychology Review, 10*(2), 177–199.

Guthrie, J.T., Hoa, L.W., Wigfield, A., Tonks, S.M., & Perencevich, K.C. (2006). From spark to fire: Can situational reading interest lead to long-term reading motivation? *Reading Research and Instruction, 45*(2), 91–117.

Guthrie, J.T., Van Meter, P., McCann, A.D., Wigfield, A., Bennett, L., Poundstone, C.C., et al. (1996). Growth of literacy engagement: Changes in motivations and strategies during Concept-Oriented Reading Instruction. *Reading Research Quarterly, 31*(3), 306–332.

Guthrie, J.T., Wigfield, A., Humenick, N.M., Perencevich, K.C., Taboada, A., & Barbosa, P. (2006). Influences of stimulating tasks on reading motivation and comprehension. *Journal of Educational Research, 99*(4), 232–245.

Hidi, S., Berndorff, D., & Ainley, M. (2002). Children's argument writing, interest and self-efficacy: An intervention study. *Learning & Instruction, 12*(4), 429–446.

Lepper, M.R., & Hodell, M. (1989). Intrinsic motivation in the classroom. In C. Ames & R. Ames (Eds.), *Research on motivation in education* (Vol. 3, pp. 139–186). New York: Academic.

Linnenbrink, E.A., & Pintrich, P.R. (2003). The role of self-efficacy beliefs in student engagement and learning in the classroom. *Reading & Writing Quarterly: Overcoming Learning Difficulties, 19*(2), 119–137.

Malloy, J.A., & Gambrell, L.B. (2009). The contribution of discussion to reading comprehension and critical thinking. In R.L. Allington & A. McGill-Franzen (Eds.), *Handbook of reading disabilities research.* Mahwah, NJ: Erlbaum.

Margolis, H., & McCabe, P.P. (2006). Motivating struggling readers in an era of mandated instructional practices. *Reading Psychology, 27*(5), 435–455.

Marinak, B.A., & Gambrell, L.B. (2008). Intrinsic motivation and rewards: What sustains children's motivation to read. *Literacy Research & Instruction, 47*(1), 9–26.

Marsh, H.W., Byrne, B.M., & Yeung, A.S. (1999). Causal ordering of academic self-concept and achievement: Reanalysis of a pioneering study and revised recommendations. *Educational Psychologist, 34*(3), 155–167.

Marsh, H.W., & Craven, R. (1997). Academic self-concept: Beyond the dustbowl. In G.D. Phye (Ed.), *Handbook of classroom assessment: Learning, adjustment, and achievement* (pp. 131–198). Orlando, FL: Academic.

Mazzoni, S.A., Gambrell, L.B., & Korkeamäki, R.L. (1999). A cross-cultural perspective of early literacy motivation. *Reading Psychology, 20*(3), 237–253.

McCombs, B.L. (2003). A framework for the redesign of K–12 education in the context of current educational reform. *Theory Into Practice, 42*(2), 93–101.

McKenna, M.C., & Kear, D.J. (1990). Measuring attitude toward reading: A new tool for teachers. *The Reading Teacher, 43*(8), 626–639.

McKenna, M.C., Kear, D.J., & Ellsworth, R.A. (1995). Children's attitudes toward reading: A national survey. *Reading Research Quarterly, 30*(4), 934–956.

Meichenbaum D., & Biemiller, A. (1998). *Nurturing independent learners: Helping students take charge of their learning.* Cambridge, MA: Brookline.

Nolen, S.B. (2007). Young children's motivation to read and write: Development in social contexts. *Cognition & Instruction, 25*(2), 219–270.

Oldfather, P., & McLaughlin, J. (1993). Gaining and losing voice: A longitudinal study of students' continuing impulse to learn across elementary and middle school contexts. *Research in Middle Level Education, 17*(1), 1–25.

Pressley, M., El-Dinary, P.B., Marks, M.B., Brown, R., & Stein, S. (1992). Good strategy instruction is motivating and interesting. In K.A. Renninger, S. Hidi, & A. Krapp (Eds.), *The role of interest in learning and development* (pp. 333–358). Hillsdale, NJ: Erlbaum.

Pressley, M., & Woloshyn, V. (Eds.). (1995). *Cognitive strategy instruction that really improves children's academic performance* (2nd ed.). Cambridge, MA: Brookline.

Renninger, K.A., & Hidi, S. (2002). Student interest and achievement: Developmental issues raised by a case study. In A. Wigfield & J. Eccles (Eds.), *Development of achievement motivation* (pp. 173–195). San Diego, CA: Academic.

Ryan, R.M., & Deci, E.L. (2000). Intrinsic and extrinsic motivations: Classic definitions and new directions. *Contemporary Educational Psychology, 25*(1), 54–67.

Samblis, K. (2006). Think-tac-toe: A motivating method of increasing comprehension. *The Reading Teacher, 59*(7), 691–694.

Schiefele, U. (1991). Interest, learning, and motivation. *Educational Psychologist, 26*(3–4), 299–323.

Skinner, B.F. (1953). *Science and human behavior.* New York: Macmillan.

Swartz, M.K., & Hendricks, C.G. (2000). Factors that influence the book selection process of students with special needs. *Journal of Adolescent & Adult Literacy, 43*(7), 608–618.

Turner, J., & Paris, S.G. (1995). How literacy tasks influence children's motivation for literacy. *The Reading Teacher, 48*(8), 662–673.

Watson, J.B. (1913). Psychology as the behaviourist views it. *Psychological Review, 20*(2), 158–177.

Wells, C.G., & Chang-Wells, G.L. (1992). *Constructing knowledge together: Classrooms as centers of inquiry and literacy.* Portsmouth, NH: Heinemann.

Wigfield, A. (1997). Children's motivations for reading and reading engagement. In J.T. Guthrie & A. Wigfield (Eds.) *Reading engagement: Motivating readers through integrated instruction* (pp. 14–33). Newark, DE: International Reading Association.

Wigfield, A., & Guthrie, J.T. (1997). Relations of children's motivation for reading to the amount and breadth of their reading. *Journal of Educational Psychology, 89*(3), 420–432.

Wigfield, A., Guthrie, J.T., Tonks, S., & Perencevich, K.C. (2004). Children's motivation for reading: Domain specificity and instructional influences. *Journal of Educational Research, 97*(6), 299–309.

Foundations of Motivation and Engagement

In preparing to craft motivating instruction and create engaging contexts for learning, it is important first to understand the nature of what motivates students to read. This section contains three articles, selected to provide a background to the "hows" and "whys" of motivation to read. The answers to "Why do students choose to participate in reading activities?" and "How do we keep them engaged when the going is tough?" are explained first in general terms in Allan Wigfield's "Children's Motivations for Reading and Reading Engagement." Then, "Is There a Bidirectional Relationship Between Children's Reading Skills and Reading Motivation?" by Paul L. Morgan and

Douglas Fuchs casts an eye on motivation for the struggling reader. Finally, with "What Teachers Can Learn About Reading Motivation Through Conversations With Children" by Kathryn M. Edmunds and Kathryn L. Bauserman turns an ear to the voices of our students.

The engagement activities and recommended readings at the end of each article are designed to provide an opportunity for you to reflect and expand on the essential readings in this section. In addition, they will prepare you for learning more about how you can support students as they find and maintain positive motivations for reading.

Children's Motivations for Reading and Reading Engagement

Allan Wigfield

Research on children's reading has a long and rich history, and much has been learned about how children learn to read. As discussed in the introduction, the focus of most of the research on reading has been the *cognitive* aspects of reading; the volumes by Adams (1990); Barr, Kamil, Mosenthal, and Pearson (1991); and Ruddell, Ruddell, and Singer (1994) provide important reviews of much of that work. Because reading is an effortful activity that involves choice (for example, when a child asks, "Am I going to read or watch television?"), *motivation* is involved in reading, along with cognition. Motivation deals with the *whys* of behavior; motivation theorists try to understand the choices individuals make about which activity to do or not to do, their degree of persistence at the chosen activities, and the amount of effort they exert as they do the activity (Eccles, Wigfield, & Schiefele, in press; Pintrich & Schunk, 1996; Weiner, 1992). Purely cognitive models of reading do not address these issues, so they do not provide a complete picture of reading. For instance, a purely cognitive perspective on reading cannot explain why some children read infrequently despite being skillful readers. In the *engagement* perspective on reading (Baker, Afflerbach, & Reinking, 1996; Guthrie, 1996; Guthrie, McGough, Bennett, & Rice, 1996) both cognitive and motivational aspects of reading are considered. This perspective provides a more complete account of how children learn to read and become engaged in literacy activities.

Work done within the engagement framework by my colleagues and me has focused on delineating the nature of children's reading motivations. We have used constructs, or concepts, from research on children's general achievement motivation and from work on motivation for reading. We believe that there are a variety of possible reading motivations that can influence children's engagement in reading and their reading performance (see Guthrie, 1996; Oldfather & Wigfield, 1996; Wigfield & Guthrie, 1995, for further discussion). The following vignettes describe children with different reading motivations.

> A fifth-grade student (whom I will call Jamal) reads in his free time an unusual mix of books, ranging from poetry books to manuals describing how to repair cars. When asked about his reading, he says that unfamiliar and difficult words sometimes stump him and threaten to disrupt his reading, but he continually strives to improve his reading. When he understands the new words and phrases, he knows his reading skills are improving. His growing skills and confidence in them help him continue to pursue his reading interests and read increasingly complex books.
>
> Cheryl, another fifth grader, reads avidly in class, keeping a book by her side to read when there are breaks in classroom activities. She often reads late into the night at home, a practice her family accepts. In explaining her interest in reading, she said she becomes very absorbed in the characters and the plot of the stories she reads. She keeps turning the pages because she wants to see what happens to the characters with whom she has become so involved. This excitement sparked by books keeps Cheryl reading even when other activities are available to her.

Reprinted from Wigfield, A. (1997). Children's motivations for reading and reading engagement. In J.T. Guthrie & A. Wigfield (Eds.), *Reading engagement: Motivating readers through integrated instruction* (pp. 14–33). Newark, DE: International Reading Association.

Bill is a fifth-grade student who will read only when others around him are reading or when he is in a group. But when peer support is removed, he stops reading. His teacher reports that much of the work Bill begins does not get finished because he does not get personally involved with his work. Although Bill keeps books around him to read in his spare time, he rarely continues his reading unless directed to by his teacher.

In these vignettes, children read to master new material, because of interest in the characters and plot in a story, for social reasons, and to comply with the teacher's directions. Each of these motivations can enhance children's reading engagement, but some of them also might interfere with children's reading engagement, a problem which will be discussed later. Further, two of the children (Jamal and Cheryl) appear to be very motivated to read, whereas Bill is not. How are these different motivations depicted in the vignettes conceptualized by motivation theorists?

Defining Motivational Constructs

Researchers who study motivation have defined a number of important motivational constructs and have assessed how these constructs relate to different achievement behaviors. However, most of their work has been on motivation in general rather than motivation for specific areas such as reading and writing. Reading researchers study the processes by which children and adults become engaged in reading but have not yet fully incorporated the constructs defined by motivation researchers (see Oldfather & Wigfield, 1996, for further discussion). I begin this section with a brief overview of the motivation constructs prominent in current motivation theories and then discuss how we have adapted them to the reading field. Some of these constructs are discussed in more detail by other authors in the first section of this volume [*Reading Engagement: Motivating Readers Through Integrated Instruction*, edited by J.T. Guthrie & A. Wigfield, International Reading Association, 1997].

Many motivation theorists propose that individuals' beliefs, values, and goals for achievement play a crucial role in their achievement-related behavior (see, for example, Bandura, 1977; Eccles et al., 1983; Nicholls, 1990; Pintrich & Schunk, 1996; Stipek & Mac Iver, 1989; Weiner, 1992; Wigfield & Eccles, 1992). Eccles, Wigfield, and Schiefele (in press; see also Eccles & Wigfield, 1985) state that the beliefs, values, and goals studied by motivation theorists can be conceptualized as different questions students can ask themselves. The questions most directly relating to motivation are "Can I succeed?" and "Do I want to succeed and why?" In terms of reading, these questions are "Can I be a good reader?" and "Do I want to be a good reader and why?"

Constructs Relating to the Question "Can I Succeed?"

The primary constructs relating the question "Can I succeed?" are children's *ability beliefs*, *expectancies*, and *efficacy beliefs*. Ability beliefs are children's evaluations of their competence in different areas. Researchers have documented that children's and adolescents' ability beliefs relate to and predict their achievement performance in domains such as reading and math (Eccles et al., 1983; Meece, Wigfield, & Eccles, 1990; Nicholls, 1979a; Stipek & Mac Iver, 1989; Wigfield et al., 1995). Expectancies refer to children's sense of how well they will do on an upcoming task, instead of their general belief of how good they are at the task (see Stipek, 1984). These beliefs also predict children's performance on different tasks.

Bandura's (1977; see also Schunk, 1991b) construct of self-efficacy also deals with individuals' expectancies about being able to do tasks; however, Bandura defines self-efficacy as a generative capacity in which different subskills are organized into courses of action. He proposes that individuals' *efficacy expectations*, or their beliefs that they can accomplish a given task or activity, are a major determinant of activity choice, willingness to expend effort, and persistence. When they think they can accomplish a task, people are more likely to choose to do it, continue working on it when they encounter difficulty, and ultimately complete the task. In work with school-aged children, Schunk and his colleagues (1991b) demonstrated that students' sense of efficacy relates to their academic performance (see also Zimmerman, Bandura, & Martinez-Pons, 1992), including their reading achievement (Schunk & Rice, 1993). They showed that training students both to be more efficacious and to believe they are more efficacious improves children's achievement in subject areas such as reading and math. An important implication of this research for motivation for reading is that when children believe they are competent and efficacious at reading they should be more likely to engage in the activity. In Chapter 2 of [*Reading Engagement*], Schunk and Zimmerman present a detailed review of the work on self-efficacy and reading comprehension.

There are several examples of ability and efficacy beliefs in the vignettes presented earlier [in *Reading Engagement*]. In the vignette in the introduction, Robert and Kantu are described as becoming more efficacious at finding information, which leads them to share their techniques with each other and experience pride in their success. Their growing skills and efficacy facilitate their continued engagement in the classroom activities. In the vignettes in this chapter, Jamal's competence and efficacy beliefs are most clearly apparent. As he successfully masters difficult words and topics, his sense of his own reading competence and efficacy increases, which leads him to read even more complicated books.

Constructs Relating to the Question "Do I Want to Succeed and Why?"

Answering the question "Do I want to succeed and why?" affirmatively and with a clear reason is critical to motivation. Even if individuals believe they are competent and efficacious at an activity, they may not engage in it if they have no reason or incentive for doing so. One construct relating to the first part of this question is *subjective task values*. Subjective task values refer broadly to individuals' incentives for doing different activities.

Eccles and I and our colleagues have done recent work on the nature of children's and adolescents' subjective task values and how their values relate to their performance and choice of different activities. We defined different components of subjective task values, including *interest value*, how much the individual likes or is interested in the activity; *attainment value*, the importance of the activity; and *utility value*, the usefulness of an activity (see Eccles et al., 1983; Wigfield, 1994; Wigfield & Eccles, 1992, for reviews of this work and further discussion of the different components of subjective task values). A major finding from this work, as mentioned earlier, is that students' ability beliefs and expectancies for success predict their performance in mathematics and language arts, whereas their subjective task values predict both intentions and actual decisions to continue taking mathematics and language arts courses (Eccles et al., 1983; Meece, Wigfield, & Eccles, 1990). This finding suggests that students' valuing of reading may be one of the more important predictors of their engagement in reading activities.

Another major construct relating to the question "Do I want to succeed?" is *intrinsic and extrinsic motivation*. Intrinsic motivation refers to being motivated and curious to do an activity for its own sake, and extrinsic motivation means being motivated for external reasons such as receiving a reward or being told to do the activity (Deci & Ryan, 1985; Harter, 1981; see Chapter 11 in [*Reading Engagement*] for further discussion of intrinsic and extrinsic motivation for reading). Intrinsic motivation has some parallels with the interest value construct defined by Eccles et al. (1983). One indicator of intrinsic motivation is total involvement in an activity. Many readers have experienced what Csikszentmihalyi (1978) describes as the "flow experience," losing track of time and self-awareness when becoming completely involved in an activity such as reading a book. Maehr's (1976) concept of continuing motivation is another important aspect of intrinsic motivation; he defines continuing motivation as individuals' engagement in a learned activity outside the context in which it was learned. He argues that schools focus too much on learning in school and not enough on promoting children's continuing motivation to learn outside the school setting.

Building on this work, Oldfather (1992) presents a social constructivist view of intrinsic motivation for learning identified as the continuing impulse to learn, an ongoing participation in learning that is motivated by the learner's thoughts and feelings that emerge from his or her processes of constructing meaning. It is characterized by intense involvement, curiosity, and a search for understanding, as the individual experiences learning as a deeply personal and continuing agenda. An important implication of Oldfather's and other theorists' work for reading is that individuals' engagement in reading will be greatly facilitated when they are intrinsically motivated to read and find personal meaning in the reading that they do. Chapter 4 in [Reading Engagement] provides further discussion of how involvement with one's own reading fosters reading engagement.

Intrinsic and extrinsic motivation constructs are illustrated in the vignettes presented earlier. As Robert and Kantu hunt for crickets and then learn more about them, they become very absorbed in the topic and show a great deal of interest in finding out more about it. Their interest and wonder promote engagement with the various activities they do to learn more about crickets. Cheryl also is a very intrinsically motivated, interested reader; she loses herself in books and becomes deeply involved with them. In contrast, Bill reads more for extrinsic reasons, such as to comply with the teacher or to be part of a group.

The second part of the question posed, "Why do I want to succeed?", can be categorized primarily by two constructs, achievement goals and subjective values, just discussed. Achievement goals refer to the purposes children have for achievement in different areas; they deal directly with the "whys" of behavior. Researchers study different kinds of achievement goals. Some (Ames, 1992b; Dweck & Leggett, 1988; Nicholls, 1979b; Nicholls et al., 1989) define different broad goal orientations toward achievement, with two goal orientations deemed most prominent: the goal to learn an activity and the goal to outperform others. These goal orientations have important consequences for motivation. When

students focus on outperforming others, they are more likely to choose to do tasks and activities they know they are able do. In contrast, children focusing on learning choose challenging tasks and are more concerned with their own progress than with outperforming others. Researchers who study children's goals argue further that children who have learning goals will be more likely to maintain positive motivation in school. An important implication of this work for reading instruction is that learning goals should be emphasized in reading instruction.

Mastery goals are evident in Robert and Kantu's study of crickets. They generate many questions, develop particular goals to pursue, and work together to achieve them. Competing against each other does not seem to occur to them; instead, the focus is on mastering the subject. Similarly, Jamal's continuing work with difficult and challenging materials shows a strong learning goal orientation; his major focus is improving his own reading.

These broad goal orientations or patterns are not the only ways researchers study goals. Some researchers (see, for example, Schunk, 1991a) look at more particular aspects of goals, such as whether they are distal or proximal, or general or specific; this work is discussed in more detail by Schunk (1991b) and in Chapter 2 by Schunk and Zimmerman in [Reading Engagement]. Still others (such as Wentzel, 1991, in press) propose that students have multiple achievement goals, including both academic and social goals (see also Urdan & Maehr, 1995).

Table 1 summarizes the different motivational constructs described in the previous two sections. The constructs listed are organized in two columns by the questions "Can I succeed?" and "Do I want to succeed and why?" The constructs in the third column under the heading "What do I need to do to succeed?" are explained in the next section.

Another Question Relating to Motivation: "What Do I Need to Do to Succeed?"

My colleagues and I (Eccles, Wigfield, & Schiefele, in press) pose the question "What do

Table 1
Defining Motivation Constructs and Dimensions of Reading Motivation

Can I Succeed?	Do I Want to Succeed and Why?	What Do I Need to Do to Succeed?
Motivation Construct	**Motivation Construct**	**Motivation-Related Construct**
Ability beliefs	Subjective task values	Strategy use
Expectancies	Interest value	Self-regulation
Efficacy beliefs	Attainment value	Volition
	Utility value	Help seeking
	Intrinsic and extrinsic motivation	
	Achievement goals	
	Mastery goals	
	Competitive goals	
	Other academic goals	
	Social goals	
Reading Motivation	**Reading Motivation**	
Reading efficacy	Reading curiosity	
Reading challenge	Involvement	
Reading work avoidance	Importance of reading	
	Reading for recognition	
	Reading for grades	
	Competition in reading	
	Social reasons for reading	
	Reading compliance	

I need to do to succeed?" as a way to conceptualize constructs such as *strategy use*, *volition*, *self-regulation*, and *help seeking*. These constructs link cognition and motivation together. Because we have not measured these constructs in our work on children's reading motivations, I will not discuss them in detail here. However, they are mentioned because of their importance to reading achievement and because they are featured by authors of Chapters 2 and 3 in [*Reading Engagement*]; also, several of the chapters in the second section discuss strategy instruction in the classroom.

These constructs are illustrated in the vignette in the introduction. Robert and Kantu's interest in crickets must be followed with effective strategy use for them to learn more about crickets. Their teacher helps them pose reasonable questions and set goals for what they want to accomplish, which are prerequisites for effective learning. Robert and Kantu learn how to search materials effectively to find more information about insects and how to work in cooperative groups to learn more and to make presentations

to the class about what they learn. In these ways their initial curiosity leads to quality learning about the topic; without the strategies for learning they may have become frustrated as they tried to learn more about crickets, perhaps losing their initial interest in the topic.

Relations Among Motivational Constructs

Because researchers often have focused on only one or two motivational constructs, we still do not have much information about how they relate to one another. However, we do know that competence beliefs, achievement values, and intrinsic motivation relate positively to one another (Eccles & Wigfield, 1995; Harter & Connell, 1984). Thus, when children think they are competent, they are more likely to be motivated for intrinsic reasons. Further, positive competence beliefs, intrinsic motivations, and learning goals lead to greater persistence, choice of more challenging activities, and higher level of engagement in different activities (Ames, 1992b; Dweck & Leggett, 1988). Similarly, if children have positive efficacy beliefs, they are likely to set more challenging goals for themselves (Schunk, 1991b).

Information about links between motivation and strategy use is beginning to emerge as well. We know that learning goals relate to the use of deeper processing strategies (elaboration) and metacognitive, self-regulatory strategies, such as planning and comprehension monitoring (Pintrich & De Groot, 1990; Pintrich, Marx, & Boyle, 1993). These links have been demonstrated in both correlational and laboratory studies. Positive efficacy beliefs relate to better strategy use and more cognitive engagement (Pintrich & De Groot, 1990; Schunk, 1991b). Personal interest relates to the use of a variety of higher order strategies and deeper level processing of material (Alexander, Kulikowich, & Jetton, 1994; Pintrich, Marx, & Boyle, 1993; Schiefele, 1991).

Pintrich and De Groot's (1990) study provides a good illustration of some of the connections between motivations and strategy use. They found that seventh-grade students' perceived self-efficacy and valuing of science and language arts learning related positively to their reported use of cognitive strategies and self-regulation in those two subject areas. Like Meece, Wigfield, and Eccles (1990), they also found that students' expectancies related more strongly to performance than did their subjective task values. However, Pintrich and De Groot note that students' cognitive strategy use and self-regulation directly predicted performance, whereas their efficacy beliefs and values did not. Pintrich and De Groot suggest that the effects of self-efficacy and values on students' performance were mediated through their use of strategies and self-regulation. They argue that students' self-efficacy may facilitate their cognitive engagement and that their subjective task values relate to their choices about whether to become engaged, but that their use of cognitive strategies and self-regulation relate more directly to performance. These results show how motivation and cognition can work together to facilitate (or impede) performance in different school subjects (see Pintrich & Schrauben,

1992, for a theoretical model describing relations between motivation and cognition). These findings suggest that students who believe they are efficacious at reading and value the activity should use more elaborate cognitive strategies as they read to become better readers.

The relations across some of the motivation and strategy constructs are evident in the vignettes in the introduction [to *Reading Engagement*] and in this chapter. Robert and Kantu's interest in crickets is followed by attempts to learn more about them. With the teacher's help and guidance, they use effective strategies to pursue this learning, which increases both their knowledge and their sense of competence about the subject. The new information they learn and their stronger sense of competence further enhance their interest in the topic, leading to even more in-depth learning. Similarly, Jamal's hard work to master difficult words increases both his reading skills and sense of competence, which allows him to pursue his reading interests in greater depth. Likewise, Cheryl's fascination with books and the time she spends reading increase her reading skills, allowing her to read more challenging and interesting materials. Through research and conversations with students we are learning much about the links among different motivations and their links to strategies, but more information about these links still is needed.

Attitudes Toward Reading and Interest in Reading

In reading research literature, some researchers discuss affective and motivational factors that can influence reading engagement. These researchers look primarily at two constructs: *attitudes toward reading* and *interest in reading*. *Attitudes toward reading* are defined generally as individuals' feelings about reading. Alexander and Filler (1976) state that these feelings about reading influence how much individuals involve themselves in reading and relate to individuals' motivation for reading (see also Mathewson, 1985, 1994; McKenna, 1994; and Ruddell & Speaker, 1985, for more specific models of how individuals' attitudes toward reading influence their reading engagement). Although Mathewson (1985) states that individuals' attitudes toward reading will differ across subject areas, scales designed to assess individuals' attitudes toward reading have remained rather general (McKenna & Kear, 1990). These scales to assess reading attitudes also have not included items to assess the different motivational constructs discussed in the previous section.

There also is a substantial body of research on *reading interest* and how interest influences reading comprehension (see Alexander, Kulikowich, & Jetton, 1994, for a recent review of the work on interest's effects on text comprehension). In discussing interest, Schiefele (1991) notes the important distinction between *individual interests* and *situational or text-based interests*. He defines individual interests as relatively stable feelings about different activity areas (such as reading); people generally tend to be interested in some activities and less interested in other activities. Individual interests seem similar to the intrinsic motivation construct discussed earlier. Situational interests are more activity specific and less stable; for example, situational interest is interest sparked by a particular text.

In one study, Schiefele (1991) assessed how college students' situational interest in text materials influenced their comprehension, when the students' prior knowledge of the materials and general intelligence were controlled. Schiefele found that college students who were interested in the text materials used in the study processed those materials more deeply and used more elaborate learning strategies while reading than did students less interested in the materials.

Shirey and his colleagues (1992) also examined how individuals' interest in reading materials affects their comprehension and task attention. Like Asher and Markell (1974) and Asher, Hymel, and Wigfield (1978), they found that children recalled more from interesting sentences than from noninteresting sentences (see also Anderson, Mason, & Shirey, 1984). Anderson (1982) also found that children paid more attention (as measured by duration of reading time) to interesting than to noninteresting materials. Renninger (1992) found in studies of fifth and sixth graders that interest in the materials read enhanced comprehension, even of materials that were quite difficult for the children (although there were some gender differences in these patterns). Overall, these results indicate that students' interest in the material they read relates clearly to the use of effective learning strategies, their level of attention, and their comprehension of reading materials. Thus interest in reading appears to be an important motivational variable influencing different aspects of reading performance.

Varieties of Reading Motivations

To explore the motivations more specifically in the reading domain, Wigfield and Guthrie (1995) developed a questionnaire measure of children's motivations for reading, deriving the different dimensions in large part from the work on motivation just reviewed. The Motivations for Reading Questionnaire (MRQ) originally was designed to assess 11 different possible dimensions of reading motivations (see Wigfield & Guthrie, 1995, for a more complete discussion of the development of the original version of the questionnaire, and Wigfield, Guthrie, & McGough, 1996, for administration and scoring instructions). These different dimensions are summarized in the bottom half of Table 1 under the heading "Reading Motivation." This table also shows how the dimensions of reading motivation connect to the general motivation constructs previously discussed, which are organized by questions. The first two dimensions in the first column—*reading efficacy* and *reading challenge*—are based on the competence and efficacy belief constructs and include the notion that reading often is an activity that requires hard work to accomplish. *Reading efficacy* is the belief that one can be successful at reading; and *reading challenge* is the satisfaction of mastering or assimilating complex ideas in text. These two dimensions are illustrated in Jamal's approach to reading: he works to master challenging material and feels more efficacious after doing so.

The set of dimensions assessed in the MRQ, listed in the second column of Table 1, is based on the work on intrinsic and extrinsic motivations, values, and learning and performance goals. Dimensions relating to intrinsic motivations and learning goals include *reading curiosity*, the desire to learn about a particular topic of personal interest, and *involvement*, the pleasure gained from reading a well-written book or article on an interesting topic. Although this construct is somewhat similar to intrinsic motivation, it captures something unique to reading, the involvement with particular kinds of texts. *Importance of reading* is a dimension taken from Eccles's and my work on subjective task values (Eccles et al., 1983; Wigfield & Eccles, 1992). In the earlier vignettes, Cheryl's approach to reading is characterized by her curiosity of and involvement with different topics and by the importance reading has to her. Robert's and Kantu's reading motivations can be characterized in similar, intrinsic ways.

Dimensions assessed in the MRQ that relate to extrinsic motivations for reading include *reading for recognition*, the pleasure in receiving a tangible form of recognition for success in reading, and *reading for grades*, the desire to be favorably evaluated by the teacher. *Competition in reading* is the desire to outperform others in reading, a dimension tied to the notion of performance goals. These three dimensions reflect the fact that children do much of their reading in school, where their reading performance is evaluated and where they may compare their performance to others' performance. Thus, recognition, grades, and competition may figure prominently in children's motivations for reading.

The other dimensions listed in the bottom half of Table 1 relate to social aspects of reading. These were included because reading often is a social activity. These dimensions are based on the work on social goals in the achievement motivation literature (Urdan & Maehr, 1995; Wentzel, 1991, 1996). One proposed dimension is *social reasons for reading*, or the process of sharing the meanings gained from reading with friends and family. Another is *reading compliance*—reading because of an external goal or requirement. The final dimension assessed in the MRQ, listed in the first column of Table 1, is a set of items that ask students what they do not like about reading; we call this set *reading work avoidance*. Bill's reading seems to be characterized by these three motivations; he reads when there are others to read with (social) and when told to do so by the teacher (compliance), and he also avoids reading in other circumstances.

The original MRQ contained 82 items intended to measure each of these different constructs. The questionnaire was given to approximately 100 fourth- and fifth-grade students twice during a school year (see Wigfield & Guthrie, 1995, for more details about this study). Various statistical analyses were run to assess the proposed dimensions of reading motivations and to determine whether the items had good psychometric qualities. These analyses show that a number of the proposed dimensions can be clearly identified and have adequate to good internal consistency reliabilities. The most clearly defined dimensions include social reasons for reading, reading competition, reading work avoidance, reading efficacy, reading recognition, reading challenge, reading curiosity, and involvement.

Based on the results of the first study, a revised 54-item version of the MRQ was created (see Table 2). This revised version of the questionnaire was given to approximately 600 fifth- and sixth-grade children who were taking part in an intervention study designed to enhance their reading comprehension. Half the children participating in the project experienced the Junior Great Books curriculum, a curriculum designed to facilitate involvement with reading and reading comprehension; the other half were in control classrooms (see Wigfield et al., 1996, for a more detailed description). The revised MRQ was given in the fall of the school year, before the program was implemented.

As in the first study, different statistical analyses were done in the second study to assess the various proposed dimensions of the MRQ. Confirmatory factor analyses showed that the different proposed dimensions of motivation could be identified empirically. The internal consistency reliabilities of these dimensions were quite similar to the reliabilities in the first study.

Table 2
Motivations for Reading Questionnaire, Revised Version

Reading Efficacy	I know that I will do well in reading next year. I am a good reader. I learn more from reading than most students in the class. In comparison to my other school subjects, I am best at reading.
Challenge	I like hard, challenging books. I like it when the questions in books make me think. I usually learn difficult things by reading. If the project is interesting, I can read difficult material. If a book is interesting, I don't care how hard it is to read.
Curiosity	If the teacher discusses something interesting, I might read more about it. I read about my hobbies to learn more about them. I read to learn new information about topics that interest me. I like to read about new things. If I am reading about an interesting topic, I sometimes lose track of time. I enjoy reading books about people in different countries.
Involvement	I read stories about fantasy and make believe. I make pictures in my mind when I read. I feel like I make friends with people in good books. I like mysteries. I enjoy a long, involved story or fiction book. I read a lot of adventure stories.
Importance	It is very important to me to be a good reader. In comparison to other activities I do, it is very important to me to be a good reader.
Recognition	My friends sometimes tell me I am a good reader. I like hearing the teacher say I read well. I am happy when someone recognizes my reading. My parents often tell me what a good job I am doing in reading. I like to get compliments for my reading.
Grades	I look forward to finding out my reading grade. Grades are a good way to see how well you are doing in reading. I read to improve my grades. My parents ask me about my reading grade.
Social	I visit the library often with my family. I often read to my brother or my sister. I sometimes read to my parents. My friends and I like to trade things to read. I talk to my friends about what I am reading. I like to help my friends with their schoolwork in reading. I like to tell my family about what I am reading.
Competition	I like being the only one who knows an answer in something we read. I like being the best at reading. It is important for me to see my name on a list of good readers. I try to get more answers right than my friends. I like to finish my reading before other students. I am willing to work hard to read better than my friends.

(continued)

Table 2		
Motivations for Reading Questionnaire, Revised Version (*Continued*)		
Compliance		*I do as little schoolwork as possible in reading.
		*I read because I have to.
		I always do my reading work exactly as the teacher wants it.
		Finishing every reading assignment is very important to me.
		I always try to finish my reading on time.
Reading Work Avoidance		I don't like reading something when the words are too difficult.
		I don't like vocabulary questions.
		Complicated stories are no fun to read.
		I don't like it when there are too many people in the story.

Note: Asterisks indicate the items were not used in scale construction for that construct.

The general conclusion from both studies is that reading motivations are multidimensional.

Connections Among Reading Motivations

In both studies using the MRQ, correlational analyses were run to determine how strongly the different scales related to one another. In general, most of the relations were positive and ranged from low to moderately high, with the exception of the work avoidance scale, which related negatively to all the scales except to competition. Three conclusions can be drawn from these correlational analyses. First, the various kinds of reading motivations relate positively to one another, which shows that children have multiple motivations for reading and are not reading for exclusively intrinsic or extrinsic reasons. Second, the *negative* relations of work avoidance to the other motivation scales suggest that children who are positively motivated for many different reasons do not want to avoid difficult and challenging reading. Third, the *positive* relations of work avoidance and competition suggest that care should be taken with competitive reading activities. Although direction of causality cannot be inferred from correlational data, the positive relation of these scales means that either too much competition leads children to avoid reading, or those who avoid reading say they are motivated for competitive reasons. In either case reading engagement may be less likely to occur.

Linking Motivations to Reading Frequency and Performance

To relate the dimensions of reading motivations to reading frequency, Wigfield and Guthrie (1995) also obtained information about children's reading frequencies from two sources: (1) the Reading Activities Inventory (Guthrie, McGough, & Wigfield, 1994), a measure that asks children to list titles of different kinds of books they read recently and to indicate how often they read different kinds of books; and (2) a measure of children's reading frequency in a school-based reading program that encouraged children to read books. The dimensions of reading motivations relating most strongly include social, reading efficacy, curiosity, involvement, recognition, grades, and reading importance. Thus both intrinsic and extrinsic reasons for reading related to children's reported reading frequencies in the study, although overall it appeared that the intrinsic motivations for reading related more strongly to reading frequency than did the extrinsic motivations. Similar measures of reading frequency were obtained in the second study, and correlational analyses done in that study in general showed similar results: both intrinsic and extrinsic motivations related to reading frequency; however, the strongest relations were with the more intrinsic reading motivations and with reading self-efficacy.

From these results it can be concluded that children are more likely to read frequently when they feel efficacious about their reading skills and are intrinsically motivated to read. However, extrinsic motivations relate to reading frequency also, so their importance should not be overlooked. Researchers now need to look at how children's intrinsic and extrinsic reading motivations relate to their engagement in reading over time.

In the second study, students also completed two subtests of the Gates-MacGinitie Reading Test (vocabulary and comprehension) and two performance assessments designed for the project (see Baker, Fernandez-Fein, & Scher, 1995, for descriptions of these assessments) in the fall and spring of the school year. Relations of reading motivations to reading performance were examined by regressing reading performance on children's motivations. The results of these regression analyses showed that the motivation scales accounted for between 6 and 13% of the variance in the performance measures. The motivation scales predicting most consistently the Gates-MacGinitie (GM) scores include reading work avoidance, social reasons for reading, and reading efficacy and recognition. Both the work avoidance and social scales negatively predicted GM scores, indicating that children with higher scores on these motivation scales had lower GM scores. Reading efficacy and recognition positively predicted GM scores; children with higher scores on these scales tended to score higher on the GM measures.

The motivation scales most consistently predicting the performance assessment (PA) measures include work avoidance and social, both of which were negative predictors. The negative relations indicate that children who scored higher on these motivation scales tended to score lower on the PA measures. Reading efficacy and recognition predicted two of the PA scales positively, which means that children with higher scores on this scale tended to have higher PA scores.

In summary, results of these two studies show that there are different dimensions of reading motivations that can be measured reliably. These dimensions include some of the important constructs identified by motivation researchers: competence and challenge, intrinsic and extrinsic motivations, and different goals for reading. For the most part these reading motivations

relate positively to one another (the major exception being reading work avoidance, which relates negatively to most of the other motivations). They also relate positively to children's reading frequency. Some of them (especially reading self-efficacy and recognition) predict positively children's performance on standardized tests, whereas others (especially reading work avoidance and social reasons for reading) predict these test scores negatively. There are many issues that remain to be studied regarding children's reading motivations; I close with a consideration of the issue of change in reading motivations.

Change in Reading Motivations

Promoting lifelong literacy engagement is an important goal for educators. A question linked to this issue is how do children's motivations change as they proceed through school? Findings from the general motivation literature suggest that many children achievement motivation declines through the elementary and middle school years. Such declines have been found in children's general interest in school (Epstein & McPartland, 1976), their intrinsic motivations (Harter, 1981), their continuing impulse to learn (Oldfather, 1992; Oldfather & McLaughlin, 1993), and their ability beliefs and expectancies for success for different school subjects (Eccles, Wigfield, Harold, & Blumenfeld, 1993; Marsh, 1989; Wigfield et al., 1995; see also Eccles, Wigfield, & Schiefele, in press, for a detailed review of this work).

Do these findings apply to the literacy area? Some of the studies (Eccles, Wigfield, Harold, & Blumenfeld, 1993; Marsh, 1989) asked children about reading and found that older elementary school children have less positive ability beliefs in reading and value reading less than do younger elementary school children. Gambrell et al.'s (1993) study also shows that third graders appear to value reading more and have more positive reasons for reading than do fifth graders. In the two studies of reading motivations discussed earlier (Wigfield & Guthrie, 1995; Wigfield et al., 1996), the evidence is more mixed: some age differences in reading motivation were found in the first study, but fewer were found in the second study. This may be because these studies did not include a wide age range of children.

Several researchers suggest that the declines in motivation observed as children proceed through school are due to changes in school and classroom environments that children experience (Eccles, Wigfield, Midgley et al., 1993, and Oldfather & McLaughlin, 1993). Although motivation often is considered a personal characteristic of students, these researchers emphasize that the kinds of school and classroom environments students encounter can influence students' motivation greatly. There are major changes in school environments following children's transition to middle school that may undermine students' motivation; they include the fact that middle schools typically are larger, less personal, and more formal than elementary schools. Middle grade teachers are often subject-matter specialists, and they teach many more students than do elementary teachers. Compared to elementary school classrooms, traditional middle school classrooms place a greater emphasis on teacher control and discipline, less personal and positive teacher-student relations, and fewer opportunities for student decision making and choice (Eccles & Midgley, 1989; Eccles, Wigfield, Midgley et al., 1993). Practices such as whole-class task organization and ability grouping between classrooms also are more common in the middle grades, and grading and evaluation become more salient and have long-term consequences for students. Eccles, Wigfield, Midgley et al. (1993) discuss in detail how these changes can lessen students' competence and efficacy beliefs, reduce intrinsic motivation for learning, and lead children to focus more on rewards and grades than on curiosity and learning.

The effect of these kinds of school and classroom environment changes on motivations for literacy should be assessed further. If similar declines are found in reading motivations (which seems likely, when the findings in the general motivation literature are considered), educators need to think of ways to redesign classrooms to continue to foster positive reading motivations. There are exciting new classroom curricula and district-based programs being designed to foster children's engagement in reading; several of these programs are described in chapters in the second half of [Reading Engagement]. These programs are having positive effects on children's reading motivations and reading engagement. For instance, Guthrie, Van Meter et al. (1996) found that nearly all the third- and fifth-grade children experiencing Concept-Oriented Reading Instruction, explained in Chapter 7 [of Reading Engagement], increased in intrinsic motivation, use of volitional strategies, and reading engagement and frequency.

Motivation theorists also have suggested ways to change classroom environments to facilitate motivation. Ames (1992a) developed one of the most influential of these programs. She uses the acronym TARGET to describe the program because it focuses on the following six aspects of the classroom: tasks, authority, rewards, grouping, evaluation, and time. She also has worked extensively with teachers to develop this program. One goal of TARGET is to focus children more on learning rather than on competitive goals. Another goal is to help both teachers and children shift the focus from ability and outcome to effort and improvement. Some of the ideas included in the program, such as making classroom activities more meaningful and authentic, using heterogeneous and cooperative classroom grouping, and allowing students choice and autonomy, are contained in the reading programs described in the second part of this book (see also Guthrie, Van Meter et al., 1996).

Conclusion

Our studies of children's reading motivations show that there are different dimensions of these motivations that correspond to constructs that are now well established in the motivation literature. These reading motivations can be measured reliably, and they relate to both children's reading frequency and their reading performance. Thus we have an emerging picture of children motivated to read for various reasons, some of which may promote lifelong literacy engagement. These motivations are psychological in nature and are greatly influenced by school and classroom contexts.

Author's Notes

I would like to thank Ann McCann for providing the vignettes of children's reading motivations used in this chapter, which she obtained through interviews with elementary school children.

The studies on reading motivation discussed in this chapter are from National Reading Research Projects of the Universities of Georgia and Maryland. They were supported under the Educational Research and Development Centers Program (PR/AWARD No. 117A2007) as administered by the Office of Educational Research and Improvement, U.S. Department of Education. The findings and opinions expressed here do not necessarily reflect the position or policies of the National Reading Research Center, the Office of Educational Research and Improvement, or the U.S. Department of Education.

References

Adams, M.J. (1990). *Beginning to read: Thinking and learning about print*. Cambridge, MA: MIT Press.

Alexander, J.E., & Filler, R.C. (1976). *Attitudes and reading*. Newark, DE: International Reading Association.

Alexander, P.A., Kulikowich, J.M., & Jetton, T.L. (1994). The role of subject-matter knowledge and interest in the processing of linear and nonlinear texts. *Review of Educational Research, 64*, 201–252.

Ames, C. (1992a). Achievement goals and the classroom motivational climate. In D.H. Schunk & J.L. Meece (Eds.), *Student perceptions in the classroom* (pp. 327–348). Hillsdale, NJ: Erlbaum.

Ames, C. (1992b). Classrooms: Goals, structures, and student motivation. *Journal of Educational Psychology, 84*, 261–271.

Anderson, R.C. (1982). Allocation of attention during reading. In A. Flammer & W. Kintsch (Eds.), *Discourse processing* (pp. 292–305). New York: North-Holland.

Anderson, R.C., Mason, J., & Shirey, L.L. (1984). The reading group: An experimental investigation of a labyrinth. *Reading Research Quarterly, 20*, 6–38.

Asher, S.R., Hymel, S., & Wigfield, A. (1978). Influence of topic interest on children's reading comprehension. *Journal of Reading Behavior, 10*, 35–47.

Asher, S.R., & Markell, R. (1974). Sex differences in comprehension of high- and low-interest reading material. *Journal of Educational Psychology, 66*, 680–687.

Baker, L., Afflerbach, P., & Reinking, D. (1996). Developing engaged readers in home and school communities: An overview. In L. Baker, P. Afflerbach, & D. Reinking (Eds.), *Developing engaged readers in school and home communities* (pp. xiii–xxvii). Hillsdale, NJ: Erlbaum.

Baker, L., Fernandez-Fein, S., & Scher, D. (1995). *Improving children's reading through the Junior Great Books Curriculum: An intervention study*. Unpublished manuscript, University of Maryland, Baltimore County.

Bandura, A. (1977). Self-efficacy: Toward a unifying theory of behavioral change. *Psychological Review, 84*, 191–215.

Barr, R., Kamil, M.L., Mosenthal, P., & Pearson, P.D. (Eds.). (1991). *Handbook of reading research, Volume II*. White Plains, NY: Longman.

Csikszentmihalyi, M. (1978). Intrinsic rewards and emergent motivation. In M. Lepper & D. Greene (Eds.), *The hidden costs of reward: New perspectives on the psychology of motivation* (pp. 205–216). Hillsdale, NJ: Erlbaum.

Deci, E.L., & Ryan, R.M. (1985). *Intrinsic motivation and self-determination in human behavior*. New York: Plenum.

Dweck, C.S., & Leggett, E.L. (1988). A social-cognitive approach to motivation and personality. *Psychological Review, 95*, 256–273.

Eccles, J.S. et al. (1983). Expectancies, values and academic behaviors. In J.T. Spence (Ed.), *Achievement and achievement motives* (pp. 75–146). San Francisco, CA: W.H. Freeman.

Eccles, J.S., & Midgley, C. (1989). Stage-environment fit: Developmentally appropriate classrooms for young adolescents. In C. Ames & R. Ames (Eds.), *Research on motivation in education* (Vol. 3, pp. 139–186). San Diego, CA: Academic.

Eccles, J.S., & Wigfield, A. (1985). Teacher expectancies and student motivation. In J.B. Dusek (Ed.), *Teacher expectancies* (pp. 185–226). Hillsdale, NJ: Erlbaum.

Eccles, J.S., & Wigfield, A. (1995). In the mind of the achiever: The structure of adolescents' academic achievement-related beliefs and self-perceptions. *Personality and Social Psychology Bulletin, 21*, 215–225.

Eccles, J.S., Wigfield, A., Harold, R., & Blumenfeld, P.C. (1993). Age and gender differences in children's self- and task perceptions during elementary school. *Child Development, 64*, 830–847.

Eccles, J.S., Wigfield, A., Midgley, C. et al. (1993). Negative effects of traditional middle schools on students' motivation. *The Elementary School Journal, 93*, 553–574.

Eccles, J.S., Wigfield, A., & Schiefele, U. (in press). The development of achievement motivation. In N. Eisenberg (Ed.), *Handbook of child psychology* (Vol. 4, 5th ed.). New York: Wiley.

Epstein, J.L., & McPartland, J.M. (1976). The concept and measurement of the quality of school life. *American Educational Research Journal, 13*, 15–30.

Gambrell, L.B. et al. (1993). *Elementary students' motivation to read*. Unpublished manuscript, University of Maryland, National Reading Research Center.

Guthrie, J.T. (1996). Educational contexts for engagement in literacy. *The Reading Teacher, 49*, 432–445.

Guthrie, J.T., McGough, K., Bennett, L., & Rice, M.E. (1996). Concept-oriented reading instruction: An integrated curriculum to develop motivations and strategies for reading. In L. Baker, P. Afflerbach, & D. Reinking (Eds.), *Developing engaged readers in school and home communities* (pp. 165–190). Hillsdale, NJ: Erlbaum.

Guthrie, J.T., McGough, K., & Wigfield, A. (1994). *Measuring reading activity: An inventory* (Instructional Resource No. 4). Athens, GA: National Reading Research Center.

Guthrie, J.T., Van Meter, P., et al. (1996). Growth of literacy engagement: Changes in motivations and strategies during concept-oriented reading instruction. *Reading Research Quarterly, 31,* 306–333.

Harter, S. (1981). A new self-report scale of intrinsic versus extrinsic orientation in the classroom: Motivational and informational components. *Developmental Psychology, 17,* 300–312.

Harter, S., & Connell, J.P. (1984). A model of children's achievement and related self-perceptions of competence, control, and motivational orientation. In J.G. Nicholls (Ed.), *Advances in motivation and achievement: Vol. 3. The development of achievement motivation* (pp. 219–250). Greenwich, CT: JAI Press.

Maehr, M.L. (1976). Continuing motivation: An analysis of a seldom considered educational outcome. *Review of Educational Research, 46,* 443–462.

Marsh, H.W. (1989). Age and sex effects in multiple dimensions of self-concept: Preadolescence to early adulthood. *Journal of Educational Psychology, 81,* 417–430.

Mathewson, G.C. (1985). Toward a comprehensive model of affect in the reading process. In H. Singer & R.B. Ruddell (Eds.), *Theoretical models and processes of reading* (3rd ed., pp. 841–856). Newark, DE: International Reading Association.

Mathewson, G.C. (1994). Model of attitude influence upon reading and learning to read. In R.B. Ruddell, M.R. Ruddell, & H. Singer (Eds.), *Theoretical models and processes of reading* (4th ed., pp. 1131–1161). Newark, DE: International Reading Association.

McKenna, M.C. (1994). Toward a model of reading attitude acquisition. In E.H. Cramer & M. Castle (Eds.), *Fostering the love of reading: The affective domain in reading education* (pp. 18–40). Newark, DE: International Reading Association.

McKenna, M.C., & Kear, D.J. (1990). Measuring attitude toward reading: A new tool for teachers. *The Reading Teacher, 43,* 626–639.

Meece, J.L., Wigfield, A., & Eccles, J.S. (1990). Predictors of math anxiety and its consequences for young adolescents' course enrollment intentions and performances in mathematics. *Journal of Educational Psychology, 82,* 60–70.

Nicholls, J.G. (1979a). Development of perception of own attainment and causal attributions for success and failure in reading. *Journal of Educational Psychology, 71,* 94–99.

Nicholls, J.G. (1979b). Quality and equality in intellectual development: The role of motivation in education. *American Psychologist, 34,* 1071–1084.

Nicholls, J.G. (1990). What is ability and why are we mindful of it? A developmental perspective. In R.J. Sternberg & J. Kolligian (Eds.), *Competence considered* (pp. 11–40). New Haven, CT: Yale University Press.

Nicholls, J.G., Cheung, P., Lauer, J., & Patashnick, M. (1989). Individual differences in academic motivation: Perceived ability, goals, beliefs, and values. *Learning and Individual Differences, 1,* 63–84.

Oldfather, P. (1992, December). *Sharing the ownership of knowing: A constructivist concept of motivation for literacy learning.* Paper presented at the 42nd Annual Meeting of the National Reading Conference, San Antonio, TX.

Oldfather, P., & McLaughlin, J. (1993). Gaining and losing voice: A longitudinal study of students' continuing impulse to learn across elementary and middle school contexts. *Research in Middle Level Education, 17,* 1–25.

Oldfather, P., & Wigfield, A. (1996). Children's motivations to read. In L. Baker, P. Afflerbach, & D. Reinking (Eds.), *Developing engaged readers in school and home communities* (pp. 89–114). Hillsdale, NJ: Erlbaum.

Pintrich, P.R., & De Groot, E. (1990). Motivational and self-regulated learning components of classroom academic performance. *Journal of Educational Psychology, 82,* 33–40.

Pintrich, P.R., Marx, R.W., & Boyle, R.A. (1993). Beyond cold conceptual change: The role of motivational beliefs and classroom contextual factors in the process of conceptual change. *Review of Educational Research, 63,* 167–199.

Pintrich, P.R., & Schrauben, B. (1992). Students' motivational beliefs and their cognitive engagement in classroom academic tasks. In D.H. Schunk & J.L. Meece (Eds.), *Student perceptions in the classroom* (pp. 149–183). Hillsdale, NJ: Erlbaum.

Pintrich, P.R., & Schunk, D.H. (1996). *Motivation in education: Theory, research, and application.* Englewood Cliffs, NJ: Prentice Hall.

Renninger, K.A. (1992). Individual interest and development: Implications for theory and practice. In K.A. Renninger, S. Hidi, & A. Krapp (Eds.), *The role of interest in learning and development* (pp. 361–396). Hillsdale, NJ: Erlbaum.

Ruddell, R.B., Ruddell, M.R., & Singer, H. (Eds.). (1994). *Theoretical models and processes of reading* (4th ed.). Newark, DE: International Reading Association.

Ruddell, R.B., & Speaker, R. (1985). The interactive reading process: A model. In H. Singer & R.B. Ruddell (Eds.), *Theoretical models and processes of reading* (3rd ed., pp. 751–793). Newark, DE: International Reading Association.

Schiefele, U. (1991). Interest, learning, and motivation. *Educational Psychologist, 26,* 299–323.

Schunk, D.H. (1991a). Goal setting and self-evaluation: A social cognitive perspective on self-regulation. In M.L. Maehr & P.R. Pintrich (Eds.), *Advances in achievement and motivation* (Vol. 7, pp. 85–113). Greenwich, CT: JAI Press.

Schunk, D.H. (1991b). Self-efficacy and academic motivation. *Educational Psychologist, 26,* 233–262.

Schunk, D.H., & Rice, J.M. (1993). Strategy fading and progress feedback: Effects on self-efficacy and comprehension among students receiving remedial reading services. *The Journal of Special Education, 27,* 257–276.

Shirey, L.L. (1992). Importance, interest, and selective attention. In K.A. Renninger, S. Hidi, & A. Krapp (Eds.), *The role of interest in learning and development* (pp. 281–296). Hillsdale, NJ: Erlbaum.

Stipek, D.J. (1984). Young children's performance expectations: Logical analysis or wishful thinking? In J.G.

Nicholls (Ed.), *Advances in motivation and achievement: Vol. 3. The development of achievement motivation* (pp. 33–56). Greenwich, CT: JAI Press.

Stipek, D.J., & Mac Iver, D. (1989). Developmental change in children's assessment of intellectual competence. *Child Development, 60,* 521–538.

Urdan, T.C., & Maehr, M.L. (1995). Beyond a two-goal theory of motivation and achievement: A case for social goals. *Review of Educational Research, 65,* 213–244.

Weiner, B. (1992). *Human motivation: Metaphors, theories, and research.* Newbury Park, CA: Sage.

Wentzel, K.R. (1996). Social goals and social relationships as motivators of school adjustment. In J. Juvonen & K.R. Wentzel (Eds.), *Social motivation: Understanding school adjustment* (pp. 226–247). New York: Cambridge University Press.

Wentzel, K.R. (1991). Social and academic goals at school: Motivations and achievement in context. In M.L. Maehr & P.R. Pintrich (Eds.), *Advances in motivation and achievement* (Vol. 7, pp. 185–212). Greenwich, CT: JAI Press.

Wigfield, A. (1994). Expectancy-value theory of achievement motivation: A developmental perspective. *Educational Psychology Review, 6,* 49–78.

Wigfield, A., & Eccles, J.S. (1992). The development of achievement task values: A theoretical analysis. *Developmental Review, 12,* 265–310.

Wigfield, A. et al. (1995). *Change in children's competence beliefs and subjective task values across the elementary school years: A three-year study.* Manuscript submitted for publication.

Wigfield, A., & Guthrie, J.T. (1995). *Dimensions of children's motivations for reading: An initial study* (Research Report No. 34). Athens, GA: National Reading Research Center.

Wigfield, A., Guthrie, J.T., & McGough, K. (1996). *A questionnaire measure of children's motivations for reading* (Instructional Resource No. 22). Athens, GA: National Reading Research Center.

Wigfield, A., Wilde, K., Baker, L., Fernandez-Fein, S., & Scher, D. (1996). *The nature of children's reading motivations, and their relations to reading frequency and reading performance* (Research Report No. 63). Athens, GA: National Reading Research Center.

Zimmerman, B.J., Bandura, A., & Martinez-Pons, M. (1992). Self-motivation for academic attainment: The role of self-efficacy beliefs and personal goal setting. *American Educational Research Journal, 29,* 663–676.

Engagement Activities

In Your Classroom

This chapter suggests that motivation can be organized around three critical questions: Can we be successful (effective) readers? Do we want to be successful (effective) readers and why? What do we need to do to be successful (effective) readers? Hold a discussion with your students about these questions and record their responses on a three-column chart similar to a K-W-L chart.

With Your Colleagues

Discuss the beliefs and behaviors of students in your classroom who are more or less motivated to read. Considering the constructs of motivation described in Table 1, what can you do to maintain the motivation of students who *are* engaged and to bolster the motivation of students who are *less* engaged?

Further Reading

Aarnoutse, C., & Schellings, G. (2003). Learning reading strategies by triggering reading motivation. *Educational Studies, 29*(4), 387–408.

Wigfield discusses the importance of developing both the *skill* and *will* to read. This study examined the effectiveness of an intervention aimed at developing both reading strategies (skills) and reading motivation (will). The findings indicate that the experimental group was more knowledgeable about reading strategies, used strategies more effectively, and was more motivated to read than the control group. The study suggests that reading instruction should include a plan to cultivate both reading strategies and motivation.

Is There a Bidirectional Relationship Between Children's Reading Skills and Reading Motivation?

Paul L. Morgan and Douglas Fuchs

Children who read frequently grow to become skillful readers (e.g., Guthrie, Schafer, & Huang, 2001; Juel, 1988; Senechal & LeFevre, 2002; Stanovich, 1986). Frequent reading contributes to growth in sight word recognition, vocabulary, verbal fluency, reading comprehension, and general knowledge (Cunningham & Stanovich, 1991; Echols, West, Stanovich, & Zehr, 1996; Griffiths & Snowling, 2002; Guthrie et al., 2001; Guthrie, Wigfield, Metsala, & Cox, 1999; Leppänen, Aunola, & Nurmi, 2005; Senechal, LeFevre, Hudson, & Lawson, 1996). For example, Leppänen et al. reported a path coefficient of .13 between children's book reading frequency in first grade and their word recognition skills in second grade. Cunningham and Stanovich (1997) found that reading practice accounted for 35% of the variance in 11th graders' vocabulary scores after their 1st grade vocabulary, nonverbal IQ, and comprehension skills were statistically controlled.

Given sufficient print resources (e.g., Neuman, 1999; Neuman & Celano, 2001), how often a child reads is explained by two factors (e.g., Cox & Guthrie, 2001; Paris & Turner, 1994). The first is initial success in acquiring reading skills (Stanovich, 1986). Cunningham and Stanovich (1997) found that measures of first grade reading ability predicted 10% of the variance in 11th graders' reading practice after statistically controlling for the children's reading comprehension skills as 11th graders. The second factor is motivation (e.g., Pressley, 2002; Wang & Guthrie, 2004). Wigfield and Guthrie (1997) reported that highly motivated children read three times as much outside of school as their less motivated peers. Guthrie et al. (1999) found that motivation significantly predicted amount of reading practice after statistically controlling for prior reading achievement. These and other results led Guthrie et al. to conclude that motivation is the "preeminent predictor" (p. 250) of frequent reading.

Unfortunately, poor readers—the children most likely to benefit from frequent practice—are often unmotivated to read (e.g., Chapman, 1988; Lepola, Vauras, & Mäki, 2000). This lack of motivation can be seen within a year or so of school entry (Chapman, Tunmer, & Prochnow, 2000; Lepola, Poskiparta, Laakkonen, & Niemi, 2005; McKenna, Kear, & Ellsworth, 1995). For example, Morgan, Fuchs, Compton, Cordray, and Fuchs (in press) found that low-skilled first graders (a) considered reading to be difficult, (b) viewed themselves as less competent readers, and (c) held more negative attitudes towards reading than high-skilled peers. Teachers rated the low-skilled readers as more avoidant of classroom reading activities. Because of its link to reading practice, poor readers' lack of motivation is increasingly suggested as an underlying cause of long-term reading difficulties

Reprinted by permission of the publisher from Morgan, P.L., & Fuchs, D. (2007). Is there a bidirectional relationship between children's reading skills and reading motivation? *Exceptional Children, 73*(2), 165-183.

28

(e.g., Baker, 2000; Gambrell & Morrow, 1996; Pressley, 2002; Quirk & Schwanenflugel, 2004; Stanovich, 1986; Wigfield, 2000). Indeed, teachers indicate one of their most pressing concerns is to find ways to boost reading motivation (Allen, Schockly, & Baumann, 1995).

One frequently studied explanation of poor readers' lack of motivation posits a bidirectional causal relationship between reading skills and motivation. Children lose motivation to read because of their repeated failure to acquire requisite skills (e.g., Aunola, Leskinen, Onatsu-Arvilommi, & Nurmi, 2002; Chapman et al., 2000). In this vein, Stanovich (1986) hypothesizes that these reading difficulties lead to "behavioral/cognitive/motivational spinoffs" (p. 389), or "negative Matthew effects" (p. 360). Because these negative Matthew effects interact to discourage children from reading frequently, they lead to a "poor-get-poorer" situation. Low motivation thus acts both as a consequence of limited skill acquisition and as a cause of later reading failure (Guthrie & Wigfield, 1999; Oldfather & Wigfield, 1996; Scarborough & Dobrich, 1994).

Are poor readers doubly disadvantaged in that they soon begin to lag behind their peers in both "skill" and "will"? If so, then their poor reading skills and low reading motivation may begin to influence each other (Stanovich, 1986). Such a negative cycle could help explain why many children with disabilities continue experiencing long-term reading failure despite receiving intensive skills-focused remediation. Understanding why many poor readers are poorly motivated to read also has important implications for early intervention. If young children are under-motivated because of repeated failure in acquiring reading skills, then this would suggest focusing primarily on remediating their skill deficits. Conversely, if poor motivation arises from altogether different factors (e.g., a parent's own views towards reading), then this would suggest a need to employ early interventions that demonstrably remediate both skill- and motivation-specific deficits.

Understanding whether and how weak reading skills and low motivation interrelate is especially pressing to help children with special needs, as so many of them are poor readers (e.g.,

National Assessment of Educational Progress, 2005; Nelson, Benner, Lane, & Smith, 2004). Moreover, children with learning and behavioral disabilities tend to be less motivated to engage in academic activities than their nondisabled peers (e.g., Chapman, 1988; Fulk, Brigham, & Lohman, 1998). The potential interaction between weak reading skills and low motivation to read is viewed as one reason why children with disabilities so consistently underperform academically (e.g., Stanovich, 1986; Torgesen, 1982; Torgesen et al., 1999).

Purpose of This Review

This review evaluated existing evidence of a bidirectional relationship between reading skills acquisition and motivation. To better weigh how well findings from the available studies indicated the possible existence of a bidirectional relationship (Cohen, Cohen, West, & Aiken, 2003; Kenny, 1979), we asked three questions:

- How strongly do children's reading skills correlate concurrently with their reading motivation?
- How strongly do (a) early differences in their acquisition of reading skills predict later differences in their motivation and (b) early differences in children's motivation predict later differences in their reading skills?
- Have the effects of potentially confounding factors been isolated in analyses of the reading skill–reading motivation relationship?

Method

Indicators of Children's Reading Motivation

It is difficult to establish an empirical relationship between growth in reading skills and reading motivation. There are at least three reasons for this. First, theoretical (e.g., Eccles, Wigfield, & Schiefele, 1998; Guthrie & Wigfield, 2000; Wigfield, 1997) and applied (e.g., Sweet,

Guthrie, & Ng, 1998; Wigfield & Guthrie, 1997) work suggests that motivation is a complex, multidimensional factor. It is hard to measure (Watkins & Coffey, 2004). Second, few studies (e.g., Baker & Scher, 2002; Gottfried, 1990) have used statistical analysis to validate that children's self-reports reflect their motivation to read rather than their willingness to engage in other academic subjects. Without establishing domain specificity, it is difficult to isolate factors that may influence children's interest in reading. Third, researchers have sometimes inadvertently complicated subsequent syntheses of their findings by (a) using different terms to refer to the same constructs (Baker & Scher), or (b) using the same terms to refer to different constructs (Guthrie & Wigfield, 2000). Our review evaluates a possible bidirectional relationship between reading and motivation by focusing on two relatively distinct and well-established indicators of reading motivation: competency beliefs and goal orientations. These two indicators are increasingly linked within dynamic models of reading motivation (e.g., Lepola et al., 2005; Nurmi & Aunola, 2005).

Competency Beliefs. Competency beliefs are "estimates of how good one is at a given activity" (Wigfield et al., 1997, p. 451). Here, they relate to whether a child considers himself or herself capable of being a good reader. Self-concept and self-efficacy are two types of competency beliefs (e.g., Linnenbrink & Pintrich, 2002). Self-concept refers to more general beliefs about one's capabilities; self-efficacy refers to more task-specific beliefs. Competency beliefs are often the first indicator of young children's motivation (Eccles et al., 1998). Gottfried (1990) argues that young children experiencing early task mastery should have higher perceptions of competence and, consequently, greater motivation. Conversely, early declines in competency beliefs should precede declines in motivation and, later, less frequent reading practice (Bandura, 1977; Chapman & Tunmer, 2003; Dweck, 1986). Some of the best evidence for domain-specific motivation comes from research on children's competency beliefs (Eccles et al., 1998; Wigfield, 1997).

Goal Orientations. Achievement goals are "the purposes children have for achievement in different areas, so they deal directly with the 'whys' of behavior" (Wigfield, 1997, p. 61). Goal orientations (as well as intrinsic motivation) relate to whether and why a child wants to be a good reader. Specifically, goal orientation marks a "set of behaviorial intentions that determines how students approach and engage in learning activities" (Meece, Blumenfeld, & Hoyle, 1988, p. 514). Differences in children's goal orientations help explain their classroom behavior (e.g., Ames, 1992; Dweck & Leggett, 1988; Meece et al., 1988; Meece & Holt, 1993; Seifert & O'Keefe, 2001) and reading performance (e.g., Graham & Golan, 1991; Meece & Miller, 1999, 2001). Goal orientations can be domain-specific (Salonen, Lepola, & Niemi, 1998); they can also be adaptive or maladaptive (Elliot & Harackiewicz, 1996; Elliott & Dweck, 1988). Adaptive goal orientations lead to task-oriented behavior, whereas maladaptive orientations lead to behaviors that are ego-defensive, socially dependent, or task-avoidant (Ames, Poskiparta, Niemi, Lepola, Ahtola, & Laine, 2003). Maladaptive goal orientations lead children to avoid reading tasks as a means of "expressing their negative attitudes toward schoolwork, avoiding failure, or coping with the constraints and demands of the learning situation" (Meece et al., p. 515).

Inclusion Criteria

The reviewed studies had to meet a priori criteria of germaneness and methodological adequacy. Given the relatively few empirical studies of young children's reading motivation (Wigfield, 1997), our criteria were deliberately modest, or inclusive (Slavin, 1986).

We accepted peer-reviewed, published studies in which authors evaluated a relationship between reading skill level and either (a) a reading-specific competency belief or (b) an achievement goal orientation in a preschool- or school-age sample. Studies evaluating only global or non-reading-specific competency beliefs (e.g., mathematics self-concept) or non-achievement goals (e.g., problem behavior, social goals) were excluded. Studies exploring the influence of nonschool factors (e.g., parental beliefs) on the relationship between reading skills acquisition and reading-specific competency beliefs or academic goal orientation also were eliminated (e.g., Aunola, Nurmi, Niemi, Lerkkanen, & Rasku-Puttonen, 2002; Lynch, 2002; Onatsu-Arvilommi, Nurmi, & Aunola, 1998; Turner & Johnson, 2003).

Because we focussed on initial acquisition of reading skills, we chose studies involving children in preschool through second grade. However, we also included investigations that began with young children and followed them into third, fourth, fifth, or sixth grade. Finally, in the selected studies, researchers used longitudinal, cross-sectional, or control group designs. Case studies and single-subject studies were not selected because of difficulties establishing statistical relationships in such research.

Literature Search

We searched for data-based studies exploring relationships between young children's reading skills and (a) their self-reported feelings of competency as readers or (b) adult ratings of their achievement goal orientations. We first generated a broad list of descriptors based on previous theoretical (e.g., Ames, 1992; Wigfield, 1997) and empirical (e.g., Valentine, DuBois, & Cooper, 2004) work: competence, competency beliefs, self-concept, self-perception, self-efficacy, motivation, engagement, goal theory, achievement goals, goal orientation, motivational orientation, task orientation, task focused behavior, mastery goals, ego-defensive goals, ego defensiveness, performance goals, social goals, task avoidant goals, task avoidant behavior, and work avoidance.

Second, we entered each descriptor into an electronic search of Education Abstracts, ERIC, Exceptional Child Educational Resources, and PsycINFO. To select relevant studies, we coupled each descriptor with the term "reading" (e.g., "competence and reading"); we set search limits to identify only those studies written in English, published after 1975 as a peer-reviewed journal

article, and involving preschool or school-age children. Our search yielded 1,429 citations. Third, we conducted an ancestral search of appropriate studies identified through the electronic search that met our inclusion criteria.

Fourth, we examined several books: *Developing Engaged Readers in School and Home Communities* (Baker, Afflerbach, & Reinking, 1996); *Engaging Young Readers: Promoting Achievement and Motivation* (Baker, Dreher, & Guthrie, 2000); *Literacy and Motivation: Reading Engagement in Individuals and Groups* (Verhoeven & Snow, 2001); *Reading Engagement: Motivating Readers Through Integrated Instruction* (Guthrie & Wigfield, 1997); and *Reading Instruction That Works: The Case for Balanced Teaching* (Pressley, 2002).

Fifth, we conducted a manual search of seven journals from January 1975 to January 2006 (or, if the journal was relatively new, from the date of inception to January 2006): *British Journal of Educational Psychology*, *Exceptional Children*, *Journal of Educational Psychology*, *Journal of Learning Disabilities*, *Journal of Special Education*, *Learning Disabilities Quarterly*, and *Reading Research Quarterly*.

We identified 15 studies that met our inclusion criteria. Seven studies (i.e., Aunola, Leskinen, et al., 2002; Chapman & Tunmer, 1995, 1997; Chapman et al., 2000; Chapman, Tunmer, & Prochnow, 2001; Tunmer & Chapman, 2002; Wilson, Chapman, & Tunmer, 1995) examined the relationship between beginning reading skills and children's reading competency beliefs. Seven studies (i.e., Gottfried, 1990; Lepola et al., 2005; Lepola, Salonen, & Vauras, 2000; Nurmi & Aunola, 2005; Onatsu-Arvilommi & Nurmi, 2000; Poskiparta et al., 2003; Salonen et al., 1998) examined the association between reading skills and children's goal orientations. One study (Lepola, Vauras, & Mäki, 2000) explored both competency beliefs and goal orientations. Table 1 displays key features of these 15 studies. (Gottfried's [1990] study of intrinsic motivation is grouped with studies evaluating children's goal orientations because intrinsic motivation is reflected by task orientation.)

Table 1
Demographics, Design, and Reliability of Measurements of Reviewed Studies

Study Authors	Sample Characteristics	Study Design	Reliability Estimates of Motivation Measures
Aunola, Leskinen, et al., 2002	N = 105; 6 to 7 years; Finnish	Longitudinal	Self-Concept of Reading Ability (test-retest reliabilities = .29 for Time 1 to 2, .55 for Time 2 to 3)
Chapman & Tunmer, 1995[a]	N = 771; 5 to 10 years; New Zealanders	Longitudinal	Reading Self-Concept Scale-30 (α range = .81-.89, full scale total sample estimate = .84)
Chapman & Tunmer, 1997	N = 118; 5 to 7 years; New Zealanders	Longitudinal	Reading Self-Concept Scale (α for age 5 = .85; age 6 = .84; age 7 = .85)
Chapman et al., 2000	N = 60; 5 years; New Zealanders	Longitudinal	Perception of Ability Scale for Students; Reading Self-Concept Scale; no reliability information reported
Chapman et al., 2001	N = 132; 5 years; New Zealanders	Longitudinal	Reading Self-Concept Scale (internal reliability = .85); Perception of Ability Scale for Students (internal reliability = .93); Adaptive Behavior Scale (internal reliability = .92) and Maladaptive Behavior Scale (internal reliability = .90) of the Child Behavior Checklist
Gottfried, 1990	N = 107; 7 to 9 years; American (longitudinal) N = 98; grades 1-3; American (cross-sectional)	Longitudinal & Cross-sectional	Young Children's Academic Intrinsic Motivation Inventory (longitudinal & cross-sectional studies combined α = .82; test-retest reliability for cross-sectional study = .73); Children's Academic Anxiety Inventory (ages 7 & 8 for both studies combined α = .67); Self Perception of Competence (α = .58 based on both studies & reading, math, & general scores)
Lepola et al., 2005	N = 100; preschool-1st grade; Finnish	Longitudinal	Task orientation in kindergarten, pre-school, and first grade (α = .83, .81, .85, respectively)
Lepola, Salnonen, et al., 2000	N = 48; 6 to 8 years; Finnish	Longitudinal	Preschool: task, social dependence, & ego-defensive orientation (α = .69, .71, & .71, respectively); coping (interrater reliability α = .70). First grade: task, social dependence orientation, & ego-defensive (α = .78, .71, & .82, respectively). Second grade: task, social dependence orientation, & ego-defensive (α = .70, .77., & .81, respectively)

(continued)

Table 1
Demographics, Design, and Reliability of Measurements of Reviewed Studies
(*Continued*)

Study Authors	Sample Characteristics	Study Design	Reliability Estimates of Motivation Measures
Lepola, Vauras, & Mäki, 2000	$N = 101$; 8, 9, & 12 years; Finnish	Longitudinal	Self-concept of attainment (no reliability information reported); task orientation (third grade $\alpha = .70$; sixth grade $\alpha = .87$), social dependence orientation (third grade $\alpha = .74$; 6th grade $\alpha = .76$), & ego-defensive (third grade $\alpha = .83$; 6th grade $\alpha = .76$)
Nurmi & Aunola, 2005	$N = 211$; 6 to 7 years; Finnish	Longitudinal	Task-Value Scale for Children ($\alpha = .72$, .83, .82, & .81 for reading-related task motivation); Self-Concept of Ability (test-retest reliability Time 1 to 2 = .50; Time 2 to 3 = .46; Time 3 to 4 = .57 for self-concept of reading ability)
Onatsu-Arvilommi & Nurmi, 2000	$N = 105$; 6 to 7 years; Finnish	Longitudinal	Teacher Ratings of Task-Irrelevant Behaviors ($\alpha = .94$ at each of 3 waves), test-retest reliability (Time 1 to 2 = .94; Time 2 to 3 = .94); Helplessness Behaviors ($\alpha = .89$, .92, & .91 at each of 3 waves), test-retest reliability (Time 1 to 2 = .92, Time 2 to 3 = .91); Lack of Persistence ($\alpha = .91$, .92, & .94 at each of 3 waves), test-retest reliability (Time 1 to 2 = .92, Time 2 to 3 = .94)
Poskiparta et al., 2003	$N = 127$; preschool-grade 2; Finnish	Longitudinal	Task orientation, social dependence orientation, ego-defensive orientation ($\alpha = .69$, .71, & .71, respectively)
Salonen, Lepola, & Nurmi, 1998	$N = 32$; 6 years; Finnish	Longitudinal	Task, social dependence, & ego-defensive orientations (rs between preschool teachers' & two experimenters' ratings = .20 & .55, .47 & .65, & .08 & .49, respectively)
Tunmer & Chapman, 2002	$N = 121$; 5 to 7 years; New Zealanders	Longitudinal	Reading self-efficacy (internal reliability = .72); Perception of Ability Scale for Students (internal reliability = .93)
Wilson et al., 1995	$N = 52$; 6 years; New Zealanders	Quasi-experimental	Reading Self-Concept Scale (no reliability information reported)

Note. α = Cronbach's alpha. Reliability information is based on the cited study's sample.

[a]Experiment 4 only.

Results

How Strongly Do Reading Skills Correlate With Reading Motivation?

Results from six studies (Chapman & Tunmer, 1995, 1997; Gottfried, 1990; Lepola et al., 2005; Lepola, Vauras, & Mäki, 2000; Salonen et al., 1998) suggest that measures of young children's reading skills correlate with concurrent measures of their motivation to read. Put another way, each of the reviewed studies that investigated this question reported a correlation between children's reading skills and their concurrent motivation. A reliable relationship emerged regardless of whether researchers relied on children's self-reports, standardized tests, teacher ratings, or direct observations. Age and gender differences appeared to moderate the correlation.

Competency Beliefs. Chapman and Tunmer (1997) tracked changes in the reading skills and self-concepts of children across the first 3 years of school. The correlation between reading skill level and reading self-concept increased steadily across three testing occasions, from .11 to .21 to .35. Whereas the children's relative reading ability was stable over the 3 years, their reading self-concepts were not. Reading Skills assessed in the 1st year correlated .69 with reading skills assessed in the 3rd year. Reading self-concept in the 1st year of school correlated only .12 with reading self-concept in the 3rd year. Children appeared to enter school with largely undifferentiated self-concepts and then, over time, begin to report self-concepts corresponding to their relative reading ability.

Lepola, Vauras, and Mäki (2000) tracked the self-concept, behavior, school grades, and reading skills of a sample of children initially assessed in second grade. The correlation between reading skills and reading self-concept was far stronger for boys ($r = .49$) than for girls ($r = .12$). By third grade, however, this correlation was more similar ($r = .56$ and .46). Reading self-concept and reading grades correlated .24 in third grade and .41 by sixth grade. Like Chapman and Tunmer (1997), Lepola, Vauras, and Mäki found that

children's reading motivation increasingly covaried with their relative progress at acquiring reading skills.

Chapman and Tunmer (1995) conducted four experiments on the development of children's reading self-concepts. The fourth one measured the relationship between children's reading skills and reading self-concepts across their 1st and 4th or 1st and 5th year of school. The reading self-concept measure included subscales of perceived competence, perceived difficulty, and attitudes towards reading. Children's scores on the reading measures increasingly correlated with their full scale reading self-concept scores. During the 1st year of school, the correlations ranged from .17 (letter identification and spelling) to .22 (word identification and pseudoword naming). By the 4th year, reading skill and reading self-concept correlated .47. The only statistically significant subscale correlation in first grade was "perceived difficulty." The correlations ranged from .22 (letter identification) to .28 (spelling). However, statistically significant correlations emerged for all three subscales by the 4th year. Subscale correlations with reading comprehension ranged from .17 (attitude towards reading) to .40 (perceived competence) to .53 (perceived difficulty). By the 5th year, subscale correlations ranged from .40 (attitude towards reading) to .43 (perceived competence) to .65 (perceived difficulty). Some children considered reading difficult by the 1st year of formal reading instruction. This perception appeared to broaden into more negative attitudes and lower feelings of competence in reading by the 4th and 5th years of school.

Goal Orientations. Lepola, Vauras, and Mäki (2000) also collected data on their sample's goal orientations. By the sixth grade, children's task orientation correlated .58 with their reading grades. The association was stronger for boys ($r = .72$) than for girls ($r = .46$). Children's ego-defensiveness and social dependency correlated negatively with their reading grades ($r = -.59$ and $-.54$, respectively). Again, these relationships were stronger for boys ($r = -.68$ and $-.65$) than for girls ($r = -.51$ and $-.34$). Reading self-concept and task orientation correlated .23 in third grade and .39 in sixth grade. Children rated by their teachers as displaying more concentration and persistence tended to report higher reading self-concepts. This relationship was stronger for boys than for girls in both third and sixth grades ($r = .36$ and .09, and .48 and .25, respectively).

Lepola et al. (2005) tracked the cognitive-linguistic skills and task orientation of a sample of children as they transitioned from kindergarten to preschool to first grade (time periods as reported by the investigators). The investigators used confirmatory factor analysis to test concurrent correlations between four latent factors: (a) letter knowledge, (b) phonological awareness, (c) rapid naming, and (d) task orientation. In preschool, the children's task orientation correlated with their letter knowledge ($r = .36$), phonological awareness ($r = .58$), and rapid naming skills ($r = -.24$). In kindergarten, task orientation correlated with phonological awareness ($r = .20$) and rapid naming skills ($r = -.47$). By first grade, the children's task orientation correlated with their phonological awareness ($r = .38$) and rapid naming ($r = -.38$). Like Chapman and Tunmer (1997), Lepola et al. found that children's reading skills were more stable than their motivation. The children's preschool phonological awareness skills correlated .78 with their first-grade skills. In contrast, their preschool task orientation correlated .45 with their first-grade task orientation.

Gottfried (1990) conducted a longitudinal and cross-sectional study of the development of children's intrinsic motivation, reading achievement, and perceptions of competence. Seven-year-old children's scores on the intrinsic motivation measure correlated both with their scores on a standardized reading measure ($r = .31$) and with teacher ratings of their reading skills ($r = .45$). Nine-year-old children's intrinsic motivation scores correlated with their scores on a standardized reading measure ($r = .21$) and teacher ratings ($r = .34$). Collectively, results from these six studies suggest that children's reading skills covary, albeit modestly, with their reading motivation.

Is There Evidence That Reading Skills Precede Motivation; That Motivation Precedes Reading Skills; or That the Two Influence Each Other?

Results from five studies (Aunola, Leskinen, et al., 2002; Chapman & Tunmer, 1997; Chapman et al., 2000; Lepola, Salonen, & Vauras, 2000; Poskiparta et al., 2003) indicate that early differences in reading skills precede later differences in reading motivation. Findings from five additional studies (Chapman et al., 2000; Gottfried, 1990; Lepola et al., 2005; Onatsu-Arvilommi & Nurmi, 2000; Salonen et al., 1998) indicate the reverse relationship: early differences in motivation precede later differences in reading skills. Findings from 10 of 11 studies (the exception, Nurmi & Aunola, 2005) are consistent with the notion of a bidirectional relationship between early reading and motivation.

Competency Beliefs. Chapman and Tunmer (1997) used path analysis to establish whether initial differences in reading skills precede later differences in reading self-concept. Results suggested that neither reading skills nor reading self-concept in the 1st year of school had a causal affect on each other in the 2nd year of school. A significant path coefficient between reading level in the 2nd year of school and reading self-concept in the 3rd year ($\beta = .27$), along with a nonsignificant path coefficient between reading self-concept in the 2nd year and reading level in the 3rd year ($\beta = .04$), suggested that reading skills "emerged as causally predominant over reading self-concept" (Chapman & Tunmer, 1997, p. 287). This apparent causal relationship developed by the middle of the 2nd school year and continued into the first half of the 3rd school year.

Aunola, Leskinen, et al. (2002) used simplex modeling, latent growth curve analysis, and cluster analysis to model the relationship between reading skills and reading self-concept. Early reading ability was a statistically significant predictor of later reading self-concept ($\beta = .29$). Multivariate latent growth curve modeling indicated that reading and reading self-concept correlated .42 across the study's three measurement periods. A statistically significant correlation of .44 between reading level and trend of reading self-concept indicated that skilled readers developed increasingly positive reading self-concepts, while low-skilled readers developed increasingly negative reading self-concepts. Cluster analysis indicated that the reading levels of children in two of the three groups correlated positively with their trends in reading self-concept.

Chapman et al. (2000) evaluated whether children with negative academic self-concepts had begun school with weaker reading skills than those with typical or positive academic self-concepts. They reported that children later identified as having negative academic self-concepts started school with consistently lower reading performance and reading self-concepts than their peers. Poor reading self-concepts became more broadly negative over time. Discriminant analyses indicated that end-of-1st-year reading performance accurately predicted positive and negative academic self-concept with an accuracy of 75% and 70%, respectively. Findings from the Chapman et al. (2000) study suggest that children who later develop negative academic self-concepts may enter school with both lower reading skills and more negative attitudes and feelings of competency than their peers.

Goal Orientations. Lepola, Salonen, and Vauras (2000) explored whether children entering school with low reading skills would later display different goal orientations than those entering with higher reading skills. Although the children did not differ on ratings of their preschool goal orientations, experimenters rated those with low preschool phonemic awareness as displaying lower task orientation through first and second grade than those with high preschool phonemic awareness. Experimenters and teachers rated the children with low preschool phonemic awareness as displaying higher social dependence in first and second grade than the children with high preschool phonemic awareness. Both experimenters and teachers rated children who

made limited progress in learning to decode as less task-oriented, more ego-defensive, and more socially dependent than children who made steady progress. These trends held regardless of the level of phonemic awareness in preschool. Differences in task orientation between low- and high-skilled readers who displayed progressive growth in word reading disappeared by second grade, suggesting that steady progress in acquiring reading skills improved task orientation.

Lepola et al. (2005) used structural equation modeling to test how children's letter knowledge, phonological awareness, rapid naming, and task orientation predicted each other across time, and, in particular, how each of these predicted children's word recognition. These relationships were tested after controlling for initial differences in nonverbal IQ. The structural model displayed both direct and indirect paths between children's reading and task orientation. The direct paths showed that children's (a) letter knowledge in kindergarten predicted task orientation in preschool ($\beta = .25$), (b) phonological awareness in preschool predicted task orientation in first grade ($\beta = .40$), (c) task orientation in kindergarten predicted preschool phonological awareness ($\beta = .31$), and (d) task orientation in the fall of first grade predicated word recognition skills ($\beta = .20$) in the spring of third grade.

The investigators also reported a set of indirect paths: First-grade task orientation mediated between preschool phonological awareness and first-grade word recognition; preschool task orientation and phonological awareness mediated between kindergarten letter knowledge and first-grade word recognition; kindergarten task orientation was indirectly related to first-grade word recognition through preschool task orientation and phonological awareness. These indirect paths suggest young children's reading skills and reading motivation begin to influence each other bidirectionally to affect later reading ability. Results from the Leponen et al. (2005) study run contrary to the notion that poor motivation emerges only as a consequence of reading failure.

Poskiparta et al. (2003) investigated whether children's goal orientations in preschool predict their status as poor readers, good decoders (i.e., children with average or above average decoding and spelling skills, but below average reading comprehension skills), and good readers in second grade. Results suggested that poor readers adopted more maladaptive goal orientations. Although poor readers, good decoders, and good readers behaved similarly in preschool, poor readers were less task-oriented and more ego-defensive than good readers in first grade. Poor readers were also more ego-defensive than good decoders. Both first- and second-grade teachers rated poor readers as less task-oriented, more socially dependent, and more ego-defensive than either good decoders or good readers.

Onatsu-Arvilommi and Nurmi (2000) researched children's cognitive abilities, reading and mathematical skills, and task orientation versus task avoidance. The children completed measures of cognitive ability prior to beginning school. They were then assessed on three occasions during the school year. Results from structural equation modeling indicated that cognitive abilities positively predicted later reading (Time 0–1, $\beta = .55$) and negatively predicted later task avoidance (Time 0–1, $\beta = -.38$). Reading skills and task avoidance influenced each other. Earlier task avoidance predicted poor reading (Time 1–2, $\beta = -.24$; Time 2–3, $\beta = -.19$). Poor reading inconsistently predicted later task avoidance (Time 1–2, $\beta = -.18$; Time 2–3, $\beta = -.07$). These results held for boys and girls. Children's performance on a reading-specific task negatively correlated with their later task avoidance (Time 0–1, $\beta = -.32$).

Salonen et al. (1998) focused on whether differences in children's preschool behavior negatively affect their development of first-grade word reading. The investigators found that first-grade word reading significantly correlated with preschool behavior such that first-grade word reading correlated .51 with preschool task orientation, $-.32$ with ego defensiveness, and $-.33$ with social dependency. When entered into a hierarchical regression, first-grade reading skills were predicted by task orientation ($\beta = .52$) and phonemic awareness ($\beta = .37$). Together, preschool task orientation and phonemic awareness

accounted for 38% of the variance in children's first-grade word reading. Task-oriented children had better (a) phonemic awareness in preschool and (b) word reading in first grade than ego-defensive or multiple non-task-oriented children. As in the Lepola et al. (2005) and Onatsu-Arvilommi and Nurmi (2000) studies, Salonen et al.'s findings suggest that subsequent development in children's reading ability is codetermined by both initial level of reading skill (i.e., phonemic awareness) and task engagement. These two factors interrelate in preschool, with task-oriented and ego-defensive children displaying significantly different levels of phonemic awareness.

Gottfried (1990) obtained mixed results on the question of whether early reading level predicted children's later reading motivation. Seven- and 8-year-old children's scores on a standardized reading measure correlated with their intrinsic motivation to read at age 9 ($r = .20$ and .24, respectively). Their teacher's ratings did not ($r = .14$ and .09, respectively). Seven-year-old children's intrinsic motivation scores also correlated with their scores as 8- and 9-year-olds on the standardized reading measure ($r = .24$ and .26, respectively). Neither standardized reading scores nor teacher ratings significantly predicted 7- and 8-year-old children's motivation at age 9 after controlling for earlier levels of motivation.

Nurmi and Aunola (2005) found no evidence for a bidirectional relationship between reading skills and reading motivation. Children's reading level at the start of first grade predicted neither their task orientation towards reading nor their reading self-concept at the end of first grade. This pattern emerged again for the children at the start and end of second grade. Furthermore, neither the children's task orientation towards reading nor their reading self-concept predicted their level of reading. This pattern held in both first and second grade.

However, two factors may have influenced these results. First, the investigators used a non-traditional "person-oriented" type of analysis, in which group membership (i.e., whether a child displayed high motivation towards school, low reading motivation, high math motivation, or low math motivation) acted as the predictor or criterion variable. Second, the researchers were conservative in their analyses (e.g., a significant level of $p < .01$, two-tailed tests, and use of autoregressor in their multinomial regression analyses).

The Nurmi and Aunola (2005) study also found that (a) boys were more likely than girls to be poorly motivated to read; (b) children reporting poor reading motivation at the beginning of first grade were likely to still be poorly motivated at the end of second grade; and (c) children with poor reading motivation were unlikely to report a high level of interest in school. However, some children reporting poor reading motivation began expressing more interest in mathematics as they moved from first to second grade. Nurmi and Aunola hypothesized that these children may have compensated for their low interest in reading by trying to become interested in a school subject in which they believed they had greater skill.

Have the Effects of Reading Skills on Reading Motivation and Vice Versa Been Isolated From Potentially Confounding Factors?

Few studies have isolated the effects of possibly confounding variables when estimating a reading-motivation relationship. Only Gottfried (1990) controlled for both IQ and socioeconomic status (SES); only Lepola et al. (2005) and Onatsu-Arvilommi and Nurmi (2000) controlled for cognitive abilities at school entry. Results from Gottfried's study indicate that IQ and SES may influence the reading-motivation relationship. Instructional factors may also moderate children's progress in acquiring reading skills and, hence, lead to differences in their reading motivation.

Level of IQ and SES. Gottfried (1990) found that the IQs of 7- and 8-year-olds correlated .27 and .31, respectively, with their reading motivation as 9-year-olds. Seven-year-old children's IQ correlated .32 with their self-reported motivation to read, while their motivation to read correlated

.27 with their IQ at age 8. Although Gottfried found significant grade differences in the longitudinal sample's total intrinsic motivation scores, the grade diminished considerably when IQ was controlled. Hierarchical multiple regression analysis indicated that IQ and SES differences predicted subsequent differences in motivation. Eight-year-old children's IQ accounted for 10% of the variance in their reading motivation at age 9. Seven-year-old children's SES accounted for 9% of the variance in their reading motivation at age 9. This suggests that IQ and SES, like reading level in Lepola, Salonen, and Vauras's (2000) study and Poskiparta et al.'s (2003) work, predict motivation. Gottfried did not assess whether reading skill remained a significant predictor of motivation after controlling for IQ and SES.

Lepola et al. (2005) found that IQ accounted for significant variance in kindergarten children's letter knowledge, rapid naming skills, and task orientation. The effect for task orientation was particularly strong. Whereas IQ accounted for 9% of the variance in letter knowledge and 5% of the variance in rapid naming, it accounted for 25% of the variance in task orientation. The investigators reported that controlling for IQ did not change the pattern of relationships among children's emergent literacy skills, task orientation, and word recognition ability. Similarly, Onatsu-Arvilommi and Nurmi (2000) found that a latent factor of cognitive competence predicted both children's reading ($\beta = .55$) and task avoidance ($\beta = -.38$) at school entry. However, the interrelation between later reading and task avoidance remained statistically insignificant.

Type of Classroom Instruction. Tunmer and Chapman (2002) investigated whether children who use text-based word identification strategies (e.g., relied on preceding content and prior knowledge to identify a word) display lower levels of reading skill and report more negative reading self-efficacy and academic self-concept beliefs than those who use word-based strategies (e.g., relied on letter-sound correspondence to identify a word). Tunmer and Chapman hypothesized that text-based strategies might prove an ineffective word identification strategy and, if relied on often, might limit children's rate of progress in acquiring reading skills and promote more negative feelings towards reading. The researchers found that children who reported using text-based strategies during their 1st year of reading instruction scored consistently lower on reading measures during their 1st and 3rd school year. They also reported holding more negative self-efficacy beliefs in reading and more negative academic self-concepts by their 3rd year than children who used word-based strategies.

Type of Remediation Program. In a similar vein, Wilson et al. (1995) evaluated whether a tutoring program emphasizing text-based strategies (i.e., Reading Recovery) would lead to improvements in poor readers' reading self-concept. Two groups of second graders were evaluated. One group was 26 children selected by their teachers for participation in the tutoring program. They scored in the bottom 20% on a text reading task. A second group of 26 children, also identified by their teachers, was judged to be making very good reading progress. The two groups were matched on sex, age, and classroom. Tutored children received individual instruction emphasizing use of text-based strategies for 12 to 20 weeks. Repeated-measures ANOVA indicated poor readers reported lower reading self-concept than skilled readers, despite receiving tutoring. Post hoc tests indicated that poor readers scored lower on both the measure's perceived difficulty and perceived competency subscales.

Chapman et al. (2001), like Wilson et al. (1995), pursued whether use of text-based strategies negatively affect the rate of progress of children's reading skill acquisition, and negatively affect their competency beliefs as readers. The researchers also investigated how using text-based strategies affect the children's classroom behaviors. Children were assessed seven times over their first 3 years in school. Teachers identified one group as having successfully completed a tutoring program (i.e., Reading Recovery) that emphasized text-based strategies. A second group was identified as having reading skills comparable to the children who subsequently entered the tutoring program. A third group was

identified as relatively skilled readers. Results indicated that the three groups had entered school with significantly different reading skills, but with similar reading self-concepts. However, by the 3rd year of reading instruction, skilled readers reported higher reading self-concepts than the tutored group and the non-tutored group with similar skills. There were no statistically significant differences in the reading self-concepts of the two groups of poor readers during the 3 years of the study. Results also indicated that tutoring in text-based strategies was largely ineffective in remediating children's phonological processing deficits. Teachers rated the children who received tutoring as working less hard, being less focused on learning, and displaying fewer appropriate behaviors during classroom instruction than the poor readers who did not receive tutoring. Chapman et al. (2001) concluded, "This finding, along with the self-concept results, is consistent with Stanovich's (1986) view that initial and specific difficulties in learning to read may result in generalized deficits in learning" (p. 172).

Discussion

Our review explored the relationships between children's reading skills and reading motivation, as measured by children's self-report and adult ratings. We asked three questions:

- How strongly to children's reading skills and motivation correlate concurrently with each other?

- Is there evidence that one precedes the other? That is, do (a) differences in children's reading skills predict later differences in their motivation and (b) differences in children's motivation predict subsequent differences in their levels of reading?

- Have the effects of potentially confounding factors been isolated in analyses of the reading-motivation relationship?

Answers to these questions have important theoretical and practical implications. For example, finding that children become poorly motivated as a result of reading failure would suggest that interventions that effectively remediate reading skill deficits should also counteract early declines in motivation. Conversely, if reading failure is not a primary cause of poor motivation, then this would suggest that poor motivation may result from something other than the quality of a child's early reading instruction. As put by Lepola et al. (2005), neglecting motivation would therefore "provide a partly misleading view of the determinants of reading acquisition" (p. 391). Finding that young children's reading and motivation influence each other to affect their later reading ability would suggest the need to provide interventions that effectively counteract initially poor reading skill and low motivation.

Evidence of a Bidirectional Relationship

Results from 15 studies consistently supported the conclusion that children's level of reading skill correlates with their reading motivation. This association held whether motivation was indicated by children's competency beliefs (e.g., Chapman & Tunmer, 1995, 1997; Lepola, Vauras, & Mäki, 2000) or goal orientations (Gottfried, 1990; Lepola, Santonen, & Vauras, 2000). For example, statistically significant correlations were obtained between children's reading skills and competency beliefs by the 2nd or 3rd year of school (e.g., Chapman & Tunmer, 1997). Children's task orientation correlated positively (and their ego-defensiveness and social dependency correlated negatively) with their reading grades (Lepola, Salonen, & Vauras). Children's competency beliefs and goal orientations also covaried (Gottfried; Lepola, Vauras, & Mäki).

Research also suggests, however tentatively, the hypothesis that children's reading achievement and reading motivation predict each other across time. Evidence of this may be found in reading self-concept and goal orientation literatures. Chapman and Tunmer (1997) and Aunola, Leskinen, et al. (2002) reported that differences in level of reading skills predicted later reading self-concept. Lepola, Salonen, and Vauras (2000) and Poskiparta et al. (2003) discovered that reading

skills predicted later goal orientation. The poor readers in Chapman et al.'s (2000) study entered school already holding more negative feelings of competency and attitudes towards reading than their peers. Finally, Onatsu-Arvilommi and Nurmi (2000) and Salonen et al. (1998) reported that children's goal orientations predicted their later reading levels.

Results from three additional studies offer more direct support for a bidirectional relationship between early reading skill and motivation (i.e., Gottfried, 1990; Lepola et al., 2005; Onatsu-Arvilommi & Nurmi, 2000). Lepola et al. indicated that kindergarten children's phonological awareness interacted over time with their task motivation to determine their first-grade word recognition skills. This study and others (e.g., Salonen et al., 1998) show that low motivation to engage in reading activities does not result only from repeated reading failure.

However, there is not causal evidence for this bidirectional relationship because (a) potentially confounding factors have infrequently been controlled and (b) true experiments have not yet been conducted. For example, differences in children's reading rarely have been separated from effects of other factors on differences in children's motivation to read, whether indicated by their competency beliefs or goal orientations.

Cohen et al. (2003) describe three methods researchers might use to isolate the effects of an independent variable: (a) removing or holding constant the effects of other variables, (b) randomly assigning different groups to different levels of an independent variable, or (c) statistically controlling for the effects of other explanatory variables. Rather than employ true experimental designs, investigators have mostly relied on causal-comparative research methods (e.g., Chapman et al., 2000, 2001; Tunmer & Chapman, 2002). This is important because (a) factors such as IQ and SES likely act as confounds in the reading skills-reading motivation relationship (e.g., Gottfried, 1990) and (b) it is difficult to determine causality from causal-comparative methods (Gall, Borg, & Gall, 1996). Still, results from the few studies that have statistically controlled for potential confounding factors are consistent with the notion of an early bidirectional reading skills-reading motivation relationship (Gottfried; Lepola et al., 2005; Onatsu-Arvilommi & Nurmi, 2000).

Although children's reading skills and motivation consistently correlated, the reported magnitude of the correlations varied substantially. Concurrent correlations ranged from a low of .11 to a high of .65, or 1% to 42% of explained variance. Because this range in correlations may reflect a developmental dynamic, we would caution against interpreting the smaller correlations as clinically insignificant. The interaction between poor reading and low motivation may "snowball," or increasingly influence each other in such a way as to lead to long-term reading failure. If so, identifying the onset of this negative feedback cycle may be critical to prevent such failure. As argued by Spear-Swerling and Sternberg (1994), "Once children have entered the 'swamp' of negative expectations, lowered motivation, and limited practice, it becomes increasingly difficult for them to get back on the road of proficient reading" (p. 101).

Methodological and Theoretical Issues

Although we focused on two relatively well-established indicators of reading motivation (i.e., reading self-concept and goal orientations), several methodological and theoretical considerations complicated our interpretation of the evidence. First, different researchers used different measures of motivation. Chapman and Tunmer (1997) and Wilson et al. (1995) used a 30-item instrument comprised of three subscales, whereas Aunola, Leskinen, et al. (2002) and Lepola, Vauras, and Mäki (2000) relied on a simple sociogram. Whether these two measures gauge the same construct—reading self-concept—remains an open question. Few researchers explored motivation with multiple measures, despite a persuasive rationale for doing so (e.g., Gersten, Baker, & Lloyd, 2000).

It is also difficult to determine if current measures of motivation are assessing children's interest in reading per se and not their interest in classroom reading activities. This is an important distinction because the interaction between reading and motivation would have its greatest impact on children's reading growth if it led them to avoid all types of reading activities. We were also unable to determine how well children's classroom materials were matched to their relative reading levels. Ignoring this might lead to a possibly mistaken conclusion that a child is uninterested in reading per se rather than simply disinclined to work on those particular reading activities that are proving too difficult.

Second, not all researchers established the validity of their motivation measures. Only Gottfried directly tested whether children might be influenced by social desirability when self-reporting on their reading motivation. Although many investigators (e.g., Chapman & Tunmer, 1995; Gottfried, 1990; Lepola et al., 2005) reported relatively strong reliability coefficients, some described weak ones (e.g., Aunola, Leskinen, et al., 2002; Salonen et al., 1998). Reliable measures are especially important in longitudinal studies.

A third problem concerns the design of the studies. Fourteen were longitudinal; one (i.e., Wilson et al., 1995) was quasi-experimental. Random selection and assignment have yet to be used in evaluating the reading-motivation relationship. This limitation, combined with the fact that so few studies used statistical means to control for the influence of possible confounding variables, weakens any causal conclusions that can be drawn (Shadish, Cook, & Campbell, 2002).

Fourth, across the 15 studies, participants were fairly homogenous, which limits generalizability. Eight of the 15 studies (Aunola, Leskinen, et al., 2002; Lepola, Salonen, & Vauras, 2000; Lepola et al., 2005; Lepola, Vauras, & Mäki, 2000; Nurmi & Aunola, 2005; Onatsu-Arvilommi & Nurmi, 2000; Poskiparta et al., 2003; Salonen et al., 1998) sampled children learning to read Finnish. The regular orthography of Finnish may affect conclusions about the nature and strength of the reading-motivation relationship for children learning to read a language with a more irregular orthography (e.g., English). Only one of the 15 investigations (i.e., Gottfried, 1990) involved American children.

Directions for Future Research and Practice

Studies that use (a) multiple measures of the same indicator (e.g., reading self-concept), (b) multiple measures of related but distinct constructs (e.g., math self-concept), and (c) exploratory factor analysis to assess whether the particular measures conform with definitions of the indicator they seek to tap (Gersten et al., 2000; Pedhazer & Schmelkin, 1991) would strengthen research on reading motivation. Future researchers might also try to build upon Gottfried's (1990) commendable attempts to establish the validity of her measure of children's intrinsic motivation.

In light of findings reported by Chapman et al. (2001), Tunmer and Chapman (2002), and Wilson et al. (1995), one promising way to explore a possible causal reading skills-reading motivation relationship would be to randomly assign poor readers to a program emphasizing strategies for word-level decoding. Establishing that those children whose decoding improves also make greater gains in reading motivation would help provide a case for the causal nature of the relationship.

Which reading deficits most strongly affect young children's motivation? Poor phonological awareness and decoding are two skills identified by Stanovich (1986) and our review and, as such, may be important to target for intervention. Researchers might also attempt to control for potentially confounding factors and involve more heterogeneous populations to improve generalizability of findings.

For practitioners, this review suggests the importance of making sure that children's motivation remains high; low motivation, like poor phonological awareness or letter knowledge, may act as an important determinant of later reading skills (Lepola et al., 2005). For example, Morgan, Farkas, Tufis, and Sperling (2006) found that first-grade children displaying low-level task orientation were three times as likely to be poor readers in third grade as first-grade peers displaying typical levels of task orientation. This was after statistically controlling for (a) poor reading ability in first grade and (b) many demographic- and SES-related characteristics. Interventions focusing on bolstering a child's reading skills, although necessary, may ultimately prove insufficient in helping him or her become a proficient reader unless they also help strengthen poor motivation.

What, then, can practitioners do to bolster a child's poor reading motivation? It may be necessary to combine scientifically-based reading interventions with motivation-building techniques. Quirk and Schwanenflugel (2004) recently detailed many of these. For example, the researchers advise practitioners to help children self-set reading goals that are challenging but reachable. A teacher might spend a few minutes each week helping a child monitor his or her progress in meeting these goals. Accomplishing these goals may bolster the child's belief that, with effort, he or she can become a better reader. Of course, it is critical to combine such motivation-building techniques with interventions that help the child meet his or her goals to become a better reader.

We suggest there is preliminary support for the hypothesis that children's early reading difficulties and low motivation interact to undermine their continued reading growth (e.g., Stanovich, 1986). Whereas results from 15 studies indicate that children's reading skills and reading motivation correlate—and that this relationship may be bidirectional across time—few of the 15 studies have eliminated plausible rival explanations of a possible causal relationship. Thus, it may be that children with specific reading deficits enter school with motivational deficits. If future research supports a bidirectional relationship between reading skills and reading motivation then researchers, practitioners, and parents may need to cultivate both "skill" and "will" if they are to help poor readers develop proficiency.

References

References marked with an asterisk indicate the studies in our review.

Allen, J., Shockley, B., & Baumann, J. (1995). Gathering 'round the kitchen table: Teacher inquiry in the NRRC School Research Consortium. *The Reading Teacher*, *48*(6), 526–529.

Ames, C. (1992). Classrooms: Goals, structures, and student motivation. *Journal of Educational Psychology, 84*, 261–271.

Aneshensel, C.S. (2002). *Theory-based data analysis for the social sciences*. Thousand Oaks, CA: Pine Forge Press.

*Aunola, K., Leskinen, E., Onatsu-Arvilommi, T., & Nurmi, J. (2002). Three methods for studying developmental change: A case of reading skills and self-concept. *British Journal of Educational Psychology, 72*, 343–364.

Aunola, K., Nurmi, J., Niemi, P., Lerkkanen, M.K., & Rasku-Puttonen, H. (2002). Developmental dynamics of achievement strategies, reading performance, and parental beliefs. *Reading Research Quarterly, 37*, 310–327.

Baker, L. (2000). Building the word-level foundation for engaged reading. In L. Baker, M.J. Dreher, & J.T. Guthrie (Eds.), *Engaging young readers: Promoting achievement and motivation* (pp. 17–42). New York: Guilford.

Baker, L., Afflerbach, P., & Reinking, D. (Eds.). (1996). *Developing engaged readers in school and home communities*. Mahwah, NJ: Lawrence Erlbaum.

Baker, L., Dreher, M.J., & Guthrie, J.T. (Eds.). (2000). *Engaging young readers: Promoting achievement and motivation*. New York: Guilford.

Baker, L., & Scher, D. (2002). Beginning readers' motivation for reading in relation to parental beliefs and home reading experiences. *Reading Psychology, 23*, 239–269.

Bandura, A. (1977). Self-efficacy: Toward a unifying theory of behavioral change. *Psychological Review, 84*, 191–215.

Chapman, J.W. (1988). Learning disabled children's self-concepts. *Review of Educational Research, 58*, 347–371.

*Chapman, J.W., & Tunmer, W.E. (1995). Development of young children's reading self-concepts: An examination of emerging subcomponents and their relation with reading achievement. *Journal of Educational Psychology, 87*, 154–167.

*Chapman, J.W., & Tunmer, W.E. (1997). A longitudinal study of beginning reading achievement and reading self-concept. *British Journal of Educational Psychology, 67*, 279–291.

Chapman, J.W., & Tunmer, W.E. (2003). Reading difficulties, reading-related self-perceptions, and strategies for overcoming negative self-beliefs. *Reading and Writing Quarterly: Overcoming Learning Difficulties, 19*, 5–24.

*Chapman, J.W., Tunmer, W.E., & Prochnow, J.E. (2000). Early reading-related skills and performance, reading self-concept, and the development of academic self-concept: A longitudinal study. *Journal of Educational Psychology, 92*, 703–708.

*Chapman, J.W., Tunmer, W.E., & Prochnow, J.E. (2001). Does success in the Reading Recovery program depend on developing proficiency in phonological-processing skills? A longitudinal study in a whole language instructional context. *Scientific Studies of Reading, 5*, 141–176.

Cohen, J., Cohen, P., West, S.G., & Aiken, L.S. (2003). *Applied multiple regression/correlation analysis for the behavioral sciences* (3rd ed.). Mahwah, NJ: Lawrence Erlbaum.

Cox, K.E., & Guthrie, J.T. (2001). Motivational and cognitive contributions to students' amount of reading. *Contemporary Educational Psychology, 26*, 116–131.

Cunningham, A.E., & Stanovich, K.E. (1991). Tracking the unique effects of print exposure in children: Associations with vocabulary, general knowledge, and spelling. *Journal of Educational Psychology, 83*, 264–274.

Cunningham, A.E., & Stanovich, K.E. (1997). Early reading acquisition and its relation to reading experience and ability 10 years later. *Developmental Psychology, 33*, 934–945.

Dweck, C.S. (1986). Motivational processes affecting learning. *American Psychologist, 41*, 1040–1048.

Dweck, C.S., & Leggett, E.L. (1988). A social-cognitive approach to motivation and personality. *Psychological Review, 95*, 256–273.

Eccles, J.S., Wigfield, A., & Schiefele, U. (1998). Motivation to succeed. In W. Damon (Series Ed.) and N. Eisenberg (Vol. Ed.), *Handbook of child psychology: Vol. 3. Social, emotional, and personality development* (5th ed., pp. 1017–1095). New York: Wiley.

Echols, L.D., West, R.W., Stanovich, K.E., & Zehr, K.S. (1996). Using children's literacy activities to predict growth in verbal cognitive skills: A longitudinal investigation. *Journal of Educational Psychology, 88*, 296–304.

Elliot, A.J., & Harackiewicz, J.M. (1996). Approach and avoidance achievement goals and intrinsic motivation: A mediational analysis. *Journal of Personality and Social Psychology, 70*, 461–475.

Elliott, E.S., & Dweck, C.S. (1988). Goals: An approach to motivation and achievement. *Journal of Personality and Social Psychology, 54*, 5–12.

Fulk, B.M., Brigham, F.J., & Lohman, D.A. (1998). Motivation and self-regulation: A comparison of students with learning and behavior problems. *Remedial and Special Education, 19*, 300–309.

Gall, M.D., Borg, W.R., & Gall, J.P. (1996). *Educational research: An introduction* (6th ed.). White Plains, NY: Longman.

Gambrell, L.B., & Morrow, L.M. (1996). Creating motivation in contexts for literacy learning. In P. Afflerbach, L. Baker, & P. Reinking (Eds.), *The engagement perspective for reading* (pp. 115–136). Hillsdale, NJ: Lawrence Erlbaum.

Gersten, R., Baker, S., & Lloyd, J.W. (2000). Designing high-quality research in special education: Group experimental design. *Journal of Special Education, 34,* 2–18.

*Gottfried, A.E. (1990). Academic intrinsic motivation in young elementary school children. *Journal of Educational Psychology, 82,* 525–538.

Graham, S., & Golan, S. (1991). Motivational influences on cognition: Task involvement, ego involvement, and depth of information processing. *Journal of Educational Psychology, 83,* 187–194.

Griffiths, Y.M., & Snowling, M.J. (2002). Predictors of exception word and nonword reading in dyslexic children: The severity hypothesis. *Journal of Educational Psychology, 94,* 34–43.

Guthrie, J.T., Schafer, W.D., & Huang, C. (2001). Benefits of opportunity to read and balanced instruction on the NAEP. *Journal of Educational Research, 94,* 145–162.

Guthrie, J.T., & Wigfield, A. (Eds.). (1997). *Reading engagement: Motivating readers through integrated instruction.* Newark, DE: International Reading Association.

Guthrie, J.T., & Wigfield, A. (1999). How motivation fits into a science of reading. *Scientific Studies of Reading, 3,* 199–205.

Guthrie, J.T., & Wigfield, A. (2000). Engagement and motivation in reading. In M.L. Kamil, P.B. Mosenthal, P.D. Pearson, & R. Barr (Eds.), *Handbook of reading research* (Vol. 3, pp. 403–422). Mahwah, NJ: Lawrence Erlbaum.

Guthrie, J.T., Wigfield, A., Mestala, J.L., & Cox, K.E. (1999). Motivational and cognitive predictors of text comprehension and reading amount. *Scientific Studies of Reading, 3,* 231–256.

Juel, C. (1988). Learning to read and write: A longitudinal study of 54 children from first through fourth grades. *Journal of Educational Psychology, 80,* 437–447.

Kenny, D.A. (1979). Correlation and causality. New York: Wiley.

*Lepola, J., Poskiparta, E., Laakkonen, E., & Niemi, P. (2005). Development of and relationship between phonological and motivational processes and naming speed in predicting word recognition in Grade 1. *Scientific Studies of Reading, 9,* 367–399.

*Lepola, J., Salonen, P., & Vauras, M. (2000). The development of motivational orientations as a function of divergent reading careers from pre-school to the second grade. *Learning and Instruction, 10,* 153–177.

*Lepola, J., Vauras, J., & Mäki, H. (2000). Gender differences in the development of academic self-concept of attainment from the 2nd to the 6th grade: Relations with achievement and perceived motivational orientation. *The Journal of Hellenic Psychological Society, 7,* 3–21.

Leppänen, U., Aunola, K., & Nurmi, J.E. (2005). Beginning readers' reading performance and reading habits. *Journal of Research in Reading, 28,* 383–399.

Linnenbrink, E.A., & Pintrich, P.R. (2002). Motivation as an enabler for academic success. *School Psychology Review, 31,* 313–327.

Lynch, J. (2002). Parents' self-efficacy beliefs, parents' gender, children's reader self-perceptions, reading achievement, and gender. *Journal of Research in Reading, 25,* 54–67.

McKenna, M.C., Kear, D.J., & Ellsworth, R.A. (1995). Children's attitudes toward reading: A national survey *Reading Research Quarterly, 30,* 934–956.

Meece, J.L., Blumenfeld, P.C., & Hoyle, R.H. (1988). Students' goal orientations and cognitive engagement in classroom activities. *Journal of Educational Psychology, 80,* 514–523.

Meece, J.L., & Holt, K. (1993). A pattern analysis of students' achievement goals. *Journal of Educational Psychology, 85,* 582–590.

Meece, J.K., & Miller, S.D. (1999). Changes in elementary school children's achievement goals for reading and writing. Results of a longitudinal and an intervention study. *Scientific Studies of Reading, 3,* 207–229.

Meece, J.L., & Miller, S.D. (2001). A longitudinal analysis of elementary school students' achievement goals in literacy activities. *Contemporary Educational Psychology, 26,* 454–480.

Morgan, P.L., Farkas, G., Tufis, P.A., & Sperling, R.A. (2006). *Are reading and behavior problems risk factors for each other?* Manuscript submitted for publication.

Morgan, P.L., Fuchs, D., Compton, D.L., Cordray, D.S., & Fuchs, L.S. (in press). Does early reading failure decrease children's reading motivation? *Journal of Learning Disabilities.*

National Assessment of Educational Progress. (2005). *2005 Reading Assessment Results.* Retrieved February 27, 2006, from National Center for Education Statistics, U.S. Department of Education Web site. http://nces.ed.gov/nationsreportcard/nrc/reading_math_2005/

Nelson, J.R., Benner, G.J., Lane, K., & Smith, B.W. (2004). An investigation of the academic achievement of K–12 students with emotional and behavioral disorders in public school settings. *Exceptional Children, 71,* 59–73.

Neuman, S.B. (1999). Books make a difference: A study of access to literacy. *Reading Research Quarterly, 34,* 202–210.

Neuman, S.B., & Celano, D. (2001). Access to print in low- and middle-income communities: An ecological study of 4 neighborhoods. *Reading Research Quarterly, 36,* 468–475.

*Nurmi, J.E., & Aunola, K. (2005). Task-motivation during the first school years: A person-oriented approach to longitudinal data. *Learning and Instruction, 15,* 103–122.

Oldfather, P., & Wigfield, A. (1996). Children's motivation for literacy learning. In L. Baker & P. Afflerbach (Eds.), *Developing engaged readers in school and home communities* (pp. 89–113). Hillsdale, NJ: Lawrence Erlbaum.

*Onatsu-Arvilommi, T., & Nurmi, J.E. (2000). The role of task-avoidant and task-focused behaviors in the development of reading and mathematical skills during the first school year: A cross-lagged longitudinal study. *Journal of Educational Psychology, 92,* 478–491.

Onatsu-Arvilommi, T., Nurmi, J., & Aunola, K. (1998). Mothers' and fathers' well-being, parenting styles, and their children's cognitive and behavioral strategies at primary school. *European Journal of Psychology of Education, 13,* 543–556.

Paris, S., & Turner, J. (1994). Situated motivation. In P. Pintrich, D. Brown, & C. Weinstein (Eds.), *Student motivation, cognition, and learning: Essays in honor of Wilbert J. McKeachie* (pp. 213–237). Hillsdale, NJ: Lawrence Erlbaum.

Pedhazer, E.J., & Schmelkin, L.P. (1991). *Measurement, design, and analysis: An integrated approach.* Hillsdale, NJ: Lawrence Erlbaum.

*Poskiparta, E., Niemi, P., Lepola, J., Ahtola, A., & Laine, P. (2003). Motivational-emotional vulnerability and difficulties in learning to read and spell. *British Journal of Educational Psychology, 73,* 187–206.

Pressley, M. (2002). *Reading instruction that works: The case for balanced teaching* (2nd ed.). New York: Guilford.

Quirk, M.P., & Schwanenflugel, P.J. (2004). Do supplemental remedial reading programs address the motivational issues of struggling readers? An analysis of five popular programs. *Reading Research and Instruction, 43,* 1–19.

*Salonen, P., Lepola, J., & Niemi, P. (1998). The development of first graders' reading skill as a function of pre-school motivational orientation and phonemic awareness. European *Journal of Psychology of Education, 13,* 155–174.

Scarborough, H.S., & Dobrich, W. (1994). On the efficacy of reading to preschoolers. *Developmental Review, 14,* 245–302.

Seifert, T.L., & O'Keefe, B.A. (2001). The relation of work avoidance and learning goals to perceived competence, externality, and meaning. *British Journal of Educational Psychology, 71,* 81–92.

Senechal, M., & LeFevre, J.A. (2002). Parent involvement in the development of children's reading skill: A five-year longitudinal study. *Child Development, 73,* 445–460.

Senechal, M., LeFevre, J., Hudson, E., & Lawson, E.P. (1996). Knowledge of storybooks as a predictor of young children's vocabulary. *Journal of Educational Psychology, 88,* 520–536.

Shadish, W.R., Cook, T.D., & Campbell, D.T. (2002). *Experimental and quasi-experimental designs for generalized causal inference.* New York: Houghton Mifflin.

Sideridis, G.D., Morgan, P.L., Botsas, G., Padeliadu, S., & Fuchs, D. (2006). Predicting learning disabilities based on motivation, metacognition, and psychopathology: A ROC analysis. *Journal of Learning Disabilities, 39,* 215–229.

Slavin, R.E. (1986). Best-evidence synthesis: An alternative to meta-analytic and traditional review. *Educational Researcher, 15*(9), 5–11.

Spear-Swerling, L., & Sternberg, R.J. (1994). The road not taken: An integrative theoretical model of reading disability. *Journal of Learning Disabilities, 27,* 91–103.

Stanovich, K.E. (1986). Matthew effects in reading: Some consequences of individual differences in the acquisition of literacy. *Reading Research Quarterly, 21,* 360–407.

Sweet, A.P., Guthrie, J.T., & Ng, M.M. (1998). Teacher perceptions and student reading motivation. *Journal of Educational Psychology, 90,* 210–223.

Torgesen, J.K. (1982). The learning disabled child as an inactive learner: Educational implications. *Topics in Learning and Learning Disabilities, 2,* 45–52.

Torgesen, J.K., Wagner, R.K., Rashotte, C.A., Rose, E., Lindamood, P., Conway, T., et al. (1999). Preventing reading failure in young children with phonological processing difficulties: Group and individual responses to instruction. *Journal of Educational Psychology, 91,* 579–593.

*Tunmer, W.E., & Chapman, J.W. (2002). The relation of beginning readers' reported word identification strategies to reading achievement, reading-related skills, and academic self-perceptions. *Reading and Writing: An Interdisciplinary Journal, 15,* 341–358.

Turner, L.A., & Johnson, B. (2003). A model of mastery motivation for at-risk preschoolers. *Journal of Educational Psychology, 95,* 495–505.

Valentine, J.C., DuBois, D.L., & Cooper, H. (2004). The relation between self-beliefs and academic achievement: A meta-analytic review. *Educational Psychologist, 39,* 111–134.

Verhoeven, L.T., & Snow, C.E. (Eds.). (2001). *Literacy and motivation: Reading engagement in individuals and groups.* Mahwah, NJ: Erlbaum.

Wang, J.H.Y., & Guthrie, J.T. (2004). Modeling the effects of intrinsic motivation, extrinsic motivation, amount of reading, and past reading achievement on text comprehension between U.S. and Chinese students. *Reading Research Quarterly, 39,* 162-184.

Watkins, M.W., & Coffey, D.Y. (2004). Reading motivation: Multidimensional and indeterminate. *Journal of Educational Psychology, 96,* 110–118.

Wigfield, A. (1997). Reading motivation: A domain-specific approach to motivation. *Educational Psychologist, 32,* 59–68.

Wigfield, A. (2000). Facilitating young children's motivation to read. In L. Baker, M.J. Dreher, & J.T. Guthrie

(Eds.), *Engaging young readers* (pp. 140–158). New York: Guilford.

Wigfield, A., Eccles, J.S., Yoon, K.S., Harold, R.D., Arbreton, A.J.A., Freedman-Doan, C., et al. (1997). Change in children's competence beliefs and subjective task values across the elementary school years: A 3-year study. *Journal of Educational Psychology, 89,* 451–469.

Wigfield, A., & Guthrie, J.T. (1997). Relations of children's motivation for reading to the amount and breadth of their reading. *Journal of Educational Psychology, 89,* 420–432.

*Wilson, M.G., Chapman, J.W., & Tunmer, W.E. (1995). Early reading difficulties and reading self-concept. *Journal of Cognitive Education, 4,* 33–45.

Engagement Activities

In Your Classroom

Consider the motivation of your struggling readers. How can you help them to set and reach challenging goals? Make a plan to confer individually with your struggling readers for a few minutes each week. Use this time to set goals and monitor progress toward meeting them.

With Your Colleagues

In what ways can you and your colleagues provide interventions for struggling readers that integrate goals for both strategy use and reading motivation?

Further Reading

Guthrie, J., Wigfield, A., Metsala, J.L., & Cox, K.E. (1999). Motivational and cognitive predictors of text comprehension and reading amount. *Scientific Studies of Reading, 3*(3), 231–256.

Just as Morgan and Fuchs recommend that interventions include both strategy use and motivation, this study found that motivation contributes to reading achievement and text comprehension. Specifically, the two studies found that motivation increased reading amount, which then increased text comprehension. In other words, comprehension instruction should include strategy modeling and practice, reading that students find interesting, and time to read for purpose and pleasure.

What Teachers Can Learn About Reading Motivation Through Conversations With Children

Kathryn M. Edmunds and Kathryn L. Bauserman

As elementary school teachers, we (the authors) have frequently heard comments such as "I hate to read" or "I never read a book." We have taught in various school settings, including urban, suburban, and rural school environments, with diverse student populations. We have employed a variety of strategies and incentives, and, like Kohn (1993), we have found that extrinsic rewards were not effective at producing lasting change. Despite our efforts, we still heard negative comments about reading from our students. After many discussions, we realized that our students' levels of reading motivation varied as much as the students themselves. We also discussed how we would much rather hear more positive comments about reading from them. Therefore, we decided it was time to talk with our students and find out how we could turn the negative comments into positive ones. We decided it was time to find out how to *really* motivate students to read.

What Does the Research Say?

Numerous research studies have been conducted to examine the role of motivation in general (Deci, 1971, 1972a, 1972b; Lepper & Greene, 1975; Lepper, Greene, & Nisbett, 1973; Loveland & Olley, 1979). Research over the past 20 years demonstrated that students' motivation is a primary concern of many teachers, and numerous

classroom teachers acknowledge that a lack of motivation is at the root of many of the problems they face in teaching (O'Flahavan, Gambrell, Guthrie, Stahl, & Alvermann, 1992; Veenman, 1984). There is a vast amount of research that supports the idea that motivation plays a major role in learning (Deci & Ryan, 1985; Dweck & Elliott, 1983; McCombs, 1989). Motivation frequently makes the difference between learning that is temporary and superficial and learning that is permanent and internalized (Oldfather, 1993).

Although there is an immense amount of research about reading, especially the cognitive aspects (Guthrie & Wigfield, 2000), few studies have been conducted to determine the role of motivation in reading (McQuillan, 1997). Even though it is believed that motivation plays a major role in reading development, a review of the *Annual Summary of Investigations Related to Reading* (International Reading Association) over several years revealed that relatively few studies had been conducted on that role. From 1985 to 1992, approximately nine studies were conducted per year on the role of motivation in literacy development (Gambrell, 1995). Gambrell (1996) reported the results of a national survey conducted by the National Reading Research Center, which showed that reading motivation was a topic that teachers would like to see investigated. There were 84 reading topics included on the survey, and teachers identified developing

Reprinted from Edmunds, K.M., & Bauserman, K.L. (2006). What teachers can learn about reading motivation through conversations with children. *The Reading Teacher, 59*(5), 414-424.

an interest in reading as their first priority for reading research. In the top 10, 3 other topics associated with motivation appeared. Those topics included increasing the amount and expanse of reading; increasing intrinsic motivation to read; and investigating teachers', parents', and peers' roles in children's reading motivation (Gambrell, 1996).

When children first enter school, they are excited about learning and are very motivated. However, their motivation to learn appears to decrease during the elementary school years in all academic subjects, including reading (Eccles, Wigfield, & Schiefele, 1998; Guthrie & Wigfield, 2000). Children's motivation to read in the school and home environment decreases as they get older (Guthrie & Wigfield). The decline in the motivation to read appears to be greatest from first through fourth grade (Wigfield et al., 1997). This decline in motivation has been attributed to children's growing awareness of their own performance as compared to others, as well as to instruction that emphasizes competition and does not address children's interests (Guthrie & Wigfield).

Teachers also recognize that motivation may be correlated to the amount and breadth of children's reading. Research conducted over the past several years suggests that elementary school children who are motivated to read spend more time reading than those who are not motivated (Guthrie, Wigfield, Metsala, & Cox, 1999; Morrow, 1992; Wigfield & Guthrie, 1997). Research has indicated that children who spend more time reading are better readers and comprehenders than children who spend little time reading. Reading motivation has also been linked to the development of lifelong readers (Morrow, 1992; Wang & Guthrie, 2004). Motivation may also influence the success of multiple strategy instruction (National Institute of Child Health and Human Development, 2000).

Because teachers are aware of the importance of motivation in reading development and achievement, they have used various educational practices to enhance reading motivation and encourage children to read (Miller & Meece, 1997; Wang & Guthrie, 2004). Like us, however,

they realized these practices are not always effective. Therefore, it was critical for us as teachers to take a more in-depth look at what really motivates children to read.

Our Study

Because we heard so many negative comments about reading and there has been very little research in this area, we decided to go to the source: we asked our students what motivated them to read. The students attended an elementary school in a midsize city in the southern United States, which had 831 students in grades pre-K through 5 and 37 teachers. Fifty-nine percent of the students were white, 38% were black, and 3% were from other ethnicities. Seventy-four percent of the students were on free or reduced-cost lunch status.

The three language arts teachers for the fourth-grade classrooms in the school agreed to participate in our study. Each teacher taught two classes of language arts. They identified their instructional program as a basal program supplemented by trade books. We asked them to rate the reading levels and motivational levels of all 91 fourth-grade students. Students were placed in the following categories: Motivated Above-Grade Level, Motivated On-Grade Level, Motivated Below-Grade Level, Unmotivated Above-Grade Level, Unmotivated On-Grade Level, and Unmotivated Below-Grade Level. Three students were randomly selected from each category, with the exception of the Unmotivated Above-Grade Level category (only one student was identified in this category).

Each child was interviewed using the Conver-sa-tional Interview portion of the Motivation to Read Profile by Gambrell, Palmer, Codling, and Mazzoni (1996). The Conversational Interview consists of 14 questions that are related to reading narrative text, expository text, and reading in general [see Figure A]. Three questions are related to the reading of narrative text, three questions are related to the reading of expository text, and eight questions are related to general reading. We asked follow-up questions to provide greater depth to student responses.

Figure A
Motivation to Read Profile

Conversational Interview

Name _____ Date _____

A. Emphasis: Narrative text

Suggested prompt (designed to engage student in a natural conversation): I have been reading a good book … I was talking with … about it last night. I enjoy talking about good stories and books that I've been reading. Today I'd like to hear about what you have been reading.

1. Tell me about the most interesting story or book you have read this week (or even last week). Take a few minutes to think about it. (Wait time.) Now, tell me about the book or story.

   Probes: What else can you tell me? Is there anything else? _____
   _____
   _____
   _____
   _____
   _____
   _____

2. How did you know or find out about this story? _____
   _____
   _____

   ☐ assigned   ☐ in school
   ☐ chosen   ☐ out of school

3. Why was this story interesting to you? _____
   _____
   _____
   _____

B. Emphasis: Informational text

Suggested prompt (designed to engage student in a natural conversation): Often we read to find out about something or to learn about something. We read for information. For example, I remember a student of mine … who read a lot of books about … to find out as much as he/she could about…. Now, I'd like to hear about some of the informational reading you have been doing.

1. Think about something important that you learned recently, not from your teacher and not from television, but from a book or some other reading material. What did you read about? (Wait time.) Tell me about what you learned.

   Probes: What else could you tell me? Is there anything else? _____
   _____
   _____
   _____
   _____

(continued)

Figure A
Motivation to Read Profile (*Continued*)

2. How did you know or find out about this book/article? _____
_____
_____

☐ assigned   ☐ in school
☐ chosen   ☐ out of school

3. Why was this book (or article) important to you? _____
_____
_____
_____

C. Emphasis: General reading

1. Did you read anything at home yesterday? _____ What?
_____
_____

2. Do you have any books at school (in your desk/storage area/locker/book bag) today that you are reading?
_____ Tell me about them.
_____
_____
_____

3. Tell me about your favorite author.
_____
_____
_____

4. What do you think you have to learn to be a better reader?
_____
_____
_____

5. Do you know about any books right now that you'd like to read? Tell me about them.
_____
_____
_____

6. How did you find out about these books?
_____
_____
_____

7. What are some things that get you really excited about reading books?
_____
_____
_____

(continued)

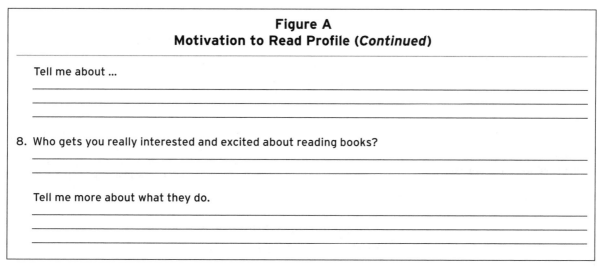

We organized and analyzed the data we collected in the Conversational Interviews using the constant comparative method introduced by Glaser and Strauss (1967). The constant comparative method of qualitative analysis allowed for the constant comparison of data. It involved comparing one incident with another incident to identify similarities and differences. We then coded the incidents into categories. Categories were changed, refined, and created throughout the analysis. The data were examined in this way to identify patterns and lead to the development of theory. Analysis of the data began with the first interview and continued simultaneously with the remainder of the data collection. Data collection was complete when new information was no longer uncovered and appropriate categories were identified. Several patterns emerged regarding children's motivation to read.

What Did the Children Say?

Our analysis of the data using the constant comparative method revealed several patterns, which we then placed into six categories. These six categories include factors that get children excited about reading narrative text, factors that get children excited about reading expository text, factors that get children excited about reading in general, sources of book referrals, sources of reading motivation, and actions of those who motivate children to read (see Figure 1).

Category 1: Factors That Get Children Excited About Reading Narrative Text

In the Conversational Interview, children were asked to talk about the most interesting story or book they have been reading recently and why the story was interesting to them. When discussing the narrative text they were reading, several factors that got them excited about reading narrative text arose. The most popular factors were personal interests, book characteristics, and choice. See Table 1 for the breakdown of raw data on narrative text.

Personal Interests. The frequent mention of personal interests indicated that children's reading motivation was influenced by their own interests. In the following comments, the children revealed that they found books interesting because of the books' relations to their personal interests:

"I like camping. They were fishing and stuff."

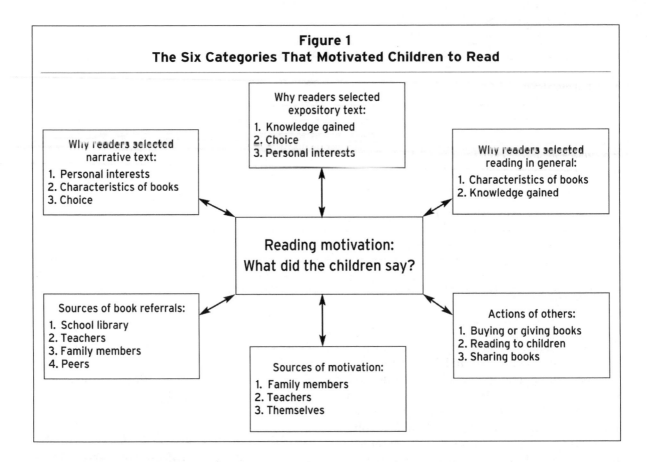

Figure 1
The Six Categories That Motivated Children to Read

Why readers selected expository text:
1. Knowledge gained
2. Choice
3. Personal interests

Why readers selected narrative text:
1. Personal interests
2. Characteristics of books
3. Choice

Why readers selected reading in general:
1. Characteristics of books
2. Knowledge gained

Reading motivation: What did the children say?

Sources of book referrals:
1. School library
2. Teachers
3. Family members
4. Peers

Sources of motivation:
1. Family members
2. Teachers
3. Themselves

Actions of others:
1. Buying or giving books
2. Reading to children
3. Sharing books

Table 1
Narrative Text: Influences on Interest

Factors Students Said Made Them Interested in Narrative Text	Number of Positive Student Responses for Each Factor (Total Population n = 16)
Knowledge gained	5
Similar personal experiences	5
Personal interests	14
Book characteristics	14
Choice	14

"It was about magic, and I like to read about magic."

"Because it is about a ferret, and I like ferrets. I like the way they chase little balls."

Characteristics of Books. When discussing narrative text, the children indicated that the characteristics of the books affected their motivation to read as well. Such things as exciting book covers, action-packed plots, and humor were frequently mentioned. The importance of the characteristics of the books was illustrated through the following types of responses.

"Because on the front cover it showed three kids, and they opened a box. The box had gold in it."

"It has funny stuff in there."

"The book seemed boring at first, but Oliver goes on a lot of adventures. The book keeps you wondering."

"Because the book had a lot of action in it, and it was funny."

Choice. The importance of choice was revealed throughout the interviews as children shared the books they were reading or had recently read. When sharing the narrative text they were reading, 84% of the children discussed books they had selected themselves, while only 16% discussed books that were assigned by the teachers. It appears the children were motivated to read when they were given an opportunity to decide what narrative text they would like to read. The following responses demonstrate the influence of choice:

"I found it in the school library."

"It is one I chose."

Category 2: Factors That Get Children Excited About Reading Expository Text

During the Conversational Interview, children were encouraged to think about something they had learned recently from a book or some other reading material. They were asked to share what they read about, what they learned, and why the book or article was important to them. When discussing expository text, the children's responses focused on the influence of the knowledge gained by reading the book, on the relationship between the book and their personal interests, and on choice. Based on the children's responses about why the expository texts were important to them, it appears that books they could read to gain knowledge, books they chose, and books related to their personal interests affected their motivation to read the most. See Table 2 for the breakdown on raw data about expository text.

Knowledge Gained. The children placed a great deal of importance on the information they could learn from reading informational books. They were excited to share facts and knowledge learned when reading expository text. Therefore, it seems the knowledge the children can gain from reading books positively affects their motivation to read, as the following examples show.

"I could learn about different animals. I see what they eat and what they look like."

"I can learn about different things like the states."

Table 2
Expository Text: Influences on Interest

Factors Students Said Made Them Interested in Narrative Text	Number of Positive Student Responses for Each Factor (Total Population $n = 16$)
Knowledge gained	13
Similar personal experiences	1
Personal interests	6
Book characteristics	4
Choice	13
Gift	1
Accelerated Reader book	1
No specific reason	1

"Because I did not know much about reptiles or animals."

Choice. The children also discussed texts they chose more frequently when they were discussing expository text they were reading or had recently read. Seventy-six percent of the children shared expository text that they had chosen themselves, and only 14% of the children shared expository text that had been assigned by the teacher. The remaining 10% could not share informational texts they had read. It appears the children were motivated to read when they were given an opportunity to decide which expository text they would like to read. The following responses reveal the effect that choice has on children's reading motivation.

"I chose the book. I got it from school."

"I chose it from the school library."

"I got it from the library at school. I picked it out myself."

Personal Interests. The children also placed a great deal of emphasis on expository text that was related to their personal interests. These responses concerning expository text supported the conclusion made from the children's responses about narrative text. The conclusion was that children's reading motivation is positively influenced by books that are related to their personal interests. The following comments show the influence of children's personal interests on their motivation to read:

> "I like dolphins. I think they are cool because they live in the ocean, and I like oceans."

> "It was important because I like different cultures."

> "Because it was about an Indian, and I am interested in Indians."

Category 3: Factors That Get Children Excited About Reading in General

After specifically discussing narrative and expository text, the children were asked questions focusing on reading in general. The children were given the opportunity to discuss other books they were reading and the things that got them excited about reading books in general. The conclusions that were made based on the responses dealing with narrative and expository text were supported by the children's responses when discussing reading in general. When discussing some of the factors that got them really excited about reading, characteristics of books and knowledge gained were patterns that repeatedly arose.

Characteristics of Books. Children enjoyed books that were funny or scary. They also chose books with great illustrations. The following responses given by the children support the conclusion that the characteristics of books had a positive effect on children's reading motivation.

> "The books, because I like them. The pictures—they are really funny."

> "When they are scary, funny, and fall stories. I like scary books because you wonder what is going to happen next.... I like funny stories because they make you laugh, and they are exciting to read. I like fall stories because they are about fall, and fall is not too hot or too cold...."

Knowledge Gained. The children also placed a great deal of importance on the information they could learn from reading books when discussing factors that got them excited about reading. They gained knowledge about many things that interested them such as travel. Thus, it seemed the knowledge children gained from reading books positively influenced their motivation to read, as the following comments show.

> "When I have not read the book before, and it has stuff about places where I have not been before. I want to find out about places you can go."

> "You can learn a lot of stuff from them."

Category 4: Sources of Book Referrals

Access to books is critical to the amount of reading children do and to their reading achievement (Gambrell & Marinak, 1997). Thus, it is valuable to examine more closely the ways in which children are exposed to books. When discussing reading in general, children were asked to share how they found out about the books they were currently reading or had recently read. While examining the ways children were exposed to books, several sources emerged, such as the school library, teachers, family members, and peers.

School Library. The importance of the school library was revealed throughout the interviews as children discussed how they found out or knew about the books they were reading. When discussing narrative and expository text, the children overwhelmingly reported that they found out about their books from the school library. Other libraries, such as the classroom library and the local or county library, were also mentioned but not as frequently. The children's responses indicated that exposure to the school library as well as to other libraries positively affected the children's motivation to read by introducing them to a variety of books.

When discussing the narrative text and the expository text they were reading, it is important to note that the children reported they found most of the books they read in the school library, but none of them referred to the school librarian as an influence in their responses. The children's repeated referral to the school library shows that the school library provided the children with a variety of books that interested them and motivated them to read. The children's omission of the school librarian also supports the fact that just having access to books facilitated their reading motivation. However, the frequent response involving the school library showed that school librarians could also have a more positive influence on children's reading motivation.

Teachers. The role the teacher plays in exposing children to books was also revealed during the interviews. When discussing the narrative text they were reading, the children frequently identified their teacher as the person who introduced books to them. The teacher was also mentioned when discussing expository text they were reading, but not as frequently. These responses highlighted the effect teachers can have on what children read and their reading motivation.

Family Members. Based on the children's responses regarding expository text, it can be concluded that family members can also greatly influence what children are currently reading and affect their reading motivation. During the interview, children reported that they found out about the expository text they were reading from various family members, such as their mothers, fathers, and cousins. It is important to note, however, that the children most frequently responded that their mother had the greatest influence on their reading choices. Various family members were also referred to when the children were describing the narrative text they were reading, but the responses were not as frequent as when discussing expository text. The children's frequent mention of family members, especially their mothers, showed that family had a positive effect on children's reading motivation by exposing them to books.

Peers. Although teachers and family were mentioned, the children most frequently responded that they had found out about books they wanted to read from their friends. This finding supports the fact that children are motivated to read by sharing books with one another.

Category 5: Sources of Motivation

When examining children's reading motivation, it is important to discover not only who *exposes* them to books but also who actually *motivates* them to read. When children were asked who got them interested in and excited about reading, the interviews revealed that the children's interest in and excitement about reading was sparked by various individuals including family members (especially mothers), teachers, and themselves.

Family Members. Once again, the children illustrated the importance of family in the area of reading motivation. The most frequent response to the question, "Who gets you interested in and excited about reading?" was their mothers. However, it is necessary to point out that other family members, such as grandmothers, siblings, and so on, were also mentioned by the children, supporting the conclusion that a variety of family members influenced children's motivation to read.

Teachers. Like the family, the teacher was a frequent response when asked, "Who gets you excited about reading?" This result showed yet again the role teachers play in children's reading motivation.

Themselves. The children also cited themselves as a source of motivation. They attributed their desire to read to their own actions. By referring to themselves as a source of motivation, the children supported the idea that their interest in reading fostered their own motivation. The effect of the children's own desire to read on their reading motivation was demonstrated through the following examples.

"Nobody gets me excited. I just like to read books."

"Nobody I know of. I just read them because I like to."

"Nobody really gets me excited about reading books because I read them because I like reading books."

Category 6: Actions of Family Members, Teachers, and Peers

After discovering who motivated the children to read, it was critical to examine the actions of these individuals. Therefore, we followed up the question about who gets them excited by asking what the individuals did to excite the children and interest them in reading. Three themes that emerged were buying or giving children books, reading to them, and sharing books with them. The two most (and equally) frequent responses were buying or giving the children books and reading to them.

Buying or Giving Children Books. Conversational Interviews showed that children valued receiving books, and that the action of giving or buying books for children motivated them to read. They enjoyed receiving books for their birthdays and for holidays, as well as other occasions.

Reading to Children. Along with the value of book giving, the value of reading to children emerged. Many of the children revealed that they enjoyed being read to by others. This finding highlighted the importance of reading to children regardless of their age.

Sharing Books. Finally, the children discussed the action of sharing books. The children enjoyed being told about books others were reading. They mentioned both formal and informal methods of sharing, such as book reports and informal discussions with peers. This was shown repeatedly by responses as simple as, "I like it when they tell me about what they are reading."

Recommendations for the Classroom Teacher

Based on the data collected during the Conversational Interviews, it is recommended that the following five approaches be used to increase children's desire to read: self-selection, attention to characteristics of books, personal interests, access to books, and active involvement of others.

Self-Selection

One way to increase children's desire to read is to let them choose their own books. During the Conversational Interview, children frequently discussed books they had chosen themselves. This finding highlighted the importance of choice when attempting to positively affect children's reading motivation. Therefore, it is recommended that teachers not only give children the opportunity to choose the books they would like to read but also allot time during the school day to read them. We recommend two activities for classroom teachers to help students in this self-discovery process.

Three-Piece Kits. The first idea is for teachers to create three-piece kits about different topics. For example, if the class is studying dolphins, then the teacher can collect an expository book, a narrative book, and a poem (all connected to the topic of dolphins) in a plastic bag labeled "Dolphins." It is important to include all three types of writing for students to explore. Kits can be added to the classroom library as new topics are studied. Students can discuss their preferences with peers or with the teacher during individual reading conferences.

Self-Discovery Bookmarks. In this activity, teachers give students bookmarks with a checklist of ideas and suggestions for reading choices by categories based on genres and personal interests. Students can take these bookmarks to the library and use them as a reminder of the types of books they might want to "discover" and check out. There is a sample in Figure 2 for teachers to copy and laminate for durability.

Attention to Characteristics of Books

In this study, two factors related to the characteristics of books appeared to influence children's interest in books and their motivation to read. These factors included characteristics of narrative books and knowledge gained by reading expository books. Thus, it is recommended that teachers consider these factors when selecting books for their classrooms. Teachers need to provide a variety of books that have different characteristics that children will desire to read—books that are scary or funny or have good illustrations. Although the children discussed narrative text more often than expository text, they frequently reported that a book was important to them because they could learn something from the book. This finding demonstrates the importance of offering expository text to children as well as narrative text when trying to increase their reading motivation.

One suggestion we have for increasing exposure to a variety of books is an activity we call Librarians Unleashed. Teachers collect all of the books students have read during the month of sustained silent reading. These books can be collected in a large box. On the last day of the month, the books are emptied onto the middle of the floor. (It should be an impressive pile for the students to admire.) Next, the students must become little librarians as they determine five categories in which to sort the pile of books they have read. Students usually have a lively discussion about the characteristics of the books they have read and the categories into which they should be sorted. Any reasonable category should be accepted as long as several books can be connected to the label, for example, Books That Made Me Laugh. The books are then distributed into five baskets and labeled by the students. Teachers can make the baskets available for sustained silent reading during the new month and then repeat the process. However, we recommend that the categories not be repeated for two consecutive months.

Figure 2
Self-Discovery Bookmark

Self-discovery bookmark

Name _____

○ Poetry
○ Expository books about
   • Animals
   • Space/planets
   • History
   • Trees/plants
   • Countries
   • Oceans/seas
   • _____
   • _____
   • _____

○ Narrative books
   • Picture books
   • Chapter books
   • Storybooks (animals)
   • Storybooks (people)
   • Mysteries
   • Funny storybooks
   • Fables
   • Fairy tales
   • Historical fiction
   • _____
   • _____
   • _____

Personal Interests

The children also chose books because they were related to their own personal interests. It is important for teachers to provide books on many different topics that match the interests of their students. Based on these themes regarding factors that influence children's interest in books, we recommend that teachers assess children's interests at the beginning and throughout the school year through reading conferences and interest inventories. We also suggest that teachers provide a variety of narrative and expository texts that address the various interests of their students. Teachers may want to consider sorting books and placing them in baskets based on their content (e.g., mystery books, animal books, and humorous books). Teachers should also rotate special book collections, such as author or themed studies, throughout the year. Another idea we suggest is a variation of Book Clubs or literature circles called Genre Gurus. Students participate in groups based on the genre they have chosen to read. For example, five students have each read a different fairy tale. In their group, the discussion revolves around the genre, not the story line of the fairy tales: How did each book fit into the genre? How are the books alike? How are they different? What did we learn about fairy tales by reading these books? Students should create a visual to share their newfound knowledge about fairy tales with the rest of the class.

Access to Books

Because children indicated that access to books positively affected their reading motivation, it is recommended that teachers not only provide extensive classroom libraries, but also that they allow students frequent access to school libraries. In this study, the children got a majority of the books they were reading or had read from the school library. Because children were getting many of the books from the school library, it is recommended that teachers give them many opportunities to go to the school library, and that school librarians establish a flexible schedule as well as an assigned schedule for classrooms. We recommend that teachers create a pass called License to Look. This license can be used during flexible library visiting times. When students finish their work early, they can use the pass to visit the library and browse for books.

The library should also provide a variety of narrative and expository books that address the interests of the children. Teachers should give librarians a list of one or two classroom topics for each week and ask the librarian to spend the first few minutes of class library time sharing some of the library resources available, being sure to include expository text, narrative text, and poetry.

Likewise, we recommend that teachers provide families access to books through inexpensive book clubs and the use of take-home literacy bags that include books for parents and children to read together, as well as interactive games, crafts, and activities that involve the books. Teachers should also encourage family members to take children on regular visits to the local library and to develop the children's personal home libraries. One idea we have used is called Saturday Read-Ins. This is an activity that can be done monthly and will help families support reading for their child. Enlist the help of the school principal and the librarian to provide a casual time on Saturday morning for children and their families to come to the library to find books and read them. Story time could be a feature. Healthy snacks could also be served. (This activity could be done one day after school instead of Saturday, again on a monthly basis.)

Active Involvement of Others

The students revealed that they were motivated to read when people read to them and when people shared what they were reading with them. Giving students books, reading to them, and sharing books with them are all practices that are recommended. Based on the frequent mention of these practices by students when asked to discuss what others do to motivate them to read, it is recommended that teachers spend time daily reading aloud to them, and that teachers allow many opportunities for them to share what they are reading with one another. Because school libraries are one of the most important resources for books, it is suggested that teachers encourage the school librarian to read to students during library time and give them an opportunity to share books they are reading with one another.

The influence of family, especially mothers, was demonstrated throughout the Conversational Interviews. Therefore, we recommend that teachers introduce family members to practices that will increase their children's reading motivation.

These practices include reading aloud to their children, sharing with their children the books they are reading, and buying or giving their children books. Best practices in reading can be modeled by teachers during open houses, parent/teacher organization meetings, or parent workshops. Tips such as the following one can also be shared with parents in newsletters.

> Reading tip of the week: Before you read a book with your child, look at the cover together and ask your child to predict what the book will be about. Ask, "What do you think this book will be about?" As you read together, check your prediction with the story and make any needed changes to your prediction.

Finally, it is recommended that teachers take advantage of the influence that peers have on children's reading motivation. The children in this study demonstrated the effect their peers have on their reading motivation by frequently mentioning them when asked how they found out about a book and when asked who motivated them to read. We suggest that teachers provide opportunities for classmates to share what they are reading with one another. This sharing can occur through book swaps (students bring in a used book to trade for another used book collected in a basket or on a shelf), literature circles, and informal discussions about the books they are reading. The following activities are some other recommendations for peer sharing of books.

- Quotable Quips: After reading a book, students are asked to write a one-sentence critique similar to those found on book jackets of adult paperbacks. (Teachers should share appropriate samples from real books and model examples after class read-alouds.) Student responses can be written on a sheet stapled inside the front cover of the book. Each critic (reader) adds his or her Quotable Quip to the running commentary. These can be used by students to help select books to read.
- Critic's Chair: After a book has been read, a critic can take the chair and share opinions about the book—both positive praise

and constructive criticism. For variation, teachers can have two students with different opinions about a book go head to head in an open discussion. This debate will give students a forum to discuss books and encourage other students in the class to read the book being discussed.

Motivation Increases Reading Achievement

Children who are motivated to read will spend more time reading (Guthrie et al., 1999; Morrow, 1992; Wigfield & Guthrie, 1997), and research supports the positive effect of increased reading on reading achievement (Mazzoni, Gambrell, & Korkeamaki, 1999; Taylor, Frye, & Maruyama, 1990) as well as the likelihood of becoming life-long readers (Morrow, 1992; Wang & Guthrie, 2004).

Based on our findings in this study, we have made five recommendations for motivating students in the classroom: self-selection, attention to characteristics of books, personal interests, access to books, and active involvement of others. We think these suggestions will help increase children's motivation to read. We would much rather hear positive comments about reading such as the following ones from students in our study: "Books are interesting and cool," and "I love to read a good story."

References
Deci, E.L. (1971). Effects of externally mediated rewards on intrinsic motivation. *Journal of Personality and Social Psychology, 18,* 105–115.
Deci, E.L. (1972a). The effects of contingent and noncontingent rewards and controls on intrinsic motivation. *Organizational Behavior and Human Performance, 8,* 217–229.
Deci, E.L. (1972b). Intrinsic motivation, extrinsic reinforcement, and inequity. *Journal of Personality and Social Psychology, 22,* 113–120.
Deci, E.L., & Ryan, R.M. (1985). *Intrinsic motivation and self-determination in human behavior.* New York: Plenum.
Dweck, C.S., & Elliott, E.S. (1983). Achievement motivation. In P.H. Mussen & E.M. Heatherington (Eds.), *Handbook of child psychology: Socialization,*

personality, and social development (pp. 643–691). New York: Wiley.

Eccles, J.S., Wigfield, A., & Schiefele, U. (1998). Motivation to succeed. In W. Damon & N. Eisenberg (Eds.), *Handbook of child psychology: Socialization, personality, and social development* (pp. 601–642). New York: Wiley.

Gambrell, L.B. (1995). Motivation matters. In W. Linek & E. Sturtevant (Eds.), *Generations of literacy: Seventeenth yearbook of the College Reading Association* (pp. 2–24). Harrisonburg, VA: College Reading Association.

Gambrell, L.B. (1996). Creating classroom cultures that foster reading motivation. *The Reading Teacher, 50,* 14–25.

Gambrell, L.B., & Marinak, B.A. (1997). Incentives and intrinsic motivation to read. In J.T. Guthrie & A. Wigfield (Eds.), *Reading engagement: Motivating readers through integrated instruction* (pp. 205–217). Newark, DE: International Reading Association.

Gambrell, L.B., Palmer, B.M., Codling, R.M., & Mazzoni, S.A. (1996). Assessing motivation to read. *The Reading Teacher, 49,* 518–533.

Glaser, B.G., & Strauss, A.L. (1967). *The discovery of grounded theory.* Hawthorne, NY: Aldine de Gruyter.

Guthrie, J.T., & Wigfield, A. (2000). Engagement and motivation in reading. In M.L. Kamil, P.B. Mosenthal, P.D. Pearson, & R. Barr (Eds.), *Handbook of reading research* (Vol. 3; pp. 403–422). Mahwah, NJ: Erlbaum.

Guthrie, J.T., Wigfield, A., Metsala, J., & Cox, K. (1999). Motivational and cognitive predictors of text comprehension and reading amount. *Scientific Studies of Reading, 3,* 231–256.

Kohn, A. (1993). Rewards versus learning: A response to Paul Chance. *Phi Delta Kappan, 74,* 783–787.

Lepper, M.R., & Greene, D. (1975). Turning play into work: Effects of adult surveillance and extrinsic rewards on children's intrinsic motivation. *Journal of Personality and Social Psychology, 31,* 479–486.

Lepper, M.R., Greene, D., & Nisbett, R.E. (1973). Understanding children's intrinsic interest with extrinsic rewards. *Journal of Personality and Social Psychology, 28*(1), 129–137.

Loveland, K.K., & Olley, J.G. (1979). The effect of external reward on interest and quality of task performance in children of high and low intrinsic motivation. *Child Development, 50,* 1207–1210.

Mazzoni, S.A., Gambrell, L.B., & Korkeamaki, R.L. (1999). A cross-cultural perspective of early literacy motivation. *Reading Psychology, 20,* 237–253.

McCombs, B.L. (1989). Self-regulated learning and academic achievement: A phenomenological view. In B.J. Zimmerman & D.H. Schunk (Eds.), *Self-regulated learning and achievement: Theory, research, and practice* (pp. 51–82). New York: Springer-Verlag.

McQuillan, J. (1997). The effects of incentives on reading. *Reading Research and Instruction, 36*(2), 111–125.

Miller, S.D., & Meece, J.L. (1997). Enhancing elementary students' motivation to read and write: A classroom intervention study. *Journal of Educational Research, 97,* 286–300.

Morrow, L.M. (1992). The impact of a literature-based program on literacy achievement, use of literature, and attitudes of children from minority backgrounds. *Reading Research Quarterly, 27,* 250–275.

National Institute of Child Health and Human Development. (2000). *Report of the National Reading Panel. Teaching children to read: An evidence-based assessment of the scientific research literature on reading and its implications for reading instruction* (NIH Publication No. 00-4769). Washington, DC: U.S. Government Printing Office.

O'Flahavan, J., Gambrell, L.B., Guthrie, J., Stahl, S., & Alvermann, D. (1992, August/September). Poll results guide activities of research center. *Reading Today,* p. 12.

Oldfather, P. (1993). What students say about motivating experiences in a whole language classroom. *The Reading Teacher, 46,* 672–681.

Taylor, B.M., Frye, B.J., & Maruyama, G.M. (1990). Time spent reading and reading growth. *American Educational Research Journal, 27,* 351–362.

Veenman, S. (1984). Perceived problems of beginning teachers. *Review of Educational Research, 54*(2), 143–178.

Wang, J.H., & Guthrie, J.T. (2004). Modeling the effects of intrinsic motivation, extrinsic motivation, amount of reading, and past reading achievement on text comprehension between U.S. and Chinese students. *Reading Research Quarterly, 39,* 162–186.

Wigfield, A., & Guthrie, J.T. (1997). Relations of children's motivation for reading to the amount and breadth of their reading. *Journal of Educational Psychology, 89,* 420–432.

Wigfield, A., Eccles, J.S., Yoon, K.S., Harold, R.D., Arbreton, A., Freedman-Doan, K., et al. (1997). Change in children's competence beliefs and subjective task values across the elementary school years: A 3-year study. *Journal of Educational Psychology, 89,* 451–469.

Engagement Activities

In Your Classroom
Interview the students in your class using the Conversational Interview from the Motivation to Read Profile (Figure A). What do your students say about what motivates them to read? How can you incorporate their beliefs and desires into your classroom reading program?

With Your Colleagues
How can you and your colleagues use the self-discovery bookmark and three-piece kit to help students select books? Discuss ways you can organize your literacy instruction to include daily read-alouds and provide students time to discuss what they are reading with one another.

Further Reading
Reynolds, P., & Symons, S. (2001). Motivational variables and children's text search. *Journal of Educational Psychology, 93*(1), 14–22.

This study investigated the effects of choice and response activity (theme boards and worksheets) on children's comprehension of informational text. The results indicate that choice and context affect how children engage with informational material. Specifically, children who were given a choice of books located information more quickly and used more efficient strategies to search than children who were not given a choice. In addition, children who created theme boards (versus recording answers on a worksheet) were more efficient in their search for information.

Crafting Instruction for Motivation and Engagement

"Excellent Reading Teachers," a position statement from the International Reading Association, opens this section to remind us that crafting instruction with motivation in mind is a recognized quality of excellence in teaching. The five articles that follow it discuss the essential elements of motivating instruction. "Intrinsic Motivation and Rewards: What Sustains Young Children's Engagement With Text?" by Barbara A. Marinak and Linda B. Gambrell focuses on the effects of different types of rewards and incentives, while in "How Literacy Tasks Influence Children's Motivation for Literacy," Julianne Turner and Scott G. Paris discuss the nature of tasks that students are asked to complete. Elaborating on tasks and activities, Mary Ryan's "Engaging Middle Years Students: Literacy Projects That Matter" offers suggestions for creating relevant reading instruction for ado-

lescents, and James F. Baumann, Helene Hooten, and Patricia White present ideas for effectively using literature to keep students engaged in meaningful reading activities in their article "Teaching Comprehension Through Literature: A Teacher-Research Project to Develop Fifth Graders' Reading Strategies and Motivation."

This section concludes with "Growth of Literacy Engagement: Changes in Motivations and Strategies During Concept-Oriented Reading Instruction," a research report on Concept-Oriented Reading Instruction by John T. Guthrie and his colleagues (abridged here with his kind permission) that highlights the procedural aspects of this well-researched model for creating reading engagement in the content areas.

Activities for discussion and engagement follow each article, along with additional recommended readings.

Excellent Reading Teachers

Every child deserves excellent reading teachers because teachers make a difference in children's reading achievement and motivation to read.

This position statement provides a research-based description of the distinguishing qualities of excellent classroom reading teachers. Excellent reading teachers share several critical qualities of knowledge and practice:

1. They understand reading and writing development, and believe all children can learn to read and write.

2. They continually assess children's individual progress and relate reading instruction to children's previous experiences.

3. They know a variety of ways to teach reading, when to use each method, and how to combine the methods into an effective instructional program.

4. They offer a variety of materials and texts for children to read.

5. They use flexible grouping strategies to tailor instruction to individual students.

6. They are good reading "coaches" (that is, they provide help strategically).

(See the chart at the end of this piece for resources that address each of these characteristics.)

In addition, excellent reading teachers share many of the characteristics of good teachers in general. They have strong content and pedagogical knowledge, manage classrooms so that there is a high rate of engagement, use strong motivation strategies that encourage independent learning, have high expectations for children's achievement, and help children who are having difficulty.

What Evidence Is There That Good Reading Teachers Have a Positive Effect on Children's Reading Achievement and Motivation to Read?

Teachers make a difference. There is a growing body of evidence that documents teacher effects on children's reading achievement scores (Jordan, Mendro, Weerasinghe, & Dallas Public Schools, 1997; Sanders & Rivers, 1996; Wright, Horn, & Sanders, 1997). Teacher effectiveness—which can be measured as scores on teacher proficiency tests (Ferguson, 1991), past records of students' improved scores, teachers' level of education, type of appointment (tenured, probationary, substitute), and years of experience (Armour, Clay, Bruno, & Allend, 1990)—is strongly correlated with children's reading achievement. Moreover, teachers have strong effects on children's motivation to read (Ruddell, 1995; Skinner & Belmont, 1993).

What Do Excellent Reading Teachers Know About Reading Development?

Excellent reading teachers know that reading development begins well before children enter school and continues throughout a child's school career. They understand the definition of reading as a complex system of deriving meaning from print that requires all of the following:

- the development and maintenance of a motivation to read
- the development of appropriate active strategies to construct meaning from print

Reprinted from International Reading Association. (2000). *Excellent reading teachers* (Position statement). Newark, DE: Author.

- sufficient background information and vocabulary to foster reading comprehension
- the ability to read fluently
- the ability to decode unfamiliar words
- the skills and knowledge to understand how phonemes or speech sounds are connected to print

(International Reading Association, 1999; see also Snow, Burns, & Griffin, 1998)

Excellent teachers understand that all components of reading influence every stage of reading, but they also realize that the balance of instruction related to these components shifts across the developmental span and shifts for individual children. Excellent teachers understand how reading and writing development are related, and they effectively integrate instruction to take advantage of the child's development in both areas. They are familiar with the sequence of children's reading development. They believe that all children can learn to read and write.

How Do Excellent Reading Teachers Assess Student Progress?

Excellent reading teachers are familiar with a wide range of assessment techniques, ranging from standardized group achievement tests to informal assessment techniques that they use daily in the classroom. They use the information from standardized group measures as one source of information about children's reading progress, recognizing that standardized group achievement tests can be valid and reliable indicators of group performance but can provide misleading information about individual performance. They are well aware that critical judgments about children's progress must draw from information from a variety of sources, and they do not make critical instructional decisions based on any single measure.

Excellent reading teachers are constantly observing children as they go about their daily work. They understand that involving children in self-evaluation has both cognitive and motivational benefits. In the classroom, these teachers use a wide variety of assessment tools, including conferences with students, analyses of samples of children's reading and writing, running records and informal reading inventories, anecdotal records of children's performance, observation checklists, and other similar tools. They are familiar with each child's instructional history and home literacy background. From their observations and the child's own self-evaluations, they draw knowledge of the child's reading development, and they can relate that development to relevant standards. They use this knowledge for planning instruction that is responsive to children's needs.

What Do Excellent Reading Teachers Know About Instructional Methods and How to Combine Them to Meet the Needs of the Children They Teach?

Excellent reading teachers know a wide variety of instructional philosophies, methods, and strategies. They understand that excellent reading instruction addresses all the essential elements of reading. They are aware that instructional strategies vary along many dimensions, including the component of reading targeted by the instruction (for example, pronouncing words, understanding text, building motivation), the degree to which the instruction is teacher- or student-directed, and the degree to which the instruction is explicit or implicit. They understand that children vary in their responses to different types of instruction, and they select the most efficient combination of instructional strategies to serve the children in their classrooms. They know early intervention techniques and ensure that children get the help they need as soon as the need becomes apparent. For example, in a single middle grade classroom, teachers have children who still recognize very few words and struggle with decoding, children who are fluent and avid readers who can and do read everything they get their hands on, and children who are fluent decoders but struggle with comprehension and motivation. In the case of a struggling reader, excellent reading teachers know enough about the child and the child's instructional history to provide access to very easy books on topics studied by the class. The teacher can work with similar children in a small group to build sight vocabulary and decoding fluency, and the teacher can provide appropriate accommodations so that these children can benefit from comprehension instruction and continue to learn critical content despite their reading difficulties.

What Kinds of Texts and Reading Materials Do Excellent Reading Teachers Use in Their Classrooms?

Excellent reading teachers include a variety of reading materials in their classrooms. Sometimes they rely on one or several reading series as the anchor of their reading program, but they also have supplemental materials and rich classroom libraries that contain at least seven books per child. They read to their students, and they provide time in class for children to read independently. They are aware of the reading abilities and interests of the children, and they constantly provide a selection of books that will be both interesting to the children and within the children's reading capabilities. Excellent reading teachers are familiar with children's literature. They include a wide variety of fiction and nonfiction genres (such as storybooks, novels, biographies, magazines, and poetry). Excellent reading teachers also use school and public libraries to ensure children's access to appropriate books.

How Do Excellent Reading Teachers Organize Their Classrooms for Instruction?

Excellent reading teachers organize their classrooms so that schedules are predictable and children know what is expected of them in a variety of activities throughout the instructional day. They use flexible grouping strategies. When

there is new and difficult information to convey that most of the class needs to learn, excellent reading teachers use large-group, direct, explicit instruction. They model the focal strategy or skill, demonstrate how and when to use it, and explain why it is important. They guide the children in their use of the skill or strategy, gradually diminishing support and assistance and requiring students to assume greater responsibility as the children become more skilled. They provide opportunities for individual practice and observe children in their use of the skill or strategy. During practice activities, they observe children closely, intervening when necessary with a question or comment that moves children forward. They also know which children will benefit from all elements of a direct instruction lesson in a particular skill or strategy and which children will need only a brief period of guided instruction or review followed by independent practice. They use efficient grouping practices to accommodate these differences.

Excellent reading teachers also understand that large-group, direct instruction is time-consuming and costly and that, often, many children in the class will not benefit from this instruction. They know when to organize children in large groups for direct, explicit instruction, when small-group or individual instruction is more appropriate, and when children will learn more efficiently on their own. They help children advance in reading by differentiating the type of instruction, the degree of support, and the amount of practice children receive. They do not allow children to spend time learning what they already know and can do.

How Do Excellent Reading Teachers Interact With Children?

Excellent reading teachers interact with individual children frequently in the course of their daily teaching activities. As they help children solve problems or practice new skills and strategies, they "coach" or "scaffold" children by providing help at strategic moments. They are skilled at observing children's performance and using informal interactions to call children's attention to important aspects of what they are learning and doing. They often help children with a difficult part of the task so that the children can move forward to complete the task successfully. It is important to note that such teaching is neither incidental or unsystematic. Excellent reading teachers know where their children are in reading development and they know the likely next steps. They help children take these steps by providing just the right amount of help at just the right time.

Recommendations for Developing Excellence in Reading Instruction

- Teachers must view themselves as lifelong learners and continually strive to improve their practice.

- Administrators must be instructional leaders who support teachers' efforts to improve reading instruction.

- Teacher educators must provide both a solid knowledge base and extensive supervised practice to prepare excellent beginning reading teachers.

- Legislators and policy makers must understand the complex role of the teacher in providing reading instruction and ensure that teachers have the resources and support they need to teach reading. Legislators and policy makers should not impose one-size-fits-all mandates

- Parents, community members, and teachers must work in partnership to assure that children value reading and have many opportunities to read outside of school.

References

Anders, P.L., Hoffman, J.V., & Duffy, G.G. (2000). Teaching teachers to teach reading: Paradigm shifts, persistent problems, and challenges. In M.L. Kamil, P.B. Mosenthal, P.D. Pearson, & R. Barr (Eds.), *Handbook of Reading Research: Volume III*. Mahwah, NJ: Erlbaum.

Armour, T.C., Clay, C., Bruno, K., & Allen, B.A. (1990). *An outlier study of elementary and middle schools in New York City: Final report*. New York: New York City Board of Education.

Briggs, K.L., & Thomas, K. (1997). *Patterns of success: Successful pathways to elementary literacy in Texas spotlight schools*. Austin, TX: Texas Center for Educational Research.

Brophy, J. (1982). Successful teaching strategies for the inner-city child. *Phi Delta Kappan, 63*, 527–530.

Duffy, G.G., Roehler, L.R., & Herrmann, B.A. (1988). Modeling mental processes helps poor readers become strategic readers. *The Reading Teacher, 41*, 762–767.

Ferguson, R. (1991). Paying for public education: New evidence on how and why money matters. *Harvard Journal on Legislation, 28*, 465–498.

Haberman, M. (1995). *Star teachers of children of poverty*. West Lafayette, IN: Kappa Delta Pi.

Hoffman, J., & Pearson, P.D. (1999). *What your grandmother's teacher didn't know that your granddaughter's teacher should*. Austin, TX: University of Texas at Austin.

International Reading Association. (1999). *Using multiple methods of beginning reading instruction: A position statement of the International Reading Association*. Newark, DE: Author.

Jordan, H.R., Mendro, R.L., Weeringhe, D., & Dallas Public Schools. (1997). *Teacher effects on longitudinal student achievement*. Presentation at the CREATE Annual Meeting, Indianapolis, IN.

Knapp, M.S. (1995). *Teaching for meaning in high poverty classrooms*. New York: Teachers College Press.

Ladson-Billings, G. (1994). *The dreamkeepers: Successful teachers of African American children*. San Francisco: Jossey-Bass.

Metsala, J.L. (1997). Effective primary-grades literacy instruction = Balanced literacy instruction. *The Reading Teacher, 50*, 518–521.

Moll, L. (1988). Some key issues in teaching Latino students. *Language Arts, 65*, 465–472.

Pederson, E., Faucher, T.A., & Eaton, W.W. (1978). A new perspective on the effects of first-grade teachers on children's subsequent adult status. *Harvard Educational Review, 48*, 1–31.

Pressley, M., Rankin, J., & Yokoi, L. (1996). A survey of instructional practice of primary teachers nominated as effective in promoting literacy. *The Elementary School Journal, 96*, 363–384.

Ruddell, R.B. (1995). Those influential literacy teachers: Meaning negotiators and motivation builders. *The Reading Teacher, 48*, 454–463.

Sanders, W.L., & Rivers, J.C. (1996). *Cumulative and residual effects of teachers on future student academic achievement: Research progress report*. Knoxville, TN: University of Tennessee Value-Added Research and Assessment Center.

Skinner, E.A., & Belmont, M.J. (1993). Motivation in the classroom: Reciprocal effects of teacher behavior and student engagement across the school year. *Journal of Educational Psychology, 85*, 571–581.

Snow, C.E., Burns, M.S., & Griffin, P. (Eds.). (1998). *Preventing reading difficulties in young children.* Washington, DC: National Academy Press.

Sweet, A.P., Guthrie, J.T., & Ng, M.M. (1998). Teacher perception and student reading motivation. *Journal of Educational Psychology, 90,* 210–223.

Taylor, B.M., Pearson, P.D., Clark, K.F., & Walpole, S. (1999). *Beating the odds in teaching all children to read.* Ann Arbor, MI: Center for the Improvement of Early Reading Achievement.

Teddlie, C., & Stringfield, S. (1993). *Schools make a difference: Lessons learned from a 10-year study of school effects.* New York: Teachers College Press.

Tharp, R.G. (1997). *The five generic principles: Current knowledge about effective education of at-risk students.* Santa Cruz, CA: Center for Research on Education Diversity and Excellence, University of California.

Thomas, K.F., & Barksdale-Ladd, M.A. (1995). Effective literacy classrooms: Teachers and students exploring literacy together. In K.A. Hinchman, D.J. Leu, & C.K. Kinzer, (Eds.), *Perspectives on literacy research and practice* (Forty-fourth Yearbook of the National Reading Conference). Chicago: National Reading Conference.

Wharton-McDonald, R., Pressley, M., & Hampston, J.M. (1998). Literacy instruction in nine first-grade classrooms: Teacher characteristics and student achievement. *The Elementary School Journal, 99,* 101–128.

Wright, P.S., Horn, S.P., & Sanders, W.L. (1997). Teacher and classroom context effects on student achievement: Implications for teacher evaluation. *Journal of Personnel Evaluation in Education, 11,* 57–67.

Characteristics of Excellent Reading Teachers: Research Support

Article	1	2	3	4	5	6
Anders, P.L., Hoffman, J.V., & Duffy, G.G. (2000)	p. 7, p. 16					p. 6
Briggs, K.L., & Thomas, K. (1997)		p. 27, p. 28, p. 33		p. 8, p. 9	p. 14	
Brophy, J. (1982)		p. 529	p. 527		p. 529	p. 527
Duffy, G.G., Roehler, L.R., & Herrmann, B.A. (1988)	p. 762	p. 763	p. 766			p. 766
Haberman, M. (1995)		p. 19				p. 19, p. 20, p. 86
Hoffman, J., & Pearson, P.D. (1999)		p. 16	p. 17			
Knapp, M.S. (1995)	p. 127, p. 128	p. 126	pp. 127-8, pp. 130-3, pp. 136-7, p. 142			
Ladson-Billings, G. (1994)	p. 123	p. 124				p. 124
Metsala, J.L. (1997)	p. 520	p. 519	p. 519, p. 520	p. 519	p. 519	p. 520
Moll, L. (1988)	p. 466, p. 468	p. 469		p. 468		p. 468
Pederson, E., Faucher, T.A., & Eaton, W.W. (1978)	p. 22					
Pressley, M., Rankin, J., & Yokoi, L. (1996)	p. 371, p. 375, p. 377				p. 373	

(continued)

Characteristics of Excellent Reading Teachers: Research Support (*Continued*)

Article	1	2	3	4	5	6
Ruddell, R.B. (1995)	p. 456	p. 455	p. 455, p. 456		p. 455	
Sweet, A.P., Guthrie, J.T., & Ng, M.M. (1998)	p. 217, p. 220	p. 218, p. 220	p. 215, p. 217, p. 220			
Taylor, B.M., Pearson, P.D., Clark, K.F., & Walpole, S. (1999)	p. 3	p. 45, p. 46	p. 3	pp. 44-6	p. 11	
Teddlie, C., & Stringfield, S. (1993)	p. 192					
Tharp, R.G. (1997)		p. 6	p. 6			p. 5
Thomas, K.F. & Barksdale-Ladd, M.A. (1995)		p. 171, p. 172	p. 171, p. 172, pp. 176-7	p. 173		
Wharton-McDonald, R., Pressley, M., & Hampston, J.M. (1998)	p. 119		p. 111, p. 112	p. 112		p. 116

Engagement Activities

In Your Classroom
Teachers can strongly influence reading motivation in their classrooms. To do so, you need information about each student's motivation to read. How can you incorporate observations and conversations about motivation while assessing students' reading?

With Your Colleagues
How can you and your colleagues increase the variety of reading materials available to students? For example, how can your classroom library and your school library be diversified to include different genres (fiction, nonfiction, poetry) in a variety of forms (picture books, comic books, short chapter books, graphic novels, newspapers, magazines, and so on)?

Further Reading
Sweet, A.P., Guthrie, J.T., & Ng, M.M. (1998). Teacher perceptions and student reading motivation. *Journal of Educational Psychology*, 90(2), 210–223.

This study examined teacher perception of students' intrinsic motivations for reading. According to the findings, teachers believe that students who take ownership of their literacy development grow more rapidly in knowledge and skills. To encourage this growth, effective teachers provide choices, interesting tasks, and cooperative activities that involve books.

Intrinsic Motivation and Rewards: What Sustains Young Children's Engagement With Text?

Barbara A. Marinak and Linda B. Gambrell

Most educators agree that motivation plays a central role in literacy development. Although phonemic awareness, phonics, vocabulary, fluency, and comprehension allow students to be skillful and strategic readers, without the intrinsic motivation to read, students may never reach their full potential as literacy learners. Many teachers voice concern about students who do not appear to be motivated to read (Hidi & Harackiewicz, 2000). According to a survey conducted by Fawson and Moore (1999), 95% of elementary teachers use some type of reward system in an effort to develop students' intrinsic motivation to read.

After five decades of intensive research, questions remain about the effect of extrinsic rewards on intrinsic motivation. Research suggests that it is not a question of whether rewards enhance or undermine intrinsic motivation (Cameron & Pierce, 1994; Deci, Koestner, & Ryan, 1999a), but rather under what conditions rewards undermine intrinsic motivation (Cameron, 2001; Deci, Koestner, & Ryan, 2001). A number of studies (Condry, 1977; McLoyd, 1979), including several meta-analyses (Cameron & Pierce, 1994; Deci, Koestner, & Ryan, 1999b; Eisenberger & Cameron, 1996; Tang & Hall, 1995; Wiersma, 1992), have examined the differential effects of variables such as interest and reward value on intrinsic motivation. Findings that have consistently emerged from these studies include the following: being rewarded for engaging in a low interest activity produces more involvement in the task (Lepper, Greene, & Nisbett, 1973; McLoyd, 1979; receiving a reward that is valued enhances interest in a task (McLoyd, 1979); and an environment that emphasizes choice of activity enhances learning motivation (Kohn, 1996; Rigby, Deci, Patrick, & Ryan, 1992).

Few studies have examined the effects of two important variables identified in reward contingency studies on intrinsic reading motivation—type of reward and choice of reward. Furthermore, the possible interaction between these two important variables has not been systematically investigated. More precisely, few studies have examined the effects of the proximity of the reward offered to the desired learning behavior (e.g., providing books as a reward for reading) (Edmunds & Tancock, 2003). In proposing the reward proximity hypothesis, Gambrell (1996) suggested that the more proximal the reward is to the desired behavior, the less undermining it will be to intrinsic motivation. For example, if the desired behavior is engagement in reading, the reward proximity hypothesis suggests that a book would be an appropriate reward to foster motivation to read. Consequently, less proximal rewards such as tokens or food, which are unrelated to the desired behavior, would undermine motivation. Although choice has been a variable in many reward contingency studies, few studies have specifically investigated the

Reprinted by permission of the publisher from Marinak, B.A., & Gambrell, L.B. (2008). Intrinsic motivation and rewards: What sustains young children's engagement with text? *Literacy Research and Instruction, 47*(1), 9-26.

effect of choice of reward on intrinsic motivation (McLoyd, 1979).

The purpose of this study was to explore the reward proximity hypothesis and the effect of choice of reward on intrinsic reading motivation of third graders. The first independent variable, reward type, consisted of a reward that was proximal to the desired behavior of reading motivation (literacy reward—book) or a reward less proximal to the desired behavior (non-literacy reward—token). Choice of reward, the second independent variable, included offering participants a choice of a proximal reward (choice of book) or a choice of a less proximal reward (choice of token). The study explored both the effect of reward type and choice of reward on intrinsic reading motivation and interactions that might exist between the two independent variables.

In this experimental study, the following research questions were investigated: (a) How does the proximity of the reward affect intrinsic motivation to read? (b) How does choice of reward affect the intrinsic motivation to read? Based on the theoretical underpinnings of this investigation, it was predicted that offering a reward that is proximal to the desired behavior would mediate the undermining effects of extrinsic rewards. Consistent with cognitive evaluation theory (Deci, 1971) and the reward proximity hypothesis (Gambrell, 1996), offering a book for reading should act as a signal of competence or success rather than being perceived as instrumental or controlling and therefore should result in sustained engagement with text. In addition, based on existing theories and research related to the role of choice in learning and motivation, it was predicted that choice of reward would enhance intrinsic motivation to read.

Theory and Research Base: Review of Literature

The theoretical underpinnings for the present study were drawn from cognitive evaluation theory (Deci, 1971, 1972a), which suggests that rewards undermine intrinsic motivation. In keeping with the theoretical orientation, intrinsic motivation was operationally defined as task persistence. Affording individuals the opportunity to return to an activity after being rewarded is consistent with task persistence procedures used in other studies of cognitive evaluation theory. Morgan (1984) noted that as long as no differential contingencies are imposed among activities, one can presume that an individual's relative intrinsic interest in a particular activity is reflected in task persistence, or the time spent engaged in the activity. Cognitive evaluation theory suggests that if individuals are intrinsically motivated by an activity and not controlled by outside forces, they are more likely to return to or continue the activity if given the opportunity.

The relationship between extrinsic rewards and intrinsic motivation has been the subject of research for decades. The results have yielded important findings and stirred an ongoing controversy regarding the effect of rewards on intrinsic motivation. The research in this area includes quantitative findings (Calder & Staw, 1975; Deci, 1971; Kruglanski, et al., 1975; McLoyd, 1979; Ryan, Mims, & Koestner, 1983) and qualitative findings (Ames, 1992; Fawson & Fawson, 1994; MacIver & Reumann, 1993-1994; Turner, 1995; Wiesendanger & Bader, 1986) as well as critical commentary (Morgan, 1981; Ryan & Deci, 2000). Because of the large volume of experimentation, a recent trend is the use of meta-analytic procedures (Cameron & Pierce, 1994; Deci, Koestner, & Ryan, 1999a); Eisenberger & Cameron, 1996; Tang & Hall, 1995; Rummel & Feinberg, 1988; Wiersma, 1992). To date, however, only a few studies have examined the specific relationship between rewards and intrinsic motivation to read (Edmunds & Tancock, 2003; McLoyd, 1979). The following section provides a brief overview of research on rewards and choice of reward.

Research on Rewards for Tasks Other Than Reading

Since the publication of the first experiment calling into question the positive and/or harmless effects of rewards on intrinsic motivation (Deci, 1971), the field has produced hundreds of empirical investigations, narrative reviews, and vigorous commentaries from behavioral psychologists and cognitive scientists. Few of these studies have focused on rewards for reading. Rather, they have focused on tasks and activities such as drawing, puzzle completion, and behavior modification. As a result of the large number of empirical studies (approximately 120 through 2005), the controversial nature of the topic, inconsistencies of the findings, and the emergence of statistical synthesizing techniques, researchers turned to the use of meta-analyses to identify trends in this body of research (Cameron & Pierce, 1994; Deci et al., 1999b; Eisenberger & Cameron, 1996; Tang & Hall, 1995; Rummel & Feinberg, 1988; Wiersma, 1992).

It is not surprising, given the lack of consistency in the research on the use of rewards to promote learning, that a number of meta-analyses have been conducted in the last 15 years. With the notable exception of the meta-analysis conducted by Cameron and Pierce (1994), all meta-analytic studies reported that rewards undermine intrinsic motivation, consistent with cognitive evaluation theory. The only reward condition reported by Cameron and Pierce (1994) that caused the undermining of intrinsic motivation was when a tangible reward was given only for engaging in a task. Cameron and Pierce (1994) found that all other types of reward conditions (verbal, tangible, expected, performance contingent, and completion contingent) did not undermine intrinsic motivation. It should be noted, however, that Lepper, Henderlong, and Gingras (1999) suggested interpretation of the meta-analytic research be approached with caution because this body of research is empirically complex and theoretically and procedurally diverse.

Research on Rewards for Reading

A number of reward contingency studies conducted with elementary or middle school students concluded that a variety of variables impact the enhancing and/or undermining effects of extrinsic rewards given for reading. According to these studies, extrinsic rewards enhance motivation to read if the rewards are given for the following: low reading motivation or low interest in

reading (McLoyd, 1979); effort, progress, and/or meaningful performance (Ames, 1992); attaining a challenging goal (MacIver & Reumann, 1993–1994; Turner, 1995); and choice of learning activity (Wiesendanger & Bader, 1986).

In reviewing the research on rewards and reading, Hidi and Harackiewicz (2000) and Harackiewicz and Sansone (2000) suggested that it may be premature to conclude that when people are intrinsically motivated, tangible extrinsic rewards will be detrimental. They point out that in most, if not all, of the studies, the effects of external rewards were examined on short and relatively simple activities. Hidi and Harackiewicz (2000) contend that it is inappropriate to assume the same relationship exists between external rewards and more complex, effortful engagements. In fact, several theorists contend that external rewards might prove beneficial under a number of conditions, such as when paired with performance feedback; when individuals have no initial interest in a task; when the task is effortful and complex; and when subjects have choice over the task and/or the reward (Hidi & Harackiewicz, 2000; Sansone & Harackiewicz, 2000; Zimmerman, 1985). Given the limited research, further investigations are warranted that examine intrinsic motivation during complex, effortful tasks such as reading.

Research on Choice of Reward

Providing task choice is widely acknowledged in the literature as a way of enhancing self-determination. Many experiments have illustrated the potential motivational and educational benefits of choice of learning activity (Cordova & Lepper, 1996; Iyengar & Lepper, 1999), although few have examined the role of choice of rewards. Both the Cordova and Lepper (1996) and the Iyengar and Lepper (1999) studies showed that allowing grade-school children to make even a trivial task choice increased learning and enhanced subsequent interest in the activity. Finney and Schraw (2003) reported increases in the affective indicators of reading motivation when choice of reading material was offered; however, they did not find gains in the cognitive indicators of reading achievement. To date, no studies have examined the reward proximity hypothesis and how intrinsic motivation might be affected by choice of reward.

To summarize, few studies exploring the role of more and less proximal rewards on reading motivation could be found (Edmunds & Tancock, 2003), and only one study (McLoyd, 1997) was located that investigated the role of choice of reward on reading motivation. Therefore, this study was designed to investigate the effects of proximity of reward (book/token) and choice of reward on the intrinsic reading motivation of third-grade students.

Method

This study employed a post-test only control. The children were randomly assigned to one of five treatment groups balanced for gender. The five treatments were: book/choice (student selected book), book/no choice (randomly selected book), token/choice (student selected token), and token/no choice (randomly selected token), and the control group (no reward/no choice).

Participants

The study was conducted at three elementary schools in a large mid-Atlantic suburban school district serving 12,000 students. There were approximately 800 students enrolled in each of the participating elementary schools. The schools reported a poverty level (as per free/reduced lunch count) ranging from 18 to 25%. The children in these schools represented a diverse population (40% Caucasian, 30% African American, 20% Asian, and 10% Eastern European). The participants were 75 third-grade students selected from a pool of 288 students who scored between the 30th and 50th percentile on the Stanford Achievement Test, Ninth Edition and for whom parent permission was granted to participate in the study.

Design of the Study

This study employed a post-test only design with a control group, allowing for the study of multiple independent variables and the examination of joint effects (Pedhazur, 1982). The first independent variable, reward type, consisted of a reward that was proximal to the desired behavior of reading motivation (literacy reward—book) and a reward less proximal to the desired behavior (nonliteracy reward—token). Choice of reward, the second independent variable, included offering participants a choice of a literacy reward (choice of a book) or a choice of a nonliteracy reward (choice of a token). The dependent variable was intrinsic motivation to read. Consistent with cognitive evaluation theory (CET) (Deci, 1971, 1972b; Deci et al., 1999b), intrinsic motivation was operationally defined as task persistence. CET suggests that if individuals are intrinsically motivated by an activity and not controlled by outside forces, they are more likely to return to or continue the activity if given the opportunity. Affording individuals the opportunity to return to an activity after being rewarded is consistent with task persistence procedures used in other studies of cognitive evaluation theory. Specifically, intrinsic motivation was measured by three indicators of task persistence: first activity selected, time spent reading, and number of words read.

Materials

There were two phases of this investigation: the library book selection activity and the observation of free-choice activity. The following section describes the books used in the library book selection activity, the rewards (books, tokens), and the books, jigsaw puzzle and math games used in the free-choice activity period, which included the option to read, do a math game, or do a jigsaw puzzle.

Books Used for the Library Book Selection Activity. To ensure that the children had never seen the books, hardcover preview titles not yet released by publishers were used for the library selection activity. Each book was at a readability level 1 full year below grade level. Readability was measured using three readability formulas: Spache, Dale-Chall, and Fry (Rodrigues, 2000). The books represented a range of interests and topics, and included three fiction titles and three nonfiction titles. Each book ranged from 1,200 to 2,000 words with a mean length of approximately 1,600 words (see Appendix A [included here as Table A] for the list of library books and corresponding readability).

Rewards for Participating in the Library Books Selection Activity.

Choice of reward involved choice of a book (more proximal reward) or choice of a token (less proximal reward). A range of books and tokens was provided for children to select from in the treatment groups where choice of reward was offered. This option was not made available to children in the no-choice treatment groups.

Books Used for Rewards.

The 25 children's literature books used as rewards included 13 fiction titles and 12 nonfiction titles. Each paperback was valued at approximately $2.50.

Token Rewards.

The 25 token rewards included Nerf balls, Pez dispensers, friendship bracelets, and key chains. Each token was valued at approximately $2.00.

Materials Used in the Free-Choice Activity Time

Books. Children were allowed to choose a book to read from the array of the six books available during the library book selection activity (see Appendix [Table] A).

Jigsaw Puzzle. The jigsaw puzzle contained 100 pieces and revealed a picture of several baby

Table A					
Readability of Library Books					
Book Title and Author(s)	Illustrator	Publisher Year	Spache* Grade Equivalent	Dale-Chall* Grade Equivalent	Fry* Grade Equivalent
Cook-A Doodle-Doo Janet Stevens Susan Stevens Crummel	Janet Stevens	Harcourt Brace and Company 1999	2.3	2.2	2.3
Locomotive: Building an Eight Wheeler David Weitzman	David Weitzman	Houghton Mifflin Company 1999	2.3	2.4	2.4
Ghost of the Southern Belle: A Sea Tale Odds Bodkin	Bernie Fuchs	Little Brown Company 1999	2.0	2.2	2.2
ABC Dogs Kathy Darling	Tara Darling	Walker Press 1997	2.0	2.1	2.2
Mud Flat Spring James Stevenson	James Stevenson	Greenwillow Press 1999	2.1	2.2	2.2
Stone Girl, Bone Girl: The Story of Mary Anning Laurence Anholt	Sheila Moxley	Corgi Children Press 2000	2.2	2.3	2.3

*Readability based on Readability Master 2000 (Rodrigues, 2000).

rabbits hidden in vegetation. The jigsaw puzzle was recommended for ages 7–10.

Math Game. The game involved a series of riddle-like problems that required rounding large numbers. The illustrations of the word problems included an astronomer counting stars and a party host counting guests, coats, and food. The mathematical concepts required for the game were taught during the second-grade curriculum.

Procedures

This study involved two phases: a library book selection activity and the observation of free-choice activity. During both phases, the researcher met with the each subject individually. Meeting with each child allowed the researcher to record data for the three measures of intrinsic motivation; first activity selected, number of words read, and number of seconds spent reading.

During phase one, the library book selection activity, each child engaged in the task of reading and recommending books for the school library. For participating in this task, they received a reward depending on treatment condition (book/choice, book/no choice, token/choice, token/no choice, no reward). In phase two, the free-choice activity, the student was given the choice of reading, doing a math game, or doing a jigsaw puzzle. Of particular interest in this study was whether the reward (book/token/no reward) or choice of reward would affect the child's subsequent reading engagement.

The Library Book Selection Activity

During the library book selection activity, the researcher asked each student to select one of six trade books to read in order to make a judgment about the question "Should this book be purchased for the school library?" First, the researcher provided a brief description of each of the six books. The child then selected a book, read a preselected 250-word sample, and made a recommendation about possible purchase of the book for the school library. The child was then rewarded (or not) based on the treatment condition (book/choice, book/no choice, token/choice, token/no choice, and no reward). After the child was given a reward (no choice condition) or selected a reward (choice condition), the researcher recorded the name of the reward on a 3×5 card. The researcher explained that she would keep the card and give the child his or her reward at the end of the school day. This procedure was implemented so that the physical reward did not serve as a distraction during the subsequent free-choice activity that followed.

To avoid disappointment, children in the control condition were invited to pick a book at the end of the school day (following the researcher's explanation that she "forgot" to offer the book while they were with her). All children who participated in the experiment were seen on the same school day to avoid contamination by children discussing their experiences.

Observation of Free-Choice Activity

Following the receipt of the reward (or not), the researcher explained that "it is not time for you to return to the classroom yet." The child was then invited to choose among a number of activities (reading, jigsaw puzzle, or a math game). Students could engage in one activity for the entire free-choice period or change activities as they wished. No specific directions were given.

While the researcher was "working" in another corner of the room, partially obscured by a wall, she observed the child's activity during the 10-minute free-choice period. Specifically, the researcher recorded the first activity selected by the child and the amount of time spent in any/all of the three activity options. If the child returned to reading at all, he or she was asked to mark the last page read.

Measures

Prior to the experiment, an assessment of children's existing motivation was completed. Six weeks before the experiment, a reading specialist administered the Motivation to Read Profile (MRP) (Gambrell, Palmer, Codling, & Mazzoni, 1996) to all the third-grade students in the elementary schools from which the random sample was drawn. The MRP was developed based on the research and theories of literacy motivation and an examination of existing surveys. The MRP consists of two subscales: self-concept as a reader and value of reading. To ascertain whether the traits measured corresponded to the two subscales, factor analyses were conducted using the unweighted least squares method and a varimax rotation. Only items that loaded cleanly on the two traits are included in the MRP. To assess reliability, Cronbach's (1951) alpha was calculated. The Cronbach's revealed a moderately high reliability for both subscales (self-concept = .75; value = .82). (Gambrell et al., 1996). Analysis of preexisting motivation was then completed on the 75 students who were randomly selected from the third-grade population for whom permission was granted.

Intrinsic motivation, for this study, was defined as task persistence. Three measures of intrinsic reading motivation were obtained: (1) first activity selected (reading, jigsaw puzzle, math game), (2) number of seconds spent reading, and (3) number of words read.

Results

This study investigated the effects of proximity of reward and choice of reward on third grade students' intrinsic motivation to read. Data were collected on the following: students' reading motivation prior to experimentation; first activity selected; number of seconds spent reading; and number of words read.

Analysis of Reading Motivation Prior to Experimentation

The MRP data was analyzed using an ANOVA to determine if statistically significant differences in reading motivation existed within or between treatment groups. An ANOVA was conducted on the total scores of the Motivation to Read Profile as well as the two subtest scores—self-concept and value of reading. The ANOVA revealed no statistically significant differences in reading motivation within or between treatment groups for the total motivation-to-read score, $F(4,74) = 2.022$, $p < .101$. In addition, no significant differences were found between or within groups for the self-concept or value of reading subtests. The ANOVA results for self concept were $F(4,74) = .663$, $p < .387$. The ANOVA results for value of reading were $F(4,74) = 1.100$, $p < .113$.

Task Persistence as a Measure of Intrinsic Reading Motivation: First Activity Selected

The first activity selected during the free-choice period was the first measure of task persistence. Descriptive statistics for the first activity selected by each child in each treatment group were examined. Table 1 reveals the frequency of the activities selected (reading, puzzle, math game) by students by treatment condition.

A chi-square analysis revealed statistically significant differences ($x = 28.420$, $p < .05$) between the students in the book groups and no reward group compared to the token groups on first activity selected. The students in the

Table 1
First Activity Selected by Treatment Group

First Activity	Book/Choice (n = 15)	Book/No Choice (n = 15)	Token/Choice (n = 15)	Token/No Choice (n = 15)	No Reward/ No Choice (n = 15)
Books	13	10	2	3	11
Math Game	1	4	8	8	1
Jigsaw Puzzle	1	1	5	4	3

book/choice, book/no choice, and no reward/no choice group selected reading as a first activity more often than students in the token (choice/no choice) groups.

To clarify the role of choice of reward, chi-square analysis of the choice/no choice treatment conditions was conducted. Table 2 displays the frequency of the first activity selected using only choice/no choice and control as the grouping variable.

The results the chi-square analysis of the choice/no choice data revealed no statistically significant differences ($x = 5.672$, $p < .05$) between the students in the choice and no choice groups. Based on these results, proximity of reward was the only significant variable for the first activity selected.

To further verify that proximity of reward was the only significant variable for first activity selected, additional chi-square analyses were conducted using regrouped treatment conditions. The regrouped treatment groups were book (choice/no choice), token (choice/no choice), and control (no reward/no choice). Table 3 contains descriptive statistics for the comparison between the book group, token group, and the control group.

Three additional chi-square analyses were completed. The results of the chi-square analysis comparing the book group and token group revealed statistically significant differences ($x = 21.78$, $p < .05$), with students in the book condition selecting reading as a first activity more often than the students in the token condition.

The results of the second chi-square analysis revealed no statistically significant differences ($x = 2.365$, $p < .05$) between the book group and the control group. The final chi-square analysis in this series compared the token group and the control group revealing statistically significant differences ($x = 15.17$, $p < .05$), with the students in the control group selecting reading as a first activity more often than the students in the token group.

Task Persistence as a Measure of Intrinsic Reading Motivation: Seconds Spent Reading

A second measure of intrinsic motivation collected during the free-choice period was the

Table 2
First Activity Selected by Choice/No Choice

First Activity	Treatment Condition		
	Choice	No Choice	Control
Books	15	13	11
Math Game	9	12	1
Jigsaw Puzzle	6	5	3
Total	30	30	15

Table 3
First Activity Selected by Proximity of Reward

First Activity	Book Group ($n = 30$)	Token Group ($n = 30$)	Control ($n = 15$)
Books	23	5	11
Math Game	5	16	1
Jigsaw Puzzle	2	9	3

number of seconds spent reading. If returning to reading was a behavior exhibited at any time during the free-choice period, the number of seconds spent reading was recorded. Students could change activities among the three choices (reading, jigsaw puzzle, math game) as desired. The number of seconds spent reading was a measure of the total time spent reading during the time available in the free-choice period.

To determine if there were significant differences across the five treatment conditions with respect to seconds reading, a one-way ANOVA with multiple comparisons (Fisher's LSD) was conducted. The means (with standards deviations in parenthesis) were as follows for seconds reading: book/choice M = 374 (237), book/no

choice M = 303 (250), token/choice M = 30 (79), token/no choice M = 67 (163), no reward/ no choice M = 365 (261).

A one-way ANOVA was conducted to determine if there were statistically significant differences across the treatment groups for the number of seconds spent reading during the free-choice period. The results of the ANOVA revealed a statistically significant difference between the treatment groups for seconds reading, $F (4,74) = 9.464, p < .000$.

To clarify the results of the one-way ANOVA, post hoc multiple comparisons using Fisher's LSD were conducted for seconds spent reading. The results of the Fisher's LSD are presented in Table 4. This analysis revealed statistically

Table 4
Fisher's LSD Test for the Number of Seconds Spent Reading

Dependent Variable	Mean Dif	Standard Error	Significance
Seconds Reading			
Book/Choice			
Book/No Choice	71.6667	76.7012	.353
Token/ Choice	344.8667*	76.7012	.000
Token/No Choice	307.8667*	76.7012	.000
No Reward	9.0000	76.7012	.907
Book/No Choice			
Book/Choice	−71.6667	76.7012	.353
Token/Choice	273.2000*	76.7012	.001
Token/No Choice	236.2000*	76.7012	.003
No Reward	−62.6667	76.7012	.417
Token/Choice			
Book/Choice	−344.8667*	76.7012	.000
Book/No Choice	−273.2000*	76.7012	.001
Token/No Choice	−37.0000	76.7012	.631
No Reward	−335.8667*	76.7012	.000
Token/No Choice			
Book/Choice	−307.8667*	76.7012	.000
Book/No choice	−236.2000*	76.7012	.003
Token/Choice	37.0000	76.7012	.631
No Reward	−298.8667*	76.7012	.000
No Reward			
Book/Choice	−9.000	76.7012	.907
Book/No Choice	62.6667	76.7012	.417
Token/Choice	335.8667*	76.7012	.000
Token/No choice	298.8667*	76.7012	.000

*Indicates a statistically significant finding.

significant differences in favor of the students in the book/choice, book/no choice, and the control conditions with respect to seconds spent reading. In other words, students in the book/choice group, the book/no choice group, and the control group spent significantly more time reading than those in the token/choice and token/no choice groups. In addition, an inspection of the post hoc multiple comparisons revealed no statistically significant differences between the book/choice group and the book/no choice group. No statistically significant differences were found between the token/choice and token/no choice groups. These results indicate that choice of reward was not a significant variable in this study.

To further verify that proximity of reward remained a significant variable for the number of seconds spent reading in the post hoc multiple comparisons, an additional one-way ANOVA and post hoc multiple comparisons were conducted

using regrouped treatment groups. The book/choice and book/no choice conditions were regrouped as a book group and the token/choice and token/no choice conditions were regrouped as a token group, resulting in three treatment conditions: book, token, and control. The means and standard deviations for the one-way ANOVA using regrouped data are in Table 5.

An ANOVA was calculated to determine if there were statistically significant differences across the regrouped treatment conditions for the number of seconds spent reading during the free-choice period. The result of the ANOVA for seconds spent reading revealed a statistically significant difference between the treatment groups, $F(2,74) = 18.607, p < .000$. To clarify the results of the one-way ANOVA, post hoc multiple comparisons using Fisher's LSD were conducted for number of seconds spent reading. The results of the Fisher's LSD are presented in Table 6. The

Table 5
Means and Standard Deviations for Number of Seconds Spent Reading by Proximity of Reward

Treatment Condition	Seconds Spent Reading	
	Mean	Standard Deviation
Book Group ($n = 30$)	339.0333	242.5441
Token Group ($n = 30$)	48.5000	127.8546
Control Group ($n = 15$)	365.8667	261.4995
Total ($n = 75$)	228.1867	253.5950

Table 6
Fisher's LSD Test for Number of Seconds Spent Reading by Proximity of Reward

	Seconds Reading		
	Mean Difference	Standard Error	Significance
Books/Tokens	290.5333*	53.8981	.000
No Reward	−26.8333	66.0114	.686
Tokens/Books	−290.5333*	53.8981	.000
No Reward	−317.3667*	66.0114	.000
No Reward/Books	26.8333	66.0114	.686
Tokens	317.3667*	66.0114	.000

*Indicates a statistically significant finding.

analysis revealed that students in the book group and the control group spent more time reading than the token group.

Task Persistence as a Measure of Intrinsic Reading Motivation: Number of Words Read

The number of words read by each student was a third task persistence measure of intrinsic motivation collected during the free-choice period. If reading was exhibited at any time during the free-choice period, the number of words read was recorded. Again, students could change activities among the three choices (reading, jigsaw puzzle, math game). Number of words read is a different measure of task persistence than number of seconds spent reading, in that all the books in the library array were picture books. Number of seconds spent reading would include time spent browsing pictures and/or reading words. Number of words read is a count of words read regardless of time spent picture browsing.

To determine if there were significant differences across the five treatment conditions with respect to number of words read, a one-way ANOVA with multiple comparisons (Fisher's LSD) was conducted. The means (with standard deviations in parentheses) were as follows for seconds reading: book/choice M = 497 (309), book/no choice M = 403 (377), token/choice M = 45 (121), token/no choice M = 78 (173), and no reward/no choice M = 483 (373).

The result of the ANOVA for number of words read is revealed a statistically significant difference between the treatment groups for number of words read, $F (4,74) = 9.464, p < .000$. To clarify the results of the one-way ANOVA, post hoc multiple comparisons using the Fisher's LSD were conducted. The results of the Fisher's LSD are presented in Table 7. The analysis revealed statistically significant differences in favor of the students in the book/choice, book/no choice, and no reward/no choice conditions with respect to number of words read. In other words, students in the book/choice group, the book/no choice group, and the no reward/no choice group read

more words than those in the token/choice and token/no choice treatment groups.

To further verify that proximity of reward remained a significant variable for the number of words read in the post hoc multiple comparisons, an additional one-way ANOVA and post hoc multiple comparisons were conducted using regrouped treatment groups. The book/choice and book/no choice conditions were regrouped as a book group. The token/choice and token/no choice conditions were regrouped as a token group, and the no reward/no choice was examined as a control group. The means and standard deviations for the one-way ANOVA using regrouped data are in Table 8.

An ANOVA was calculated to determine if there were statistically significant differences across the regrouped treatment conditions for the number of words read during the free-choice period. The results of the ANOVA for words read revealed a statistically significant difference between the treatment groups for number of words read, $F (2,74) = 144.29, p < .000$. The results of the Fisher's LSD are presented in Table 9. The analysis found that students in the book group and the control group read more words than those in the token group.

Discussion and Conclusions

This study explored the conditions under which rewards influence reading motivation. The theoretical underpinnings of the study were primarily grounded in the cognitive evaluation theory (CET) proposed by Deci and his colleagues (Deci, 1971, 1972b; Deci et al., 1999b). CET proposes that under certain conditions, rewarding students for engaging in an activity or behavior will decrease subsequent engagement in that activity. In addition, the study was designed to test the reward proximity hypothesis (Gambrell, 1996) that suggests that type of reward may play an important role in whether motivation is undermined by rewards. Specifically, the reward proximity hypothesis posits that rewards that are proximal to the desired behavior may mediate the undermining effects of extrinsic rewards.

Table 7
Fisher's LSD Test for Number of Words Read

Dependent Variable	Mean Differences	Standard Error	Significance
Words Read			
Book/Choice			
Book/No choice	93.9333	106.2457	.380
Token/Choice	452.1333*	106.2457	.000
Token/No choice	419.6000*	106.2457	.000
No Reward	14.600	106.2457	.891
Book/No choice			
Book/Choice	−93.9333	106.2457	.380
Token/Choice	358.2000*	106.2457	.001
Token/No choice	325.6667*	106.2457	.003
No Reward	−79.333	106.2457	.458
Token/Choice			
Book/Choice	−452.1333*	106.2457	.000
Book/No choice	−358.2000*	106.2457	.001
Token/No choice	−32.5333	106.2457	.760
No Reward	−437.5333*	106.2457	.000
Token/No choice			
Book/Choice	−419.6000*	106.2457	.000
Book/No choice	−325.6667*	106.2457	.003
Token/Choice	32.5333	106.2457	.760
No Reward	−405.0000*	106.2457	.000
No Reward			
Book/Choice	−14.6000	106.2457	.891
Book/No choice	79.3333	106.2457	.458
Token/Choice	437.5333*	106.2457	.000
Token/No choice	405.0000*	106.2457	.000

*Indicates a statistically significant finding.

Table 8
Number of Words Read by Proximity of Reward

	Number of Words Read	
Treatment Condition	Mean	Standard Deviations
Book Group (*n* = 30)	450.833	342.8089
Token Group (*n* = 30)	61.9333	147.8865
Control Group (*n* = 15)	483.2000	373.9872
Total (*n* = 75)	301.7467	346.5348

Table 9
Fisher's LSD Test for Number of Words Read by Proximity of Reward

Treatment Condition	Words Read		
	Mean Difference	Std. Error	Significance
Books/Tokens	388.9000*	74.5380	.000
No Reward	−32.3667	91.2901	.724
Tokens/Books	−388.9000*	74.5380	.000
No Reward	−421.2667*	91.2901	.000
No Reward/Books	32.3667	91.2901	.724
Tokens	421.2667*	91.2901	.000

*Indicates a statistically significant finding.

The present study examined the effects of a reward that was proximal to the desired behavior of reading (books), a reward that was less proximal to the desired behavior (tokens), and no reward on third graders' intrinsic motivation to read. In addition, the effect of choice of reward on intrinsic reading motivation was explored. Intrinsic motivation was assessed through a series of task persistence measures: first choice of activity (reading, puzzle, math game), time spent reading, and number of words read. Time spent reading and number of words read reflect actual engagement with reading during the free-choice period.

The major finding of this study is that the students who were given a book (proximal reward) and students who received no reward were more motivated to engage in subsequent reading than the students who received a token (less proximal reward). Although the intrinsic motivation of the book group and the control group was comparable, the intrinsic motivation of the token group was lower on the three measures of intrinsic motivation; first activity selected, number of seconds spent reading, and number of words read. Thus, the findings of this study suggest that the proximity of the reward to the desired behavior is a particularly salient factor in enhancing motivation to read.

Generalizability of this study is limited to the reward conditions used in the experiment (type of reward and choice of reward). In addition, the results of the study can be generalized only to children of approximately the same age and levels of reading achievement. It is acknowledged that the reading motivation of young children is influenced by a number of factors not included in this study.

The results of the present study support the reward proximity hypothesis (Gambrell, 1996) and Rigby et al.'s (1992) differentiated concept of extrinsic motivation within cognitive evaluation theory (Deci, 1971). Rigby and his colleagues (1992) suggest that rewards do not necessarily undermine intrinsic motivation if the reward condition invites children into self-determination. The results of this study suggest that receiving a reward (book) proximal to the desired behavior (reading) was perceived by the students as sufficiently positive and supporting competence (Rigby et al., 1992). In accordance with the reward proximity hypothesis, the reward of a book was sufficiently proximal to the desired behavior of reading, therefore intrinsic motivation was not undermined.

Three conclusions drawn from the present study are consistent with both the reward proximity hypothesis (Gambrell, 1996) and cognitive evaluation theory (Deci, 1971). The first is that rewards proximal to the desired behavior, such as books to reading, do not undermine intrinsic motivation to read. Specifically, when offering extrinsic rewards for reading, books are less undermining to intrinsic motivation than rewards less proximal to reading, such as tokens. The second conclusion is that less proximal rewards, such as tokens, do serve to undermine intrinsic motivation to read. When offering extrinsic rewards for reading, tokens are more undermining to intrinsic motivation than rewards more proximal to reading such as books or no reward at all. The third conclusion is that although choice has been demonstrated to be a powerful aspect of intrinsic motivation (Rigby et al., 1992; Gottfried, 1985; Guthrie & Wigfield, 1997), choice of reward was not found to be a salient factor in this study. Choice of a book or choice of a token neither enhanced nor undermined subsequent reading motivation.

This study has implications for the practice of using rewards as a means of motivating children to read. It seems likely that classroom teachers will continue to make use of rewards in an attempt to motivate uninterested and/or struggling readers (Hidi & Harackiewicz, 2000). Regardless of why or when educators employ the use of rewards, the findings of this study are interpreted as support for the reward proximity hypothesis and have significant implications related to increasing and sustaining reading engagement.

Using Rewards That Are Proximal to Reading Supports Intrinsic Motivation to Read

This study indicates that the type of reward—specifically the proximity of the reward to the desired behavior—should be carefully considered when using rewards in the classroom. If the desired behavior is reading, rewards that are proximal to engaging with books should be offered (e.g., books, increased read-aloud time, increased time for self-selected reading, increased library time, and increased number of books available).

Consistent with cognitive evaluation theory and reward proximity hypothesis, in this study the reward of a book did not undermine intrinsic motivation to read. Using literacy-related rewards may increase students' sense of personal competence and signals task mastery, thereby increasing the likelihood of sustained reading engagement.

Type of Reward Is More Important Than Choice of Reward

Although the research on learning clearly indicates that task choice is a powerful influence on motivation, the results of the present study suggest that choice of reward is not as salient as type of reward. Instead of focusing on reward choices, educators who want to promote intrinsic motivation to read should be encouraged to consider reward alternatives that are proximal to reading. It may be that providing reading-related rewards sends a message about the value of reading and sustained engagement with text.

Carefully Chosen Rewards Can Foster a Culture of Reading Motivation

Turner (1995) urges teachers to be aware of what is done in classrooms in the name of literacy and how it affects children. What and how children learn, she notes, are intimately intertwined. So, too, the case can be made that rewards and the classrooms in which they are offered are inseparable. If this is true, rewards offered for reading should be a natural extension of a literacy-rich classroom culture (Gambrell & Marinak, 1997). This study provides clear support for the reward proximity hypothesis and the use of books as appropriate reading rewards. However, the importance of reading-related rewards may go beyond recognizing the relationship between reward proximity and the desired behavior. It could be that the real value of using books to reward reading and foster intrinsic motivation is that both the desired behavior (reading) and the reward (books) define a classroom culture that supports and nurtures intrinsic motivation to read.

Acknowledgments

This study is based on the dissertation of the first author. The dissertation received the College Reading Association's Dissertation Research Award, 2005, and was recognized as a finalist for the International Reading

Association's Outstanding Dissertation of the Year Award for 2006. A brief abstract of the study is scheduled to be published in 2006 College Reading Association Yearbook in acknowledgement of the award. The authors thank Mariam Jean Dreher, William Henk, Wayne Slater, and Alan Wigfield who served on the dissertation committee of the first author.

References

Ames, C. (1992). Classrooms: Goals, structures, and student motivation. *Journal of Educational Psychology*, *84*(3), 261–271.

Calder, B., & Staw, B. (1975). Interaction of intrinsic and extrinsic motivation: Some methodological notes. *Journal of Personality and Social Psychology, 31*, 76–80.

Cameron, J. (2001). Negative effects of reward on intrinsic motivation—a limited phenomenon: Comment on Deci, Koestner, and Ryan (2001). *Review of Educational Research, 71*(1), 29–42.

Cameron, J., & Pierce, W.D. (1994). Reinforcement, reward, and intrinsic motivation: A meta-analysis. *Review of Educational Research, 64*, 363–423.

Condry, J. (1977). Enemies of exploration: Self-initiated versus other-initiated learning. *Journal of Personality and Social Psychology, 18*, 105–115.

Cordova, D., & Lepper, M. (1996). Intrinsic motivation and the process of learning. Beneficial effects of contextualization, personalization, and choice. *Journal of Educational Psychology, 88*, 715–730.

Cronbach, L. (1951). Coefficient alpha and the internal structure of tests. *Psychometrika, 16*, 297–334.

Deci, E.L. (1971). Effects of externally mediated rewards on intrinsic motivation. *Journal of Personality and Social Psychology, 18*, 105–115.

Deci, E.L. (1972a). Intrinsic motivation, extrinsic reinforcement and inequity. *Journal of Personality and Social Psychology, 22*, 113–120.

Deci, E.L. (1972b). The effects of contingent and noncontingent rewards and controls on intrinsic motivation. *Organizational Behavior and Human Performance, 8*, 217–229.

Deci, E., Koestner, R., & Ryan, R. (1999a). The undermining effect is a reality after all extrinsic rewards, task interest, and self-determination: Reply to Eisenberger, Pierce, and Cameron (1999) and Lepper, Henderlong, and Gingras (1999). *Psychological Bulletin, 125*, 692–700.

Deci, E., Koestner, R., & Ryan, R. (1999b). A meta-analytic review of experiments examining the effects of extrinsic rewards on intrinsic motivation. *Psychological Bulletin, 125*, 627–668.

Deci, E., Koestner, R., & Ryan, R. (2001). Extrinsic rewards and intrinsic motivation in education: Reconsidered once again. *Review of Educational Research, 71*(1), 1–28.

Edmunds, K., & Tancock, S. (2003). Incentives: The effects on the reading motivation of fourth grade students. *Reading Research and Instruction, 42*(2), 17–38.

Eisenberger, R., & Cameron, J. (1996). Detrimental effects of reward: Reality or myth? *American Psychologist, 51*, 1153–1166.

Fawson, P.C., & Fawson, C. (1994). *Conditional philanthropy: A study of corporate sponsorship of reading programs*. Paper presented at the annual meeting of the International Reading Association Toronto, Canada.

Fawson, P., & Moore, S. (1999). Reading incentive programs: Beliefs and practices. *Reading Psychology, 4*, 325–340.

Finney, S., & Schraw, G. (2003). Self-efficacy beliefs in college autistics courses. *Contemporary Education Psychology, 28*, 161–186.

Gambrell, L. (1996). Creating classrooms cultures that foster reading motivation. *The Reading Teacher, 50*, 4–25.

Gambrell, L., & Marinak, B. (1997). Incentives and intrinsic motivation to read. In J.T. Guthrie & A. Wigfield (Eds.), *Reading engagement: Motivating readers through integrated instruction*. Newark, DE: International Reading Association.

Gambrell, L., Palmer, B., Codling, R., & Mazzoni, S. (1996). Assessing motivation to read. *The Reading Teacher, 49*(7), 518–533.

Gottfried, A.E. (1985). Academic intrinsic motivation in elementary and junior high school students. *Journal of Educational Psychology, 77*, 631–645.

Guthrie, J.T., & Wigfield, A. (1997). *Reading engagement: Motivating readers through integrated instruction*. Newark, DE: International Reading Association.

Harackiewicz, J., & Sansone, C. (2000). Rewarding competence: The importance of goals in the study of intrinsic motivation. In C. Sansone & J. Harackiewicz (Eds.), *Intrinsic and extrinsic motivation: the search for optimal performance*. Burlington, MA: Academic Press.

Hidi, S., & Harackiewicz, J. (2000). Motivating the academically unmotivated: A critical issue for the 21st century. *Review of Educational Research, 70*, 151–179.

Iyengar, S., & Lepper, M. (1999). Rethinking the value of choice: A cultural perspective on intrinsic motivation. *Journal of Personality and Social Psychology, 76*, 349–366.

Kohn, A. (1996). By all available means: Cameron and Pierce's defense of extrinsic motivators. *Review of Educational Research, 66*, 1–4.

Kruglanski, A., Riter, A., Amitai, A., Margolin, B., Shabtai, L., & Zaksh, D. (1975). Can money enhance intrinsic motivation?: A test of the content-consequence hypothesis. *Journal of Personality and Social Psychology, 31*, 744–750.

Lepper, M., Greene, D., & Nisbett, E. (1973). Undermining children's intrinsic interest with extrinsic reward. *Journal of Personality and Social Psychology, 28*(1), 129–137.

Lepper, M., Henderlong, J., & Gingras, I. (1999). Understanding the effects of extrinsic rewards on intrinsic motivation-uses and abuses of meta-analysis: Comment on Deci, Koestner, and Ryan. *Psychological Bulletin*, *125*, 669–676.

MacIver, D.J., & Reuman, D.A. (1993–1994). Giving their best. *American Educator*, 24–31.

McLoyd, V. (1979). The effects of extrinsic rewards of differential value on high and low intrinsic interest. *Child Development*, *50*, 636–644.

Morgan, M. (1981). The overjustification effect: A developmental test of self-perception interpretations. *Journal of Personality and Social Psychology*, *40*, 809–821.

Morgan, M. (1984). Reward-induced decrements and increments in intrinsic motivation. *Review of Educational Research*, *54*, 5–30.

Pedhazur, E. (1982). *Multiple regression in behavioral research: Explanation and prediction*. New York: Harcourt Brace.

Rigby, C.S., Deci, E.L., Patrick, B.C., & Ryan, R.M. (1992). Beyond the intrinsic-extrinsic dichotomy: Self-determination and motivation in learning. *Motivation and Emotion*, *16*(3), 165–185.

Rodrigues, M. (2000). *Readability master 2000*. Brookline, MA: Brookline Books.

Rummel, A., & Feinberg, R. (1988). Cognitive evaluation theory: A meta-analytic review of the literature. *Social Behavior and Personality*, *60*, 158–161.

Ryan, R., & Deci, E. (2000). When rewards compete with nature: The undermining of intrinsic motivation and self-regulation. In C. Sansone & J. Harackiewicz (Eds.), *Intrinsic and extrinsic motivation* (pp. 14–48). Burlington, MA: Academic Press.

Ryan, R., Mims, V., & Koestner, R. (1983). Relation of reward contingency and interpersonal context to intrinsic motivation: A review and test using cognitive evaluation theory. *Journal of Personality and Social Psychology*, *45*, 736–750.

Sansone, C., & Harackiewicz, J. (2000). *Intrinsic and extrinsic motivation: The search for optimal motivation and performance*. Burlington, MA: Academic Press.

Tang, S., & Hall, V. (1995). The overjustification effect: A meta-analysis. *Applied Cognitive Psychology*, *9*, 364–404.

Turner, J. (1995). The influence of classroom contexts on young children's motivation for literacy. *Reading Research Quarterly*, *30*(3), 410–441.

Wiersma, U. (1992). The effects of extrinsic rewards in intrinsic motivation: A meta-analysis. *Journal of Occupational and Organizational Psychology*, *65*, 101–114.

Wiesendanger, K., & Bader, L. (1986). The university based reading clinic—practices and procedures. *The Reading Teacher*, *39*, 698–702.

Zimmerman, B. (1985). The development of "intrinsic motivation": A social learning analysis. *Annals of Child Development*, *2*, 117–160.

Engagement Activities

In Your Classroom
How can you make rewards for reading more proximal to the desired behavior of engaging with books? For example, can you reward reading by offering students more reading time, a basket of new books to choose from, or the opportunity to lead a discussion about one their favorite books?

With Your Colleagues
Make a list of the ways that you and your colleagues currently recognize or reward reading. Now brainstorm a list of ways that you can create reading incentive programs that reward children with books they can own.

Further Reading
Pachtman, A.B., & Wilson, K.A. (2006). What do the kids think? *The Reading Teacher*, *59*(7), 580–584.

This study asked fifth graders to reflect on past classroom practices that contributed most to their reading engagement. The results indicate that proximity and access to books, choice, and reading-related goals are important dimensions of a reading program. For example, the students felt it was "very important" to have lots of books in their library, to choose their own books, and to work toward a reading goal.

How Literacy Tasks Influence Children's Motivation for Literacy

Julianne Turner and Scott G. Paris

It is 10:45 on Tuesday morning, time for first-grade literacy instruction.

Mike's teacher has just completed a lesson on rhyming words and has distributed two worksheets to the children for practice in decoding. Mike glances at the first worksheet requiring him to use rhyming words to complete a sentence. He quickly decodes the word choices, *Jam, ham,* and *Sam,* and places them in the sentence blanks, *Sam* put grape *jam* on his *ham.* Then he moves on to a worksheet on short *u.* He begins by coloring and cutting. Fifteen minutes later, he is still laboriously decorating cups, tubs, and other objects on the sheet. When the teacher reminds the children that they have only 5 minutes left for morning work, he hurriedly matches several pictures to words on the worksheet and hands it in. Later, when asked what he was supposed to learn that morning, Mike replied, "vowels." When queried about why vowels were a good thing to learn, he shrugged his shoulders with an "I don't know."

Across the hall, the teacher is reading *Clifford's Birthday Party* (Bridwell, 1988) and discussing plans for celebrating his birthday in class. On easel paper, she lists various activities and labels each one as "reading," "writing," "planning," or "thinking." One of the activities, writing a story about Clifford, is required. But students may choose other activities that include writing invitations to Clifford's party, making a list of the needed preparations, designing and writing a birthday card for Clifford, following directions to make Clifford's cake, and reading and listening to other Clifford stories.

Lauren takes out paper to begin her story, thinks for a while, then asks Susan about her plans. Susan replies, "When Clifford goes swimming." Lauren suggests that it would be funny if he got everyone wet, then begins to write, saying the words as she writes them. Unable to spell a word, she walks to the easel where some Clifford books are displayed. She copies the word and continues writing. Several minutes later, she asks if Megan knows how to spell *house.* Together they construct a phonetic approximation, *hos.* When she finishes, she reads her story to Megan, then makes two changes. When asked what she was supposed to learn from this activity, Lauren replied, "What Clifford does, and why he is funny." When pressed about why this might be a good thing, she answered, "I want to be an author when I grow up."

What distinguishes how Mike and Lauren approach, engage in, and understand their literacy activities? It is not ability; both are average readers. Nor is it experience, because both own books and have enjoyed them with their families. The biggest difference between these two children is their classroom literacy contexts, specifically the activities they complete during literacy instruction. Although both are progressing as readers and writers, they are developing different conceptions of literacy from their classroom tasks.

Mike understands that his instructional work is important and that he must do it accurately, neatly, and turn it in on time. He is pleased to

Reprinted from Turner, J., & Paris, S.G. (1995). How literacy tasks influence children's motivation for literacy. *The Reading Teacher, 48*(8), 662–673.

get frequent stickers and gold stars on his papers and thinks he is a good reader. However, he is often bored by the rote nature of his work and completes it quickly with little thought.

Lauren, on the other hand, thinks about her work, plans, and discusses it with others. She visualizes how literacy will play a part in her future. She is effortful and she tries a variety of strategies as she works. She is seldom bored because her classroom offers choices that are challenging, meaningful, and related to her interests. Although Lauren wants the teacher to evaluate her work positively, she also strives to meet her own standards of quality.

In this article, we discuss how classroom tasks affect students' motivation for literacy. We propose that tasks influence students' affect, such as desire to read and write, understanding of the goals of literacy, and self-regulation as readers and writers. We illustrate our proposition with examples gathered during a study of motivation for literacy in 12 classrooms of 6-year-olds (6 integrated language-arts and 6 skills-based) (Turner, in press). The first author observed 84 children during literacy instruction over 5 days in each classroom. After observations, students were interviewed to determine their understanding of and value for literacy.

A variety of other data were gathered to provide as complete a picture of classroom instruction as possible. These included daily field notes, verbatim transcripts of literacy lessons, and descriptions of all the tasks the children completed. Literacy tasks were classified as *open* or *closed*. In open tasks, students were in control of both the products they created and the processes they employed. There was no one correct answer, nor was there a specified procedure to use. Open tasks required students to set goals, select and organize information, choose strategies, and assess the final results. For example, if students were composing, they decided what information about the topic interested them, how to organize it to create a theme, and what they wanted the final message to be. Because there were many "correct" answers to open tasks, students approached tasks as problems to solve rather than as exercises to complete.

Closed tasks were those in which either the product (e.g., there is one correct answer), the process (e.g., sound out the word), or both were specified. For example, in many worksheet activities, students were given cloze sentences and directed to fill in the blanks with selected vocabulary words. Closed tasks afforded students fewer opportunities to control their learning and explore their interests because these tasks did not permit students to make choices and decisions.

The major finding of the study was that the most reliable indicator of motivation was not the type of reading program that districts follow, but the actual daily tasks that teachers provided students in their classrooms. Tasks that provided opportunities for students to use reading and writing for authentic purposes (like reading trade books and composing), that conveyed the value of literacy for communication and enjoyment, and that allowed students to be actively involved in constructing meanings and metacognitions about literacy were most successful in motivating students.

Creating Contexts for Motivation

Why did open-ended tasks have such a powerful effect on students' engagement? We can summarize the influence of open tasks on students' motivation with six *C*s, an easy mnemonic to remember critical features of motivating tasks (e.g., Ames, 1992; Lepper & Hodell, 1989). First, open-ended tasks allow students to make personal *choices* among literacy activities. Second, these activities provide *challenge* for all students. Third, they allow students to take *control* over their own learning through planning, evaluation and self-monitoring. Fourth, they foster the sharing of expertise through *collaboration*. Fifth, open activities foster *constructive comprehension* or making meaning through reading and writing. Sixth, the *consequences* of open activities promote feelings of competence and efficacy. In the sections that follow, we describe how teachers can use these characteristics of open tasks as a guide for designing literacy activities that engage and support their students' learning.

Choice

Research has shown that choice is a powerful motivator. When students can choose tasks and texts they are interested in, they expend more effort learning and understanding the material (Schiefele, 1991). Similarly, when students are allowed to select the tasks that have personal value, they are more likely to use learning strategies like summarizing or backtracking rather than shortcuts like memorizing, copying, or guessing. Open-ended activities provide students with opportunities to mold tasks to interests and values, thus supporting their efforts to make meaning while engaging them affectively.

Students in the study who were allowed to choose among activities and who had options about how to organize and plan showed more personal responsibility for their literacy learning because the activities themselves required such behaviors. For example, when selecting texts, students decided what their interests were, whether they were of the appropriate level, and how the text supported their reading progress. Similarly, in writing, students selected an approach to the topic, organized information, and monitored their execution. How did teachers provide choices and how did those choices affect students' learning?

Providing Choices During Literacy Instruction

In many of the classrooms observed, teachers structured the morning literacy time to encourage students to make personal choices. They wanted to demonstrate to students that literacy means pursuing personal aesthetic and informational goals. There are many ways that choices can be offered as part of the literacy curriculum. For example, students can select from a variety of tasks appropriate for their learning needs and interests. Interest can also be stimulated in reading and writing through the integration of literacy activities with science, art, and music, or in relation to classroom themes like chocolate,

bears, or the March wind. For instance, in some classrooms students wrote and followed recipes for chocolate milkshakes and read, wrote, and listened to bear stories. These choices involved meaning making and learning goals, while capitalizing on individual interests and familiarity.

Another kind of choice that students can make is selecting their own texts for oral reading practice. Unlike traditional approaches in which all students read the same basal stories, students can be encouraged to think about choosing texts based on interest and level. Sometimes children may select texts in order to improve fluency or gain mastery, but at other times, they may select them for the pure enjoyment of the language. If children select inappropriate books, teachers can suggest more (or less) challenging texts. Then students take responsibility for evaluating texts to set new reading goals.

This approach to oral reading not only creates a greater interest in reading, it also encourages wider reading. Because children are expected to select books for free reading and reading with the teacher, they frequently browse in the classroom library. As a result, they become familiar with many books, and, as they exchange evaluations of books with their peers, they regularly discover new books. Compared to children whose daily reading experiences are confined to basal stories, these children have rich experiences in selecting, evaluating, and enjoying literature.

Another crucial element of choice is that it can encourage students to take personal responsibility for their tasks by setting goals and deciding how to reach those goals. For example, in one class, students read a text about the life cycle of the butterfly. The composition assignment was to use the text as a source of ideas. Students were expected to decide which ideas in the text interested them and how they wanted their final product to represent those ideas. Thus, students chose both process and product.

Liza, fascinated by the life cycle, composed this text: "I would fly away and find a mate. We will lay eggs and have children. It would start again so I would be a grandma and I will die and that would be my life. And then the little ones would be a mother and its mom will die and we will start over again."

Butterflies inspired Joanna to write an action story: "One day I pretended to be a butterfly. I jumped in. I hit my head on the ceiling. Then I landed on the couch. My brother tried, too, but he didn't land on the couch, but instead landed on the floor."

In contrast, in classrooms where teachers assigned identical topics for composition, students had limited opportunities to integrate their interests with the topics. Closed tasks denied students the chance to make decisions about organizing information and creating unique products. In one class, the teacher told the children to write about "what I did at the farm today." Instead of personal elaborations, many students' efforts were mechanical, like these compositions: "We went to the farm. We had some food" [Betty]. "I did not like the farm kos it is sikey (stinky). I liked it a little" [Andrew].

Allowing students to make choices encourages them to develop an interest in literacy, and it provides students an opportunity to plan and regulate their literacy learning.

Challenge

Some teachers, especially those in first grade, are justifiably wary of tasks that may overtax young students and cause frustration or failure. The solution is to assign tasks that children can master easily, thinking that such tasks will inspire confidence. However, we found that students showed scant enthusiasm for such literacy activities. The most motivated students were those who were engaged in moderately challenging tasks that led them to make new discoveries and to reorganize their understandings.

Moderately challenging tasks lead to positive feelings because they provide feedback to students about what they are learning and how they are progressing. If tasks are too easy, students become bored. If they are too difficult, students are likely to become frustrated. However, open tasks can be used to provide enough flexibility so that students can tackle a problem and use their competencies to solve it. In other words,

open tasks allow all students to work at their fullest capacity by adjusting the goals and relative difficulty of the tasks.

Interviews with talented and successful people support the motivational value of moderately difficult tasks. When asked about their deep commitment to their work, chess masters, rock climbers, basketball players, musical composers, and surgeons report that the exhilaration of operating at one's optimum level is all the reward they need for their efforts (Csikszentmihalyi, 1990). The real compensation in such "peak" experiences is receiving accurate information about what they can do and how they can improve. Where do these experts acquire the information they use to improve? They cull it from their errors. Unlike many school children, they do not look upon their errors as failures, but as a way to diagnose what went wrong and how to improve (Clifford, 1991). As a result, the next time they engage in that activity, they adjust the challenge to skills so that they can continue to advance.

How can teachers accomplish such a feat? In the classrooms that successfully promoted challenge, teachers designed tasks that required reflection and planning and that could not be accomplished in a rote or automatic fashion. An additional feature of these tasks was that they could be accomplished in a variety of ways. Because solutions were not obvious, children drew on the resources they had and were developing. Thus challenging tasks tended to "pull" learning in a variety of ways. They prompted students to use more organizational and self-monitoring strategies, such as arranging the pieces of a game ahead of time; to use more and varied reading strategies, such as using title, picture, and sound-symbol cues simultaneously; and to persist longer at an activity.

Challenging Tasks

One example of a challenging task that all students can accomplish successfully is the text scramble. Teachers reproduce text from stories or nursery rhymes on oaktag, cutting the sentences into individual words. Students reconstruct the sentences in a meaningful way. The task requires students to design a plan; monitor for decoding, meaning, punctuation, and upper and lower case letters; attend to sequencing; and use rehearsal for text memory. The task is accessible to students at various developmental levels. Students can solve it using a variety of strategies (i.e., they can use meaning or punctuation clues or both), and there are several solutions (i.e., students can recreate the original sentences from the text or create sentences of their own). This task encourages persistence. Instead of giving up, asking for answers, or going on to a new activity, students use their errors diagnostically (Clifford, 1991).

Steve, a below-average reader, made more than 25 attempts to arrange the words in one sentence so that they made sense. He tried many arrangements, rereading and checking each time to determine if it "sounded right." He also used teacher hints ("What does a sentence start with?") to introduce new strategies. After Steve finally completed the task, the teacher congratulated him. Steve smiled proudly and then asked for another sentence to complete.

Most closed or rote tasks lack personal challenges. In tasks where children fill in words, match sounds with pictures, or underline key words, there is little need to use learning strategies or maintain concentration. Many students complete such tasks as if they are operating on "automatic pilot." The skills-focused tasks that provide the staple fare in their classrooms do not seem to provide students with opportunities for adjusting the tasks to make them personally challenging. As a consequence, meaning making, self-regulation, and pride in accomplishment suffer.

Control

A third feature of open-ended activities is that they provide students some control over their learning. A significant goal of literacy education is to support learners' independence and versatility as readers. When teachers and students share control, students learn to make crucial literacy decisions themselves.

Sharing control has consequences for motivation as well. When teachers completely control classroom tasks and processes, students are likely to perceive that they are being pressured to think or perform in a certain way. However, when teachers share control (e.g., invite children to sequence tasks, choose partners, or design a strategy), students interpret instruction as information they can use to learn and improve (Deci, Vallerand, Pelletier, & Ryan, 1991). For example, research has shown that children in shared-control classrooms reported more interest in their schoolwork and perceived themselves as more competent than those in teacher-controlled classrooms (Ryan & Grolnick, 1986).

Students want to see themselves as originators of plans and ideas, not as followers in a grand scheme they may not understand. Tasks and classroom structures that are overly controlling unwittingly undermine intrinsic motivation by removing the element of student participation, standard setting, and decision making. Shared control provides students with both the tools and the opportunities to take responsibility for their learning. They select strategies to reach their goals and protect their intentions by avoiding distractions (Corno, 1992). For example, one student clearly communicated her need to concentrate when she said, "Shut up, Jason, I am *trying* to work. Do you mind?"

Open Tasks Facilitate Student Control

Because open tasks are more cognitively complex than closed tasks, they require students to think strategically and to monitor and evaluate their learning. When students are actively involved in controlling their learning, they feel greater ownership of their performance and achievement. Typical open tasks include trade book reading, composition, partner reading, and games or interactive activities in which students manipulate text to create meaning or solidify skills. For example, when students compose, they can use wall charts of vowel sounds and lists of favorite vocabulary that the class has generated as sources for spelling and ideas.

Another activity that promotes student control is sequencing sentence strips from a favorite story. Students paste the strips in sequence and then illustrate the accompanying text. In this activity, students have to plan how to accomplish the task. When Susan completed this task, she followed these steps. First, she drew on her memory of the text to sequence the strips in the appropriate order. Then she used text features to check her work (in the story, characters appeared in a logical order). Finally, she compared her version to the actual text which she got from the classroom library.

However, during closed tasks children have fewer opportunities to select, monitor, and evaluate their strategy use. These tasks mostly require automatized responses or repeated application of the same response as opposed to active strategy use. For example, one common task required students to decode two words and decide which one has a certain sound. In another typical closed task, students read a sentence and decided which of two words correctly completed the sentence.

Although the goal of using sound-symbol knowledge is an important one, the tasks used to meet this goal are very limiting. Children do not have to devise a plan or organize information. As a result, they have few opportunities to see how sound-symbol knowledge facilitates reading comprehension. Indeed, many closed tasks (such as those in some workbooks) are so repetitive that after several months of first-grade reading instruction students recognize the pattern and little thinking is required to accomplish them. Less active involvement in literacy activities leads to disempowerment and ultimately to disinterest for many students.

Interviews with children further illuminate how students use their problem-solving skills to gain control over tasks. In this study, when students engaged in open tasks were asked about the learning difficulties they had encountered and how they handled those difficulties, they were likely to respond by naming a specific difficulty, such as "I knew they had the same letter, but not the same sound" and by saying that they heightened their effort to solve the difficulty. By contrast, students who were engaged in mostly closed tasks were more vague about their problems, often saying that the words were hard or that they had trouble following directions. In addition, they

often responded that when they had learning difficulties they "guessed" or "just did it."

The difference in the students' responses appears to indicate that those who spend time in open tasks are more self-directed and aware of how learning processes can be used, whereas those in closed tasks are more narrowly focused either on meeting the expectations of the teacher or on the task.

Collaboration

Although previous conceptions of teaching and learning emphasized the teacher's role in transmitting knowledge, more recent ideas have emphasized the social and interactional nature of learning. Some have described the desired relationship between teachers and students (as well as among students) as an apprentice ship in which a more able companion guides, supports, and challenges another's understanding (e.g., Newman & Schwager, 1993). In addition to cognitive benefits, social guidance and cooperation in classrooms are also fundamental to motivation.

Social interaction is motivational in several ways. First, peer comments and ideas can pique students' curiosity and spark further interest. Second, children's observations of their classmates' progress may increase their confidence in their own ability to succeed (Schunk, 1989). Third, research in cooperative learning has shown that working with others promotes student engagement in work and group consciousness (Slavin, 1987). Collaboration can increase both effort and persistence. Situations that encourage productive social interaction offer ways for students to develop competence and efficacy as readers and writers.

Modeling and coaching were two activities we observed in classrooms that supported student motivation. In many classrooms, mixed-ability groups worked together on related tasks. Children in these groups could observe that there were multiple ways of planning and executing tasks, and they could borrow strategies that seemed useful. At the same time, children could develop more refined understandings of tasks and procedures by observing others more expert than they (Collins, Brown, & Newman, 1989). For example, Shannon profited from the clues Kate provided when they were working on flash cards together. When Shannon mispronounced words, Kate read a sentence from the back of the card to provide context, asked questions like "Does this have an *s* in it?", and prompted with "What is the opposite of *slow*?"

In addition, students often adopted a coaching role, integrating cognitive and motivational strategies to support successful completion of tasks. For example, Anna, an able reader, shared the oral reading of a story with Matt, a less able reader. When Matt accidentally skipped a page, Anna reminded him, "That doesn't make sense yet; it happened later. Go back." When Matt stumbled on a word, Anna said, "Don't ask me for help. Try to sound it out." Matt dutifully (and successfully) did so.

Students in classrooms where collaboration was encouraged gave and received help routinely, but because tasks differed, the help rarely consisted of giving answers. For example, during a Bingo game, one child helped her peers by pronouncing, then spelling, bingo words. One of the players requested help, asking, "Is *listen* spelled l-i-s-t-e-n?" These activities supported learning, encouraged continued persistence and engagement, and helped students feel like competent readers and writers.

In classrooms where students completed mostly closed activities, children remained at their desks working on identical tasks. Although teachers did not actively discourage collaboration on seatwork (indeed, in some classrooms, desks were in work groups of four), there was a premium on quiet because teachers met with reading groups at that time. Also, students had fewer models. They worked at the same desks with the same peers day in and day out. The same was true in reading groups. In some classes, reading groups were formed by ability, so the models available were limited both in number and in expertise. Finally, because all children completed identical tasks, it appeared that children in classes doing closed activities regarded help seeking more as cheating than helping a peer learn. Thus, there were more behaviors like veiled glances at a neighbor's work as well as shielding papers from prying eyes. When students perceive situations as competitive, they focus less on effort and learning and more on appearing able or outperforming their peers (Ames, 1992).

Opportunities to Learn From and With Others

Collaboration can be encouraged in several ways. First, in classrooms where students have a choice of tasks, they can select activities and join groups of children with the same interests at various centers around the classroom. Because most children complete several tasks during reading time, they have opportunities to work with many other children. Moreover, the students in the interest groups can be encouraged to help peers and to provide explanations of goals and processes. Additionally, when appropriate, teachers can redirect students' questions to a peer who has successfully completed a similar activity. Finally, students can be asked to demonstrate to peers or to explain an important understanding they have gained.

In one classroom where students frequently generated prediction questions about text, the teacher asked students to help her spell as she wrote the questions on the easel. As students spelled, she asked them to explain their thinking processes in selecting the letters for the words or where they had learned the words. Modeling how to request and give help and then providing opportunities for students to assist each other will encourage children to regard literacy as an opportunity for engagement and improvement rather than a search for the correct answer or a race to completion. Thus, open tasks in collaborative classrooms are more likely to foster intrinsic interest in learning through help seeking, help giving, and child discussions about ideas and strategies.

Constructing Meaning

Open and closed tasks offer students different opportunities to construct meaning. When they complete open tasks, students have more chances to construct meaning in text as well as to build a rationale for the meaningfulness of literacy activities.

Constructing meaning promotes motivation by assisting children in making sense of their learning—the tasks in which they engage and the strategies they employ (Paris & Byrnes, 1989). They use information gleaned from their daily tasks in literacy to construct purposes for reading and writing and how they may be entertaining, informational, and useful. If children find that literacy allows them to solve interesting problems, they will associate reading and writing with thinking, challenge, and personal growth. If, however, they associate literacy with completing exercises, they may interpret it simply as manipulating symbols or solving abstract puzzles (Resnick, 1987). Increasingly, national assessments like the National Assessment of Educational Progress (Mullis, Campbell, & Farstrup, 1993) suggest that many children continue to separate learning to read and write in school from out-of-school uses of reading and writing.

Children's responses to the interview question "What are you supposed to learn from your reading activity?" provides clear evidence of the effect of tasks on students' understanding of and appreciation for reading and writing. After completing open tasks, children frequently responded that they were learning new information (e.g., "About the life cycle of a butterfly" or "Where the wind goes") and monitoring their self-improvement ("So I can read second-grade books"). However, children who completed mostly closed tasks typically took a more limited view. They often responded that they were learning word parts (e.g., "short *a*") or that they "didn't know" what they were supposed to learn from their activities. Apparently their tasks did not provide enough information for them to set meaningful literacy goals.

Literacy Tasks Support the Construction of Meaning

How did teachers in this study promote students' motivation through meaning making? In one classroom, the children and teacher created thematic lists of favorite vocabulary words on large charts. There were color words, Halloween words, apple words, words about birds, and others. Sean used the charts to add some words to his personal word bank. However, in the process he had many opportunities to construct meaning. As he read the sentences on the "black" chart, he was aided by the context: "Blackberries are black. A scary bat is black. A bowling ball is black. A crayon can be black. A blackbird is black. The sky is black at night. A witch's hat is black. Watermelon seeds are black." Compared to the limited vocabulary and decontextualized sentences that most worksheets offer (e.g., "Can a goat float in a boat?"), this task provided opportunities to use meaning as an aid both in building a rich vocabulary and in learning to use many decoding strategies.

During free reading time in one classroom, two students retreated to the puppet theater to share a story. As they read, they spontaneously picked up puppets and began to act out the story. This task allowed students to use various ways to create meaning. Compared to the typical exercise of reading short paragraphs and answering comprehension questions, this open task supported students' creative responses to text and generated enthusiasm for personal and meaningful interpretations. However, tasks alone cannot facilitate meaning making. Students must have an understanding of how to approach literacy tasks if they are to solve them meaningfully. Therefore, instruction is an important factor in providing students tools to use in constructing meaning.

Instruction Supports the Construction of Meaning

Teachers who are most successful in motivating their students introduce, model, and provide opportunities for students to use many reading strategies. In addition to teaching sound-symbol correspondences and the use of sentence context for decoding, they teach comprehension skills such as predicting, question-asking, relating stories to prior knowledge, and making inferences. For example, one teacher demonstrated how students could use a combination of strategies by covering up key words in a big book with self-sticking notes and asking students to use the context to predict the words and then use sound-symbol cues to confirm or revise.

Teachers can introduce both instructional and recreational texts by asking students what they know about the topic and asking them to predict what the author would say. When asked to predict what the text *Noisy Nora* (Wells, 1973) would be about, students suggested: "A little mouse that makes a lot of noise," "She gets in trouble for making things fall down," and "She is annoying." Before studying the text *A House Is a House for Me* (Hoberman, 1978), the teacher asked what kinds of houses creatures live in. Children's responses ranged from the conventional (e.g., cement, mansion, wood, apartment) to the imaginative (e.g., cave, tree house, mouse hole, gingerbread, cage). During reading, children delighted in discovering their contributions in print. After reading, children added to their original lists of dwellings.

In addition to teaching a variety of reading/thinking strategies, successful teachers foster metacognition about learning and reading. Reflectiveness can be encouraged by inviting students to plan and evaluate their learning. In this study, in classes where students engaged in many open tasks, students were guided to make and sequence choices and to evaluate their decisions.

Some teachers regularly conducted a discussion at the end of literacy activities in which students were invited to describe both more and less successful strategies and to help each other by making suggestions for "working smarter." One teacher emphasized the importance of self control for learning by helping her students maintain attention. Used judiciously, her brief question "Are you focused?" reminded students that they needed to redirect attention to stay in control of their learning. Other tactics, such as asking students "How do you know?" and requiring them to explain the process they use to complete an activity reminds students that they have a major role in deciding which information is useful and valuable.

In classrooms where strategy teaching is largely confined to decoding sound-symbol correspondences, there may be little emphasis on comprehension or on how strategies can be used in reading extended text. This approach to literacy instruction not only limits students' strategic repertoires, but it also restricts opportunities to use reading strategies in meaningful situations. Unless students have many chances to use reading strategies in authentic reading and writing, they may begin to doubt their usefulness and value.

Consequences

Open and closed tasks also have different consequences for students. Closed tasks direct attention to correct answers, often reported by numbers, red pencil, stars, or smiley faces. Children may be forced to judge their performance by the number of stars they receive, whether their paper was hung on the board, and how they compare to other students. In contrast, open tasks seldom have one correct answer, allowing students to focus on whether they achieved their purposes, whether they used good tactics, and whether they tried to do their best. Rather than stars or stickers, students can base their self-assessments on the effort they expended, their enjoyment, or the meaningfulness of the activity. The consequences of this latter focus are usually positive feelings about effort, ownership, achievement, and responsibility.

The motivational outcomes of literacy tasks influence how students interpret their roles in learning to read. Those interpretations can affect their desire to persist and to remain involved in literacy. Tasks affect the consequences of literacy in two ways.

First, open tasks support a constructive approach to failure (Clifford, 1991). If a task can be approached at an appropriate difficulty level, miscues or errors evoke a strategy orientation in which students interpret "failures" not as evidence of insufficient ability or effort but as temporary setbacks caused by less than optimal strategy use. In these situations, students adapt their strategies rather than give up. When students are moderately challenged, they are likely to show such positive responses to failure as increased persistence, more varied strategy use, greater task interest, and increased task performance.

Second, when students see tasks as controllable, they are more likely to take personal responsibility for them (Weiner, 1979). In addition, they have confidence that they can adjust their effort and strategy use appropriately. They do not interpret all situations in a similar manner, such as the student who says, "I'm not good at reading" or "I'll never figure this out." Instead, with open tasks and appropriate support from cognitive and metacognitive strategy instruction, students are able to maintain a belief in their ability to succeed as readers and writers.

In fact, students define failure differently in open and closed tasks. In closed tasks, if students cannot get the correct answer, they may become frustrated or discouraged because the one avenue to success is blocked. However, in open tasks, if one approach does not work, another can be tried. Errors are regarded as information about what one does or doesn't know or what one has or hasn't tried. In either case, this information can be used to adjust goals or strategies.

For example, when Steve was engaged in the text scramble, he ran into several obstacles. He had rearranged the sentence "Then she felled some chairs" several ways. Each time, the word *some* was inappropriately placed. Finally, Steve revealed that he did not know that word. With some cues and strategy support, he decoded *some* and completed the sentence. Similarly, after he failed to use a teacher cue, "What does a sentence start with?", Steve asked what the difference between upper- and lowercase *t* was. In both cases, he used the information not as signals of his low ability, but as clues to help him reach a meaningful solution.

In summary, open-ended tasks are more likely to provide appropriate challenges, genuine choices, some student control over learning, opportunities to collaborate with others and to construct meaning through reading and writing. These activities support student motivation through positive, affective consequences and by fostering students' determination, effort, and thoughtful engagement.

The classroom observations and examples reported in this article suggest that motivation for literacy is not necessarily a quality that children bring to instruction. That is, motivation does not reside solely in the child; rather it is in the interaction between students and their literacy environments (Paris & Turner, 1994). This finding underscores the considerable role that instruction plays in influencing children's motivation for literacy. Because children come to know and understand literacy primarily through the activities in which they engage, literacy tasks have enormous potential to influence students' feelings and attitudes toward literacy as well as their use of learning strategies and self-regulation.

Teachers who foster motivation in literacy classrooms:

1. *Provide authentic choices and purposes for literacy.* They recast activities to emphasize the enjoyment and the informational values of literacy. Instead of referring to daily tasks as work, these teachers rename them by emphasizing their function, such as "Today we are going to plan for *Clifford's* birthday party by writing invitations, composing stories about what the party will be like, and making lists of guests."

2. *Allow students to modify tasks so the difficulty and interest levels are challenging.* They demonstrate to students the many ways that a task can be done. Students are given concrete examples of successful, but different, approaches to tasks. Students are taught to assess whether a task is too easy or difficult for them and how to adjust goals or strategies for appropriate difficulty. Such teachers point out how students have molded tasks to their interests and assign tasks that can be modified in many ways.

3. *Show students how they can control their learning.* They teach students how to evaluate what they know, and how to monitor and evaluate their learning. Reminders such as "Are you staying focused?" and "What's more important—that you made a mistake or what you learned?" guide students' inner speech so they can self-monitor.

4. *Encourage collaboration.* These teachers emphasize the positive aspects of help seeking and help giving. They design

activities so that students have opportunities to work with many different peers. They teach students how to help each other by emphasizing the giving of clues, not answers. Some individual activities are recast as collaborative ones. For example, students work on flash cards together. One student gives hints, such as putting the word in context or giving a synonym or antonym. Similarly, individual reading is sometimes done in pairs.

5. *Emphasize strategies and metacognition for constructing meaning.* Students need a repertoire of strategies in order to respond flexibly in reading and writing situations. Extensive applications of comprehension (as well as decoding/encoding) strategies assist students in acquiring an understanding of what literacy is as well as how to use and understand it.

6. *Use the consequences of tasks to build responsibility, ownership, and self-regulation.* Group evaluation is a regular part of literacy instruction. Students are encouraged to share their successes and their failures. These teachers help students see that errorless learning is not learning at all. Real learning comes about through error, since errors provide information about needed improvement. Such teachers emphasize the value of effort and honing strategies. These tools equip students to attempt more and more challenging tasks.

Our purpose in this article was to share the motivational strategies of some expert teachers in literacy instruction. These teachers were successful in helping their students develop an interest in reading, in encouraging wide reading in the classroom and at home, and in instilling an intrinsic desire for learning and reading in many of their students. They did this by molding literacy instruction to the needs, interests, and skills of their students. If students are to be motivated readers and writers, we must give them the tools and the reasons to read and write and allow them to discover the many paths to literacy—paths that fit the diverse goals, purposes, interests, and social needs of children.

References

Ames, C. (1992). Classrooms: Goals, structures, and student motivation. *Journal of Educational Psychology, 84*, 261–271.

Bridwell, N. (1988). *Clifford's birthday party.* New York: Scholastic.

Clifford, M.M. (1991). Risk taking: Theoretical, empirical and educational considerations. *Educational Psychologist, 26*, 263–297.

Collins, A., Brown, J.S., & Newman, S. (1989). Cognitive apprenticeship: Teaching the crafts of reading, writing, and mathematics. In L.B. Resnick (Ed.), *Knowing, learning, and instruction.* Hillsdale, NJ: Erlbaum.

Corno, L. (1992). Encouraging students to take responsibility for learning and performance. *Elementary School Journal, 93*, 69–83.

Csikszentmihalyi, M. (1990). Literacy and intrinsic motivation. *Daedalus, 119*, 115–140.

Deci, E.L., Vallerand, R.J., Pelletier, L.G., & Ryan, R.M. (1991). Motivation and education: The self-determination perspective. *Educational Psychologist, 26*, 325–346.

Hoberman, M.A. (1978). *A house is a house for me.* Bergenfield, NJ: Viking Press.

Lepper, M.R., & Hodell, M. (1989). Intrinsic motivation in the classroom. In C. Ames & R. Ames (Eds.), *Research on motivation in education* (Vol. 3, pp. 73–105). San Diego: Academic Press.

Mullis, I.V.S., Campbell, J.R., & Farstrup, A.E. (1993). *Executive summary of the NAEP 1992 reading report card for the nation and the states.* Washington, DC: U.S. Department of Education.

Newman, R.S., & Schwager, M.T. (1993). Students' perceptions of the teacher and classmates in relation to reported help seeking in math class. *Elementary School Journal, 94*, 3–17.

Paris, S.G., & Byrnes, J.P. (1989). The constructivist approach to self-regulation. In B.J. Zimmerman & D.H. Schunk (Eds.), *Self-regulated learning and academic achievement* (pp. 169–200). New York: Springer-Verlag.

Paris, S.G., & Turner, J.C. (1994). Situated motivation. In P. Pintrich, D. Brown, & C.E. Weinstein (Eds.), *Student motivation, cognition, and learning: Essays in honor of Wilbert J. McKeachie* (pp. 213–237). Hillsdale, NJ: Erlbaum.

Resnick, L.B. (1987). Learning in school and out. *Educational Researcher, 16*, 13–20.

Ryan, R.M., & Grolnick, W.S. (1986). Origins and pawns in the classroom: Self-report and projective assessments of individual differences in children's perceptions. *Journal of Personality and Social Psychology, 50*, 550–558.

Schiefele, U. (1991). Interest, learning, and motivation. *Educational Psychologist, 26*, 299–323.

Schunk, D.H. (1989). Social cognitive theory and self-regulated learning. In B.J. Zimmerman & D.H. Schunk (Eds.), *Self-regulated learning and academic achievement* (pp. 83–110). New York: Springer-Verlag.

Slavin, R.E. (1987). Cooperative learning: Where behavioral and humanistic approaches to classroom motivation meet. *Elementary School Journal, 88*, 29–37.

Turner, J. (in press). The influence of classroom contexts on young children's motivation for literacy. *Reading Research Quarterly.*

Weiner, B. (1979). A theory of motivation for some classroom experiences. *Journal of Educational Psychology, 71*, 3–25.

Wells, R. (1973). *Noisy Nora.* New York: Scholastic.

Engagement Activites

In Your Classroom
Reflect on the authenticity of the reading tasks offered in your classroom. Think of ways you can offer students opportunities to choose books and modify their reading tasks. How can you model and encourage collaboration about reading?

With Your Colleagues
Modeling how students regulate their learning and practice can be challenging. In the final section of their article, Turner and Paris offer reminder questions—Are you staying focused? What's more important—that you made a mistake or what you learned?—to show students how they can control their learning. Discuss how you and your colleagues can encourage self-regulated reading and how you can model talking about books and monitoring comprehension.

Further Reading
Lutz, S.L., Guthrie, J.T., & Davis, M.H. (2006). Scaffolding for engagement in elementary school reading instruction. *Journal of Educational Research, 100*(1), 3–20.

This study investigated student engagement during fourth-grade reading lessons. The results indicate that engagement and motivation are high when students participate in complex, integrated reading and writing tasks (in this case, involving literacy and science). In addition, classrooms that demonstrated high levels of engagement and motivation showed greater gains in reading comprehension. The researchers attributed these gains to effective teacher scaffolding. Several helpful rubrics are presented, including rubrics for literacy task complexity, student engagement, and teacher scaffolding.

Engaging Middle Years Students: Literacy Projects That Matter

Mary Ryan

Sarah is in her second year of teaching at an urban middle school in Australia. This is her first teaching post from university. Student attendance is low, and the students seem to be disengaged from the curriculum. She does a situational analysis of her class and finds the following:

- There are 27 students (ages 11–12).
- There are 25 different cultures from 24 suburbs in the school—a highly diverse representation.
- There are 6 different cultures in the class, including 1 ESL student.
- There are 19 boys and 8 girls.
- There are 6 boys who are working with behavior management staff. One was recently diagnosed with attention deficit disorder.
- This class holds more than half of the total citations in the whole school for unacceptable behavior. Sixteen students are repeat offenders.
- There are 12 students identified through standardized tests as below satisfactory standard, 9 students in every area.
- There are 6 students receiving funded literacy support.

Sarah knows that she needs to try something new, both for the students' sake and her own! She

asks herself, How do I engage these students and improve their literacy skills at the same time?

Students often enter my undergraduate literacy curriculum and pedagogy classes with conflicting and certainly varied notions about which literacy practices "matter" in middle years classrooms. Media debates in Australia and elsewhere promote different viewpoints about the importance of making learning interesting and relevant versus teaching students the basics of spelling, grammar, sentence structure, comprehension, and so on (see, for example, Donnelly, 2006). These preservice teachers say that they can see why we need to engage middle years students in authentic learning activities. Yet many of their experiences during the practicum seem to suggest that basic skills are more important, particularly given the time constraints in an already crowded curriculum.

I introduce students to an approach to planning that suggests that these debates about what matters in literacy are moot. We can successfully plan authentic literacy projects that have basic skills as integral to the practices required for the success of the authentic outcomes. The skills (which span a variety of modes) are explicitly unpacked to ensure that students have the resources they need to be successful in all literacy practices and to address the skills scope and sequence charts of syllabus documents. This approach to planning is based upon a multiliteracies pedagogic framework (Kalantzis & Cope, 2005; The New London Group, 2000), which favors authentic projects as vehicles for learning

Reprinted from Ryan, M. (2008). Engaging middle years students: Literacy projects that matter. *Journal of Adolescent & Adult Literacy*, *52*(3), 190-201.

key skills and knowledge processes. These projects matter in all of the ways that are relevant for middle years students. They are community based, cross-curricular, and connected to students' complex textual lives, which make them authentic. They cater to diverse needs and build upon diverse strengths so that not all students need to achieve the outcomes in exactly the same way. They raise the intellectual bar as deep, substantive issues are introduced, analyzed, and incorporated into the outcomes. They support students as learners by giving them real responsibility for their learning and by explicitly teaching them key academic skills. All of these conditions matter if we are to engage students in the middle years as successful and motivated learners.

This article begins by briefly defining the phenomenon of the "middle years" in schools, followed by an explanation of the multiliteracies designs of meaning and pedagogic framework. Finally, some practical planning snapshots are included to illustrate how these authentic projects can be designed for classrooms.

Middle Years Students

Education for early adolescents (typically ages 10–14, known as the middle years) has been a locus of reform for countries such as the United Kingdom, New Zealand, the United States, Australia, and Singapore (Carrington, 2002). These reforms have typically challenged the notion of adolescents as incapable of difficult and analytic thinking (see, for example, Carnegie Council on Adolescent Development, 1989; Jackson & Davis, 2000). The middle years are seen as significant in terms of the changes that young people experience, their increasing awareness of the world around them, and their increased susceptibility to alienation. Middle years policies often suggest that students in these years should be engaged through connectedness to the world, intellectual stimulation, and the recognition of difference and diversity (Carrington, 2002; Education Queensland, 2003; Ministerial Advisory Committee for Educational Renewal, 2003).

For youths in a contemporary, globalized society, life is characterized by change. There is nothing startling about such a statement—indeed, any generation of youths from the baby boomers to post-1970s youth could be described in this way. What is of significant interest is the multitude of ways in which contemporary youth respond to and negotiate such change, growing up as they are in drastically different social conditions. In a society characterized by risk and individualism (Bauman, 2001; Beck & Beck-Gernsheim, 2002), with increasing levels of responsibility and choice (Furlong & Cartmel, 2007; Wyn & Woodman, 2007), young people face new imperatives to perform identities and to generate new forms of expression and participation.

Less predictable life pathways (Côté, 2002) mean that young people must continually make choices about what is salient for them at particular times (Wright, Macdonald, Wyn, & Kriflik, 2005). Sometimes such choices may be at odds with the expected attributes or behaviors of the phase of life that is applied to them by adults and society, and as such they are marginalized or tagged as problem cases. Social, cultural, economic, and institutional factors can influence their performances at school; hence, assuming that all young people want and need the same experiences at school needs to be reconsidered. So how can we engage middle years students so that they feel involved, are stimulated intellectually, and are also supported academically to develop the skills and knowledge that they need? A multiliteracies pedagogic framework offers much potential for such goals.

Multiliteracies Designs and Pedagogy

In 1996, the New London Group met to discuss the emerging literacy needs for a new world that emphasizes the complex potential of language as a productive and innovative meaning-making system in culturally diverse "new times" (Hall, 1992). They argued that the young people of today operate within what they came to call "multiliteracies," a complex set of communication media involving many different kinds of text, including video, CD, truncated language forms used in computer speak, SMS/MMS communication (short text or visual messaging on mobile phones or computers), alternative verbal communication with hybrid words and sentences (for example, making new words or phrases by merging existing ones), gestural communication, audio literacies, and more. Kress and van Leeuwen (2006) suggested that forms of communication that are based solely on written language are untenable in this new knowledge society. Kist (2003) argued that literacy achievement in these new times includes fluency in multiple forms of representation, critical thinking and talking about the work, collaboration, and engagement. He argued that students must be active participants in authentic curricula, where student achievement equals student engagement.

Cope and Kalantzis (2000b) captured the essence of multiliteracies when they described it as creating a different way of learning or coming to know "in which language and other modes of meaning are dynamic representational resources, constantly being remade by their users as they work to achieve their various cultural purposes" (p. 5). Cope and Kalantzis (2000a) indicate that these various modes of representation that learners access include linguistic, visual, audio, gestural, and spatial with combinations of these as multimodal design (see Figure 1). These design areas have been represented as overlapping, as there is not always a clear distinction between different designs. For example, perspective and layout on a page could be considered part of both visual and spatial design.

Kalantzis and Cope (2005) have more recently developed the multiliteracies model as

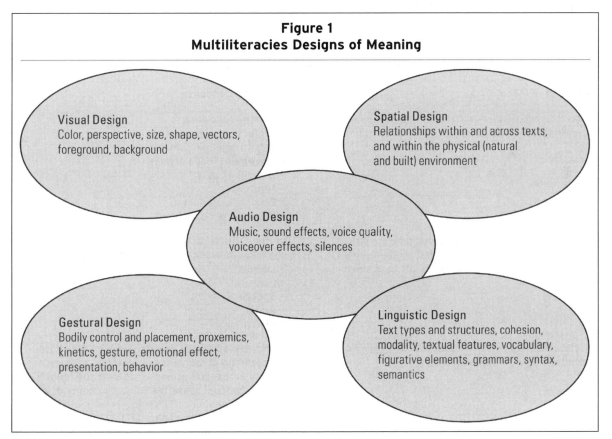

Figure 1
Multiliteracies Designs of Meaning

Visual Design
Color, perspective, size, shape, vectors, foreground, background

Spatial Design
Relationships within and across texts, and within the physical (natural and built) environment

Audio Design
Music, sound effects, voice quality, voiceover effects, silences

Gestural Design
Bodily control and placement, proxemics, kinetics, gesture, emotional effect, presentation, behavior

Linguistic Design
Text types and structures, cohesion, modality, textual features, vocabulary, figurative elements, grammars, syntax, semantics

Note. Adapted from Cope, B., & Kalantzis, M. (2000). Designs for social futures. In B. Cope & M. Kalantzis (Eds.), *Multiliteracies: Literacy learning and the design of social futures* (pp. 203–234). Melbourne, Australia: Macmillan.

a pedagogic framework through their understanding of meaning making as a combination of knowledge processes— that is, we learn by doing. They suggest that learners or novices (where the teacher or instructor is seen as a learner alongside the students) need the opportunity to engage in four broad knowledge processes: *experiencing* the known and the new, *conceptualizing* by identifying and theorizing, *analyzing* functionally and critically, and *applying* appropriately and creatively. These knowledge processes constitute what they term a *transformative curriculum*, which differs from inquiry learning in that it emphasizes different sequences for different learners and areas of knowledge. Student diversity and multiple ways of thinking and learning are paramount in this approach.

Working from a research question that is pertinent to student lives and that addresses issues and interests in society is central to new learning theory and the notion of longer term curriculum projects. This approach has been used variously in classrooms across Australia (see, for example, Healy, 2004; Mills, 2006), Singapore (Tan, 2008), Canada and the United States (Kist, 2003), and Malaysia (Pandian & Balraj, 2005). Mills's (2006) findings suggest that the implementation of multiliteracies projects must include a focus on an inclusive classroom, where meaning making and cultures are seen as dynamic and changing rather than as stable and regular. Pandian and Balraj (2005) argued that teacher professional preparation must include aspects of this type of planning and implementation if it is to have long-term success.

I turn now to some practical manifestations of a multiliteracies approach to learning in the middle years. I provide some snapshots of a three-step model of contextualized planning. See Table 1 for an outline of the model.

Table 1
A Three-Step Planning Model

Three-step Model	Organizing Concepts
Step 1: *Conceptualize* (with students) the ideas and knowledge base for authentic project outcomes.	Include the following: • Project title or question • Key knowledge domains • Movement focus groups • Outcome tasks • Mentors • Flexible sequencing • Knowledge objectives
Step 2: *Unpack* the ideas to determine specific literacy skills and knowledge that students need to experience or be explicitly taught to achieve the outcomes.	Use the multiliteracies designs to unpack literacy skills and knowledge, including the following: • Linguistic • Gestural • Spatial • Audio • Visual
Step 3: *Strategize* the pragmatics of the project: detailed short-term planning.	The three-step model can also be used for short-term planning of sequences of lessons or learning episodes across the project, including the following: Step 1: Conceptualize the topic, the context, and the platform. Step 2: Unpack the design skill. Step 3: Strategize how these new skills and knowledge can be applied in authentic ways.

This type of planning suggests that students are investigators who are putting their skills to work to solve a problem or address an issue that is relevant to them. Thus, the projects should start with a question. Catering for diverse interests and needs is also a key element for engaging middle years students. Within the project, it is desirable that groups of students work on different facets of the project to build their strengths and to develop their skills and knowledge. In this sense, not all students need to produce exactly the same outcome, nor do they necessarily require explicit instruction in the same skills. Students can achieve literacy and subject content or disciplinary literacies (Moje, 2007; Stull, 2007) objectives by taking different pathways through transdisciplinary projects. Moje's (2007) notion of socially just pedagogy for subject matter instruction fits nicely with a multiliteracies framework. She argued that students should learn not only about established knowledge, but also how to question it and be given opportunities to relate it to their lives and to offer alternatives. She posited a view of subject matter instruction that focuses on ways of *producing* knowledge, using language, across multiple disciplines. This too is a goal of a multiliteracies approach, albeit with greater focus on multiple design elements rather than just on written language. Assessment of such projects can be conducted using the knowledge processes and design elements to create rubrics and to guide development of portfolios and group assessments (see Kalantzis & Cope, 2005).

In the following project snapshot, I outline a project idea using the three steps outlined in Table 1. I do not include the full gamut of planning for the project; rather, I provide illustrative snapshots for each step. I have used a project centered on socially just disciplinary literacies (Moje, 2007) of health and physical education (HPE), which are grouped together in the Queensland curriculum. This project is timely and relevant in the Australian context, with health issues dominating media debates in relation to Indigenous communities and the so-called "obesity epidemic" in Australian children that is used as opportunistic political capital (Gard, 2004; Gard & Wright, 2001). It is important to plan projects that are contextually relevant to the community and to the young people in the class. See Ryan and Healy (2008) for projects related to the arts curriculum.

Project Snapshot: Health and Physical Education Focus

Step 1: Conceptualize

Project Question. How can we promote and develop independent and lifelong physical activity for health in our community (adapted from Ryan & Rossi, 2008)?

Key Knowledge Domains. The project task will determine which key learning areas or knowledge domains from school curricula will be integrated. This project may include the following:

- Health and physical education—health, healthy communities, development of physical skills
- English—reading, writing, viewing, shaping, speaking, and listening in operational, cultural, critical strands of learning
- Studies of society and the environment (or similar)—diverse communities, cultural groups, influences on individuals, participation in decision making, showing evidence over time, explaining causes and effects
- Information and communication technology—manipulation of materials, design challenges, use of interactive systems, accessing different sources of material

Movement Focus Groups. Movement focus groups are integral to this project; however, they are not relevant for all projects. Students work in focus groups within the project, where they undertake an ongoing program of physical activity across the school term. I suggest that the teacher may set parameters of realistic activities, subject to the local community—for example, a beach community could prompt quite different activities than an inner-city or a rural community—from which students could choose, with criteria developed by the class to guide selection. Such criteria may include the following:

- Try an activity that includes at least one unfamiliar skill.
- Choose an activity that you believe you will continue to pursue after the project is completed.
- Consider any health issues that may affect your performance.
- Join a group with at least one person with whom you have rarely worked before.

Possible movement focus groups follow. Note the breadth of activities that cater to diverse physical, financial, and cultural situations.

- Group #1—team activities (e.g., focus game)
- Group #2—walking/hiking
- Group #3—spiritual/muscular activities (e.g., yoga or Pilates)
- Group #4—dancing
- Group #5—cycling (e.g., road or trail)

Outcome Tasks. Each group has a major outcome task to produce, which contributes to the overall project task. Other tasks may also be assigned to the whole class, and during the course of the project many lead-up tasks and focused teaching episodes should be undertaken that contribute to the production of the final tasks. Table 2

Table 2
Outcome Tasks for Movement Focus Groups

Group Number	Outcome Task
All	Performance log—includes documentation of physical activities, progress, changes in general fitness and attitudes. May include artifacts such as digital photos, time/duration improvements, comments from mentor, and drawings. May be digital or print.
All	Contribution to school website—develop a community health page, load outcome tasks or representations (photos or film footage) as ongoing class responsibility, and appoint web director to maintain page.
1	Film documentary of the focus game—includes information about rules of the game and how to play, segments of game play with voice-over depicting functional analysis with tips for improved performance related to timing, spatial and motor skill elements of the game, interviews with community players, and so forth.
2	Montage—includes photographs, scale maps of walking tracks, scale models showing gradients of particular hiking trails, and descriptions and displays of appropriate clothing and equipment, including explanations of "breathable" or "moisture-wicking" fabric technology, and so forth.
3	Movement demonstration—planned sequence of hierarchical muscle control, introducing levels of meditation, breathing, and equipment use. Voice-over or PowerPoint presentation that provides information and commentary about the activity accompanies demonstration.
4	Choreographed dance demonstration—specific attention to gestural, spatial, and visual aspects of body movement, along with audio components to introduce mood and tempo. Voice-over that explains the functional analysis of the movements and provides the community with information about the activity accompanies demonstration.
5	Information booklet—mass-produced for distribution in the community. Liaise with local printing/copying company. Focus on creative visual impact, spatial layout, and appropriate linguistic forms. Include photographs, advertisements for local sponsors (e.g., bike shops), and scale maps of suitable road/trail routes graded for difficulty. Explain technology of lightweight titanium or carbon materials used for high-performance bicycle construction, advantages and disadvantages of click-in pedals, and so forth.

shows suggested outcome tasks for the movement focus groups listed earlier. The individual group tasks may be presented and displayed at a community event or in a community focal point on a designated day. The tasks may include research findings about the relevant movement activity, information about community facilities, associated costs, necessary and optional equipment, physical mobility requirements, significant cultural impacts pertaining to the suitability of the activity, possible risks or barriers, current participation rates in the local school or community, and survey results to suggest typical clientele and reasons for participation or nonparticipation.

Mentors. Each group would be assigned a mentor to guide the movement program. Mentors can be recruited from within the school—senior students, HPE teachers, or other staff with experience in the activities—or from experts in the community, such as yoga instructors, who may be encouraged to donate their time for one or two hours per week during the project. Many sporting or activity clubs have development officers who are willing to provide such services, and the students' first activity may be to contact relevant groups or individuals to invite them to participate. It makes sense to plan projects that are feasible in the local community.

Each group would be guided by an additional mentor for their outcome task. For example, a group producing a film documentary could work with a local filmmaker or media specialist either in person or in an e-mail. Media departments in secondary schools or universities may be useful contacts. The variety of outcome tasks can be reduced if school or community resources are limited. Some teachers plan one major outcome task for the whole class, with different groups taking responsibility for different sections (e.g., designing a product, marketing the idea, developing a website, planning finances).

Flexible Sequencing. I have seen a number of teachers harness the organizational skills of their students to plan timelines and keep everyone on track in their text outcomes. Pasting a large term calendar on the wall can keep everyone in the loop in terms of targets and deadlines. Broad targets, such as when the website will go live or when the documentary will be filmed, can be posted, then lead-up activities can be planned. Student groups can brainstorm their sequences of activities with time frames to achieve their outcome tasks and then add them to the calendar. Notes about booking times with media departments can also be added.

It is useful for project groups to come together regularly for whole-class meetings during which they can report progress, share what they have learned, and outline what their next target is. This level of responsibility can motivate students to achieve their goals.

Knowledge Objectives. It is essential that teachers provide opportunities throughout the project for students to learn by doing. Kalantzis and Cope's (2005) four broad, overlapping knowledge processes will be used here as a guide in Table 3 for facilitating such opportunities.

Step 2: Unpack

It is important to note here that not all students need explicit instruction in all of the knowledge and skills that are required for specific literacy practices. Small groups or individual students might be targeted for some focused episodes, while other episodes can be directed at the whole class. Literacy skills and knowledge for this project may include the following.

Linguistic Design

- Vocabulary development including content glossaries and metalanguage of texts
- Recognition of top-level text structures to aid comprehension, such as comparison/contrast, cause/effect, time/order, problem/solution, argument
- Research skills including locating, organizing, and synthesizing information
- Functional grammar as a critical tool of representation and analysis

Table 3
Concepts and Knowledge Within the Project

Experiencing the Known	Experiencing the New
• Use familiar texts or contexts as a catalyst to the project (e.g., book, movie, media report, major sporting event) • Practice familiar movement activities • Access students' prior knowledge of digital text production, cultural insights, text structures and features	• Introduce new movement activities and associated metalanguage • Try extended levels of muscle control • Practice decision making based on visual or spatial clues during movement activities • Teach elements of digital text production (e.g., editing and splicing film, uploading documents onto a web interface; aspects of ratio for scale maps and drawings; audio textual features of information voice-over or commentary, including intonation, pitch and pausing; use of effective visual grammars such as vectors, color, space, or perspective) • Conduct functional analyses (e.g., effectiveness of text layout, ball distribution during a game, use of space in text or movement) • Analyze critically text and movement activities (e.g., omissions; inclusions; determining those who benefit or are marginalized by texts or movement activities; recognizing multiple viewpoints or motor actions that are influenced by social, cultural, and historical discourses; mapping the relationships between individual choices and social influences or structures)
Conceptualizing by identifying • Metalanguage associated with students' tasks and activities • Vocabulary and glossary lists of new terms and concepts • Correct labels or captions on display texts or components of drawings or maps • Correct subject terminology related to texts or movements • Correct terminology of analysis	**Conceptualizing by theorizing** • Why a "twist" is different from a "turn" • Why particular movements are appropriate in different situations • Connections between the practice of particular motor actions or movements and the broader movement activity such as the game or the dance. Decontextualized drills and skills in physical activity (or in linguistic activity) are of no use if students do not understand how they contribute to enhanced performance • How and why students have used space, what effect it had and how this differed from the effect that they anticipated • Connections between different information and knowledge using diagrammatical representations such as concept maps, graphic outlines, structured overviews, and labeled drawings • Written synopses of overall tasks that show the inter-relating components
Analyzing functionally • Functional analysis *by students* of associated lead-up tasks, necessary resources, and possible timelines • Functional analysis of key texts in terms of structure; effective use of visual, spatial, or audio elements; appropriate	**Analyzing critically** • Helping students to frame their competencies gained within the learning context in social, political, ideological, historical, and value-centered ways (e.g., How do expectations of society affect their activities?) • Understanding that visual modes of meaning in health should be viewed as problematic and alternative images

(continued)

Table 3
Concepts and Knowledge Within the Project (*Continued*)

Analyzing functionally

use of language. Interaction of design elements and readability can be used to inform students' own constructions of similar texts

- Functional analysis of physical activity by viewing a visual representation of a game or an event so that key moments, movements, or decisions can be analyzed with a view to improvement

Analyzing critically

of "healthy bodies" should be juxtaposed against stereotypical visages (e.g., What do we make of wheelchair athletes or Sumo wrestlers? Not exactly the conventional picture of health and fitness, but nonetheless they perform at the highest level.)

Applying appropriately

- Use new skills and knowledge (from experiencing the new) in outcome tasks. Aspects of assessment are related to the appropriate use of these skills and knowledge
- Transform practices in game play with improved technical competence, knowledge, and understanding
- Transform life practices through meaningful health-related physical activities
- Document applications of new skills or abilities to show evidence of *ongoing* application. In this project, the performance log task will enable students to document such applications

Applying creatively

- Students should not just be trained to construct prescriptive texts or perform prescriptive movements
- Students can be encouraged to combine and recombine their knowledge and skills in new and different ways to achieve multiple purposes
- Students can make decisions about creative presentation of texts or movement demonstrations, creative inclusions in their tasks, and innovative ways to persuade the community to engage in lifelong physical activity for health
- Teachers need to liberate the capacities of students to take risks in the production of texts and should create conditions during physical activity in which students make decisions based on their ability to assess the context of the activity and try new moves or new sequences of known moves

- Contextual and textual features of several text types to be read and written by some or all students, with varying levels of expertise, including the following:

  ○ Reflective log writing
  ○ Annotations
  ○ Captions
  ○ Film/documentary scripts
  ○ News articles
  ○ Descriptions
  ○ Explanations
  ○ Analytical comments
  ○ Advertisements
  ○ Information reports
  ○ Commentaries

Gestural Design

- Body positioning, size, and meanings generated in different contexts
- Linking of bodily sequences
- Elements of body control in different contexts for different purposes
- Movement activities related to changes in body
- Movement skill improvement related to physical activity performance

- Bodily response to different stimuli, such as music, visual image and film, physical activity
- Presentation skills of posture, voice, facial expression, eye contact, absence of eye contact, silences, use of hands
- Effective listening techniques

Spatial Design

- Placement of hyperlinks embedded in digital texts
- Cohesive layout and connective techniques of website, booklet, log, montage, and PowerPoint presentation
- Development of organizational flowcharts of texts
- Placement of print text and images in texts
- Use of space in texts and in physical contexts
- Ratio of elements on a page or components of a model

Audio Design

- Voice-over and commentary including intonation, pitch, volume, pace, pausing
- Insertion of audio links in digital texts
- Choice of music to denote attitudes and tastes or overall mood through tempo, beat, style

Visual Design

- Development of graphic organizers for improved comprehension
- Film editing and splicing
- Use of color, line, shape, size, perspective, foreground, background, shot style in visual texts
- Meanings portrayed by visual contours of the body, for example muscle definition, body shape, facial features
- Editing and loading digital photos and scanned images
- Type colors and icons

Step 3: Strategize

Short-Term Planning of Strategies and Activities. An important shift from traditional pedagogic practices concerns the creation of opportunities for students to express their knowledge, try different approaches to text construction, and identify what they know and don't know about information and communication technologies (ICTs) and meaning repertoires well before teachers begin to teach from their own knowledge or exemplars. Teacher "silence"—that is, not putting teacher knowledge up front as a model to follow—can provide, in many cases, opportunities for students to take risks and to be more innovative. This does not mean that teacher demonstration or modeling is not pedagogically effective, but that in many instances, we should access student knowledge first.

In the following steps, I provide examples for explicit lesson or episode planning that also follow the contextualized three-step model for project planning as outlined earlier.

Step 1: Conceptualize the Topic, the Context, and the Platform. First, provide a context for the episode by refocusing students on the topic at hand—the *content knowledge*. This can be a long or short step, depending upon the goals of the episode. Then, explore the *design platform* for the focus design element. The knowledge processes (indicated in parentheses) can be enacted in many ways, such as the following:

- Immerse students in sharing personal experiences and artifacts and making sense of them through discussion (experiencing, conceptualizing).
- Explore ways in which meaning is made accessible for others in the immediate or wider community, and why different people take different views from one another (analyzing).
- Connect personal knowledge (the known) to the knowledge of local others and to the wider community (experiencing, conceptualizing).

- Use K-W-L (what I *k*now, what I *w*ant to learn, and what I've *l*earned) charts, Y-charts, SWOT (*s*trengths, *w*eaknesses, *o*pportunities, *t*hreats) analyses, or other conceptual maps to chart knowledge (conceptualizing, analyzing).
- Conceptualize and see knowledge as problematic (conceptualizing, analyzing).
- Deepen student knowledge of the subject through research and exploring new resources (experiencing, analyzing).
- Ensure that students work from a cluster of texts that centers on the topic or specific interest targets. The cluster should include texts from different modes, of different media, and which contain different viewpoints (conceptualizing, analyzing).
- Deepen knowledge through problem solving and scenarios (conceptualizing, analyzing, applying).

In the following linguistic design element example—teaching a new text type—strategies and activities that use the four knowledge processes are shown.

- Provide a variety of real-life examples of the text type so students can conceptualize and analyze their common or different features and choose a structure that suits their purpose, audience, and mode (experiencing, conceptualizing, analyzing).
- Provide opportunities for students to experiment with ways that the text type could change according to audience, medium—such as a newspaper, brochure, or website—or mode—such as oral, written, or visual (experiencing, conceptualizing, analyzing, applying).

Step 2: Unpack the Design Skill. This is where the explicit teaching and guiding can happen. Once students have established a workable text structure as indicated in Step 1 on page 108, explicit teaching of specific elements can occur using example texts. For example, textual features, such as paragraphing, grammar, sentence

structure, top-level structure, and so forth, can be taught in context. Students in the middle years need to be taught to notice relationships within and across texts, to check the purposes of textual features, and to develop strategies for engaging with and producing texts. Following are some examples:

- Discover cause-and-effect patterns in reports (e.g., about nutrition and health) and represent them visually. Then outline the three major implications from the text (e.g., weight gain/loss, heart disease, low/high energy levels) and note the consequences of each (e.g., low energy—inability to concentrate, less motivated to be active, headaches).
- Compare/contrast structures of traditional texts and multimedia texts. How do texts change for different subject matter, audiences, platforms, or modes?
- Show how explanations use action verbs to explain phenomena. Ask students to sketch the main objects from the text, name them (e.g., asthma attack), then list the associated action verbs (e.g., wheeze, cough, gasp).
- Understand that narratives accessed by middle years students can be quite complex. Developing plot profiles, character profiles, and sociograms can aid comprehension.
- Teach paragraphing explicitly, as it can be difficult to grasp. Cut up sentences from a paragraph and ask students to classify them as topic sentences, elaborating sentences, or synthesizing sentences. Students can also be encouraged to retell the paragraph orally in their own words using a similar structure.
- Use popular song lyrics to show how language is used to position people and groups. Students identify the participants (nouns) and the attributes (adjectives) and processes (verbs) that are associated with the participants to develop a comparison chart of how the characters are positioned in the text according to gender, race, sexual orientation, group identity, and so forth.

- Teach students to use coding strategies to annotate their work. For example, when writing a new text type, they can label the sections and the key textual features down the side. This can also work when reading—students can use sticky notes to code sections of the text that relate to other sections or sections that they don't understand or about which they want to ask a question.
- Link written and visual text. For example, if a cause/effect or comparison/contrast cohesive relationship is found in a text, how could we represent that graphically (e.g., in a diagram or graph)? If a time/order cohesive structure is present, could we create a timeline or story map?

Step 3: Strategize How These New Skills and Knowledge Can Be Applied in Authentic Ways. Students are given opportunities to apply new skills and knowledge in an achievable lead-up task to the overall project outcome. For example, in one teaching episode, students might produce the introductory paragraph of their information report, show the first two slides of their PowerPoint presentation, or take notes from several sources using keywords.

Tips

Additional tips for implementing multiliteracies projects include the following:

- Diverse cultural and social backgrounds are implicit in these projects. Token "multicultural days" are not seen as authentic; rather, the students continually engage with texts and experiences that reflect the diversity of our communities and viewpoints. Some communities may have different emphases in some modes, such as the absence of eye contact and the use of silence in Indigenous Australian communities (Martin, 2008).
- Students for whom English is a second or additional language benefit from both the authentic tasks (to which they can bring their own backgrounds and knowledge)

and the explicit teaching of skills (Dooley, 2008). Vocabulary and texts can include English as well as other languages represented in the classroom.
- The teacher doesn't need to be an expert in every facet of the project. I have worked with teachers who learned alongside their students how to create film documentaries or claymation effects. Access information from the Internet and from a variety of community resources, including human resources and physical resources.

Back to the Opening Example: What Did Sarah Do?

Sarah thought back to the multiliteracies unit she did at university—could she try this with such a challenging class? Nothing else seemed to be working, so she decided it was worth a shot; if students started coming to school again, it would be worth it. Sarah planned a multiliteracies, problem-based project to engage and intellectually stimulate her students. The project involved the planning and development of a local skate park. She figured that this would go a long way toward improving engagement and, therefore, behavior. An unexpected outcome was that the standardized test scores for the class improved dramatically because students were engaged more often and for longer periods of time in sustained literacy tasks.

Multiliteracies projects, such as the ones I have described in this article, have much to offer teachers of middle years students. The standardized, print-centric assessment required by government policy seems to be unavoidable, at least for now. However, as teachers, we must not be held ransom to such traditional views of learning and knowledge that promote "sameness," "correct" answer (singular), and print-based skills (Kalantzis & Cope, 2005). Teachers can still include the old "basics" in their programs, but they must be part of the new "basics" of multimodal texts, multiliteracies, technologies, collaboration, new ways of knowing, innovation, problem solving, and creativity. As Kist (2003) suggested, "a print-centric focus for student achievement in our schools may be holding some of our adolescent readers and writers back from achieving to their utmost capabilities and developing meaningful literacy lives that will last them well into this century" (p. 10).

References

Bauman, Z. (2001). *The individualized society*. Malden, MA: Polity.

Beck, U., & Beck-Gernsheim, E. (2002). *Individualization: Institutionalized individualism and its social and political consequences*. London: Sage.

Carnegie Council on Adolescent Development. (1989). *Turning points: Preparing American youth for the 21st century: The report for the task force on education of young adolescents*. New York: Carnegie Corporation.

Carrington, V. (2002). *The middle years of schooling in Queensland: A way forward*. Brisbane, QLD, Australia: Education Queensland.

Cope, B., & Kalantzis, M. (2000a). Designs for social futures. In B. Cope & M. Kalantzis (Eds.), *Multiliteracies: Literacy learning and the design of social futures* (pp. 203–234). Melbourne, VIC, Australia: Macmillan.

Cope, B., & Kalantzis, M. (2000b). Introduction: Multiliteracies: The beginnings of an idea. In B. Cope & M. Kalantzis (Eds.), *Multiliteracies: Literacy learning and the design of social futures* (pp. 3–8). Melbourne, VIC, Australia: Macmillan.

Côté, J.E. (2002). The role of identity capital in the transition to adulthood: The individualization examined. *Journal of Youth Studies, 5*(2), 117–134. doi:10.1080/13676260220134403

Donnelly, K. (2006, January 31). Let's go back to basics, beginning with the three R's. *The Australian,* p. 12.

Dooley, K. (2008). Multiliteracies for students of English as an additional language. In A. Healy (Ed.), *Multiliteracies and diversity in education: New pedagogies for expanding landscapes* (pp. 102–125). South Melbourne, VIC, Australia: Oxford University Press.

Education Queensland. (2003). *The middle phase of learning: State school action plan*. Retrieved May 2, 2006, from education.qld.gov.au/etrf/middle.html

Furlong, A., & Cartmel, A. (2007). *Young people and social change: New perspectives* (2nd ed.). Maidenhead, England: Open University Press.

Gard, M. (2004). An elephant in the room and a bridge too far, or physical education and the "obesity epidemic." In J. Evans, B. Davies, & J. Wright (Eds.), *Body knowledge and control: Studies in the sociology of physical education and health* (pp. 68–82). London: Routledge.

Gard, M., & Wright, J. (2001). Managing uncertainty: Obesity discourses and physical education in a risk society. *Studies in Philosophy and Education, 20*(6), 535–549. doi:10.1023/A:1012238617836

Hall, S. (1992). The question of cultural identity. In S. Hall, D. Held, & T. McGrew (Eds.), *Modernity and its futures* (pp. 273–326). Cambridge, England: Polity.

Healy, A. (2004). *Text next: New resources for literacy learning*. Newton, NSW, Australia: Primary English Teaching Association.

Jackson, A., & Davis, G. (2000). *Turning points 2000: Education of adolescents in the 21st century*. New York: Teachers College Press.

Kalantzis, M., & Cope, B. (2005). *Learning by design*. Altona, VIC, Australia: Common Ground.

Kist, W. (2003). Student achievement in new literacies for the 21st century. *Middle School Journal, 35*(1), 6–13.

Kress, G., & van Leeuwen, T. (2006). *Reading images: The grammar of visual design* (2nd ed.). London: Routledge.

Martin, K. (2008). The intersection of Aboriginal knowledges, Aboriginal literacies, and new learning pedagogy for Aboriginal students. In A. Healy (Ed.), *Multiliteracies and diversity in education: New pedagogies for expanding landscapes* (pp. 58–81). South Melbourne, VIC, Australia: Oxford University Press.

Mills, K. (2006). "Mr Travelling-at-will Ted Doyle": Discourses in a multiliteracies classroom. *Australian Journal of Language and Literacy, 29*(2), 132–149.

Ministerial Advisory Committee for Educational Renewal. (2003). *The middle phase of learning: A report to the minister*. Brisbane, QLD, Australia: Education Queensland.

Moje, E.B. (2007). Developing socially just subject-matter instruction: A review of the literature on disciplinary literacy teaching. *Review of Research in Education, 31*(1), 1–44. doi:10.3102/0091732X07300046

The New London Group. (2000). A pedagogy of multiliteracies: Designing social futures. In B. Cope & M. Kalantzis (Eds.), *Multiliteracies: Literacy learning and the design of social futures* (pp. 9–38). Melbourne, VIC, Australia: Macmillan.

Pandian, A., & Balraj, S. (2005). Approaching *Learning by Design* as an agenda for Malaysian schools. In M. Kalantzis & B. Cope (Eds.), *Learning by Design* (pp. 285–314). Altona, VIC, Australia: Common Ground.

Ryan, M., & Healy, A. (2008). 'Art'efacts of knowing: Multiliteracies and the arts. In A. Healy (Ed.), *Multiliteracies and diversity in education: New pedagogies for expanding landscapes* (pp. 82–101). South Melbourne, VIC, Australia: Oxford University Press.

Ryan, M., & Rossi, T. (2008). The transdisciplinary potential of multiliteracies: Bodily performances and meaning making in health and physical education. In A. Healy (Ed.), *Multiliteracies and diversity in education: New pedagogies for expanding landscapes* (pp. 30–57). South Melbourne, VIC, Australia: Oxford University Press.

Stull, M. (2007, November 30). *Conceptions of responsibility for disciplinary literacy instruction: A study of secondary, preservice teachers in history and the social sciences*. Paper presented at the National Reading Conference, Austin, TX.

Tan, J. (2008). Closing the gap: A multiliteracies approach to English language teaching for "at-risk" students in Singapore. In A. Healy (Ed.), *Multiliteracies and diversity in education: New pedagogies for expanding landscapes* (pp. 144–167). South Melbourne, VIC, Australia: Oxford University Press.

Wright, J., Macdonald, D., Wyn, J., & Kriflik, L. (2005). Becoming somebody: Changing priorities and physical activity. *Youth Studies Australia, 24*(1), 16–21.

Wyn, J., & Woodman, D. (2007). Researching youth in a context of social change: A reply to Roberts. *Journal of Youth Studies, 10*(3), 373–381. doi:10.1080/13676260701342624

Engagement Activities

In Your Classroom
Think of ways you can integrate different forms of communication media in your classroom and model how they can be used. How can your students demonstrate comprehension visually, spatially, through gesture, in sound, or by creating a new representation using words?

With Your Colleagues
Brainstorm topics for cross-curricular projects. Then plan how students can demonstrate their knowledge through different communication media. (See the health and physical education outcome tasks in Table 2 for examples.)

Further Reading
Kasten, W.C., & Wilfong, L.G. (2005). Encouraging independent reading with ambience: The Book Bistro in middle and secondary school classes. *Journal of Adolescent & Adult Literacy, 48*(8), 656–664.

In this study, the researchers created a Book Bistro in an attempt to nurture motivated, independent reading in older students. The Book Bistro, held once a month in elementary and middle school reading classes, was a free-choice period during which students could linger over books in a café atmosphere. Students could select, share, and discuss books. Surveys taken before the Book Bistro indicated that 3% of the students felt positive about independent reading. After a year of Book Bistro, 97% of the participating students felt positive about independent reading.

Teaching Comprehension Through Literature: A Teacher-Research Project to Develop Fifth Graders' Reading Strategies and Motivation

James F. Baumann, Helene Hooten, and Patricia White

Well … I have a confession to make. I didn't really like reading until we started to do this program. And now this has gotten me into reading and I like reading now … umm … a lot. And I do it at home.… I didn't know what reading was about and why you should read until we started this program.… And my mom says, the more you read the more you know. And I just like reading now. (Kenneth)

It was rewarding to hear Kenneth's testimony near the end of our program of teaching reading strategies through trade books. It felt good to learn that the books he had been reading and the strategy instruction we had been providing him encouraged him to read more and with greater enthusiasm. But how did Kenneth reach this point? What about the other students in the program? Was Kenneth's testimony really reflective of his growth in comprehension skills and motivation to read? We address these questions by describing a yearlong, teacher action research study involving fifth-grade students at Cedar Elementary School. (To protect the privacy of the children, all students' names and the school name are pseudonyms.) In our project, Helene and Pat, fifth-grade teachers at Cedar Elementary, and Jim, an education professor, explored the implementation of a program in which we introduced trade books into the curriculum and used them to teach students various reading comprehension strategies.

Background to the Investigation

Prior to our inquiry, Helene and Pat referred to themselves as "contemporary traditional" in their reading instruction. They used the adopted basal reading program as the foundation of their literacy instruction, finding the literature selections generally to be engaging and of high quality. In addition, Helene and Pat read aloud to their students daily, engaged them in process writing, and had their students read thematically related trade books that accompanied the basal program.

Helene and Pat were not satisfied, however, with the comprehension performance of prior and current fifth-grade students. They saw a pattern of comprehension skills in their students that reflected national trends as reported in National Assessment of Educational Progress (NAEP) data for 9-year-olds (Campbell, Voelkl, & Donahue, 1997). Specifically, they found that most of their students could identify simple facts from paragraphs, make inferences based on short passages, and understand specific or sequentially related ideas (NAEP Level 200).

Reprinted from Baumann, J.F., Hooten, H., & White, P. (1999). Teaching comprehension through literature: A teacher-research project to develop fifth graders' reading strategies and motivation. *The Reading Teacher, 53*(1), 38–51.

In contrast, many students had difficulty when it came to searching for specific information in text, interrelating ideas, and making generalizations (NAEP Level 250), and understanding complicated information (NAEP Level 300) was more challenging yet. Further, given the diversity in the Cedar population, they were concerned about disparity between the performance of minority children and their mainstream counterparts (Campbell et al., 1997).

Prior to the study, Helene and Pat had begun investigating their own classroom practices as part of the School Research Consortium, a teacher-research community sponsored by the University of Georgia site of the National Reading Research Center. In one inquiry, they collaborated with a second-grade teacher and the school media specialist at Cedar Elementary on a cross-grade-level, writing buddies project. During one of the regularly scheduled, after school research meetings, they talked with Jim, a university liaison to the School Research Consortium, about their frustrations in the area of reading comprehension. This led to subsequent meetings and the initiation of the literature and comprehension strategies project we report here.

Background and Purpose for the Study

We began by looking at relevant theoretical and applied literature and decided to ground our study in three key constructs: a literature-based framework, contextually based comprehension instruction, and culturally relevant teaching. We considered the rationale behind a literature-based, trade book program (e.g., Heald-Taylor, 1996; Hiebert & Colt, 1989; Zarillo, 1989) and examined examples of how it might be implemented in elementary classrooms (e.g., Cox & Zarillo, 1993; Cullinan, 1987, 1992; Hancock & Hill, 1988; Tompkins & McGee, 1993; Wood & Moss, 1992). We decided that we would use a variety of trade books to read, discuss, and enjoy, and that the books would provide the medium for teaching comprehension strategies.

We also explored the research and theory on teaching reading comprehension strategies within the context of literature and found that most literature-based perspectives accounted for reading strategy instruction (e.g., McMahon, Raphael, Goatley, & Pardo, 1997; Routman, 1988, 1991; Tompkins & McGee, 1993; Yopp & Yopp, 1992). Routman emphasized, however, that effective literature-based skill or strategy instruction must be crafted carefully: "Application of a skill to another context is far more likely to occur when the skill has been taught in a meaningful context that considers the needs of the learners" (1991, p. 135). Thus, we were committed to teaching important, high-utility reading comprehension strategies as they could be applied in the trade books students would read.

Given the low income of many Cedar Elementary families and the diverse nature of students in Helene's and Pat's classes, we also planned on heeding what we were learning about culturally responsive teaching (Ladson-Billings, 1994; Strickland, 1994). We believed it was important to provide students a mix of explicit instruction to give them access to power code literacy (Delpit, 1988) along with more spontaneous instruction that emerged from authentic reading tasks. Delpit (1995) reminded us that "students must be *taught* the codes needed to participate fully in the mainstream of American life, not by being forced to attend to hollow, inane, decontextualized subskills, but rather within the context of meaningful communicative endeavors" (p. 45).

The purpose of our inquiry was to integrate comprehension strategy instruction into literature reading and response activities. Although we hoped to develop the students' reading comprehension skills and strategies, we did not wish to do so at the expense of their interest in or attitude toward reading and books. Therefore, we posed two research questions: (a) What is the nature of fifth graders' reading comprehension development as a result of our literature strategies program? (b) What is the nature of fifth graders' attitudes toward reading and literature as a result of our literature strategies program?

Research Perspective and Setting

We grounded our study in teacher research (Cochran-Smith & Lytle, 1993; Patterson, Santa, Short, & Smith, 1993). Like other teacher researchers, we identified methods that were practical and efficient for addressing our research questions, and we selected, adapted, or created qualitative research methods for collecting and analyzing data (Baumann & Duffy-Hester, in press). We found Hubbard and Power's (1993) *The Art of Classroom Inquiry* particularly useful in this process. Our data included videotapes of lessons and research-team meetings; a teacher-research journal; lesson plans; students' reading journals that included literary responses and strategy-related activities; student interviews; an informal survey we constructed that probed students' in- and out-of-school reading habits, attitudes, and interests; and various artifacts such as students' projects and our teaching charts and handouts.

Cedar Elementary School is located in a lower middle-class neighborhood of a southern U.S. community of about 65,000 residents. The median per capita income was less than US$16,000, and over one fourth of the households had incomes of less than US$10,000. Cedar Elementary served 514 children in Prekindergarten through Grade 5 at the time of our study, 60% of whom received free or reduced-price lunch. Approximately half of the students were bussed to school from low-income housing projects. The school population, reflected in Helene's and Pat's classes, was 61% African American, 35% European American, 3% Asian, and 1% Hispanic. Helene and Pat each averaged 23 students in their classes during the school year, and all students participated in one or more phases of the yearlong instructional program.

Three Types of Strategy Lessons

We decided to include in our program what Durkin (1990) referred to as planned and unplanned instruction. *Planned instruction* involved lessons we prepared in advance and taught directly to students within the context of trade books they were reading. *Unplanned instruction* involved on-the-spot lessons, which allowed us to respond to teachable moments as they occurred within literature discussions. Specifically, we taught three types of literature-based, reading comprehension lessons (Baumann, Hooten, & White, 1996).

Elaborated strategy lessons were planned, teacher-directed lessons within which we introduced a comprehension skill or strategy. We explained the strategy, modeled it, and provided guided and independent practice, all within a meaningful story context. For example, in conjunction with the book *Man From the Sky* (Avi, 1980), we taught an Elaborated strategy lesson on predicting and verifying. We began by introducing the strategy and displaying on a chart a five-step process for predicting and verifying (read, predict, check predictions, change or make new predictions, repeat the steps). We modeled the strategy using the beginning of *Man From the Sky* and had the students apply it as they read the remainder of the first chapter under our supervision. For independent application, students wrote predictions in their journals describing what they anticipated occurring in the next chapter of *Man From the Sky*.

Brief strategy lessons were planned review or extension lessons in which we revisited a previously taught strategy and provided reinforcement. For instance, when reading *Man From the Sky*, several predict/verify Brief strategy lessons followed the Elaborated strategy lesson described above. Another example involved the book *Yellow Bird and Me* (Hansen, 1986), with which we taught an Elaborated strategy lesson on retelling as a means to understand and clarify the meaning of a text. The next day, we taught a Brief strategy lesson on this same skill. We began by reviewing the guidelines for retelling which we had on a chart:

To retell ...

- Put the story in your own words.
- Say ideas in the order in which they happened in the story.
- Include all the most important events and ideas.

We then had the students practice retelling with a partner by alternating with sections of a chapter they had read for homework.

Impromptu strategy lessons were unplanned lessons in which we seized an instructional moment by engaging in an on-the-spot lesson that flowed from the reading or discussion of a selection. These were unlike the Elaborated and Brief strategy lessons, which were planned in advance. For example, while practicing retelling sections of *The Not-Just-Anybody Family* (Byars, 1986), we realized that students were confusing a retelling with a summary. This led to an Impromptu lesson in which we drew a diagram on the board to represent a summary (the word *Main Idea* in a circle with *Detail* written on rays emanating from it) and then discussed how these strategies differed (e.g., a retelling tells about most or all of the selection whereas a summary contains only the main points; a retelling is usually oral whereas a summary is usually written).

Three Phases of the Instructional Program

The literature strategies program consisted of 42 lessons organized into three phases, which encompassed about 17 weeks of the school year. Lessons were 50 minutes long and occurred two to four times per week during each phase. The literature strategy lessons were scheduled during the regular morning reading and language arts period, within which Helene and Pat team-taught lessons from the basal reading program and accompanying trade books. Helene and Pat continued with basal instruction between phases and on days when the literature strategy lessons were not scheduled. Thus, our program complemented and extended the existing reading curriculum and instruction rather than supplanted it.

Phase 1: Strategy Lesson Trials

In Phase 1 (October), we assessed the structure, nature, and focus of the integrated literature and strategy lessons. During Phase 1, Jim worked with eight students from Helene's and Pat's classrooms as they read *Man From the Sky*, the story of Jamie, an 11-year-old boy, who sees a criminal parachuting from an airplane and becomes entangled with the criminal's attempted escape. Helene and Pat observed and critiqued several of the Phase 1 lessons.

Because this was a trial phase, we decided to restrict our lessons to the broadly based, generic comprehension strategy of making and verifying predictions. *Man From the Sky* was well suited for this objective, for the text was short and the suspenseful nature of the story lent itself well to instruction in prediction. Phase 1 consisted of one Elaborated strategy lesson on predicting and verifying, followed by several Brief Lessons on this same strategy.

Part of our objective for the trial phase was to strike an appropriate balance between comprehension strategy instruction and enjoyment of the books themselves. At the end of Phase 1, we came up with a tentative 20%–80% rule. This was derived from our experience that, in each 50-minute period in Phase 1, we found ourselves spending approximately 80% of the time reading, discussing, analyzing, responding to, and enjoying the trade books, with about 20% of the time being spent on strategy instruction. Stated differently, on average, about 40 minutes of each lesson involved trade book literary engagement and appreciation activities with about 10 minutes spent on strategy instruction and practice.

Phase 2: Expansion of Strategy Lessons

Our objective in Phase 2 (November, January, early February) was to expand the lessons to include additional comprehension strategies. During November Jim and 23 students from Helene's and Pat's classes read *Yellow Bird and Me*, a realistic fiction story by an African American author who depicts diverse preadolescents struggling with school and personal challenges. We taught six strategies along with *Yellow Bird*: (a) self-questioning to promote and monitor comprehension, (b) retelling to clarify meaning, (c) writing to construct understanding, (d) summarizing and identifying main ideas to understand a story line, (e) predicting and verifying information in a text, and (f) using a story map to organize narrative comprehension. We introduced and taught these lessons with the help of a fictional superhero, Clark Canine— Super Reporter (Baumann, Jones, & Seifert-Kessell, 1993). We used Clark Canine to show that readers interact with text in ways similar to how reporters interact with people. For example, when teaching self-questioning, we compared how reporter Clark Canine interviewed people to get his story to how a reader can interview the author by asking questions to get the meaning of a reading selection.

In January and early February, Helene and Pat taught additional comprehension strategies to their classes using the humorous story of a family of endearing misfits, *The Not-Just-Anybody Family*. Pat focused on five strategies: three review strategies in which she determined that her students needed further instruction (retelling, summarizing, and prediction and verification), and two new strategies that were suited to this particular title (having students assume the role of story characters and aesthetic response). Helene also focused on the three review strategies stated above, and a new one (using story boards to construct and reconstruct the meaning from a narrative).

As in Phase 1, we planned together and observed and critiqued one another's lessons. For example, 3 days into Pat's teaching of *The Not-Just-Anybody Family* in early January, she and Jim met to evaluate the students' progress and to determine subsequent instructional emphases. After this meeting, Jim commented in the research journal: "As we reflected on these [the strategies to teach with *The Not-Just-Anybody Family*], we thought that they nicely covered various cognitive levels.... Pat will focus on these strategies with the kids, blending instruction into reading and discussion of the story. She will, however, do enough 'formal' instruction so the kids know explicitly what the strategies are so she can discuss, model, and guide students in strategy use."

As Pat taught, Jim observed and provided feedback about the lessons and students' progress. For example, on January 24 he wrote:

"Issue: Maybe talk w/P about having the kids spend more time during the hour actually reading? Maybe some paired or individual silent reading? I wonder if the discussions don't drag a bit?" Jim and Pat talked about this issue, and over the next several days they experimented with a more balanced independent reading/discussion ratio. Pat came down with laryngitis, so she asked Jim to teach the next couple of lessons, which she observed. Jim tried, although not very successfully, to provide more time for reading, but Pat picked up on this when she resumed teaching. Jim commented on January 26 that "P gives the kids a fairly extensive [independent] reading assignment" and on January 27 that "P assigns the rest of the book for tomorrow.... She will give them time to read with a buddy if they wish." This kind of give-and-take between teaching and critiquing helped us reflect on and adapt our instruction.

We also used our observations to acquire insight into students' learning. For example, we noted in late January that "Kizzie and Lakesha are an interesting pair. They sit next to one another and don't talk a lot, but they communicate in various ways." We decided that we'd "like to get them both into the discussion more [because] they have much to offer." These observations and reflections led us to adapt our instruction and discussion strategies to be more inclusive of all students.

Phase 3: Refinement of Strategy Lessons

In Phase 3, which began in late March and extended through April, we strove to refine the literature strategies program. We worked with groups of students who each read two additional titles: *One More River to Cross: The Stories of Twelve Black Americans* (Haskins, 1992), a collection of biographies of famous African Americans, and *The 18th Emergency* (Byars, 1973), the humorous story of a likable but eccentric 12-year-old who imagines various emergencies and escape procedures. These titles allowed us to explore new comprehension topics such as genre (we contrasted the nonfiction biography to the dramatic and humorous realistic fiction stories we had read) while revisiting other strategies (e.g., self-questioning) and expanding on others (we added new ways to teach story structure and retelling). We used these final titles to continue to evaluate our instruction and the students' learning. The following research journal excerpts illustrate some of the issues that came up while reading these books:

- "Neat discussion of the conclusion of "Malcolm X" [from *One More River to Cross*]. The kids had clearly read it carefully and had some wonderful insights. Quentin and Jarvis had some particularly interesting comments from their perspectives as African American students. We moved on and talked about genre and completed some of the chart.... The kids really got into it.... They thought the word *genre* was neat— highfalutin' language." (March 30)
- "We discussed the story [*The 18th Emergency*], talking about how the author steps you out of the story and into Mouse's mind on occasion. We also talked about some of the vocabulary. For example, the kids acted out in pantomime the section of the story where Mouse is fleeing from Hammerman." (April 15)

As a culmination to Phase 3 and the entire project, we provided students opportunities to read books of their choice in small groups. Students could select one of four books (*Skinnybones*, Park, 1982; *Me, Mop, and the Moondance Kid*, Myers, 1988; *The Blossoms Meet the Vulture Lady*, Byars, 1985; *Philip Hall Likes Me, I Reckon, Maybe*, Greene, 1974) and join a reading study and discussion group, a form of book club (McMahon et al., 1997) or literature-response group (Spiegel, 1998).

Data Analysis

We employed an adapted version of content analysis (Lincoln & Guba, 1985) to analyze our qualitative data. This involved four steps. First, we compiled data sources in a notebook. These included lesson plans, teacher-research journal entries, copies of students' reading journals, summarized results of the informal reading habit and attitude survey, lists of artifacts (e.g., teaching charts, students' projects and assignments, still photos), and transcribed portions of lessons, student interviews, and research-team meetings.

Second, we coded data by research question. This involved two substeps: (a) marking evidence related to the comprehension research question in one color and evidence related to the attitude question in another; and (b) consolidating evidence into data index summaries, one for each question. These summaries enabled us to bring together information related to each research question and examine the data for trends. They also facilitated access back to the raw data for elaboration and verification. Table 1 presents excerpts from the data index summary for the comprehension research question.

Third, we examined the data in detail, looking for evidence of strategic reading development and aesthetic reading growth. This involved using the index summaries to identify potential themes which could then be checked against the data. For example, for the comprehension research question, we color coded the summaries by type of comprehension strategy. We then used the summaries to return to the data to confirm student growth in each strategy. We illustrate this in Table 2, which presents several of the 38 data points that document that students acquired skill in prediction and verification, both under teacher direction and in their independent reading and writing.

Fourth, we went back and tested the emerging themes against the data, revising the categories as necessary. For example, an initial theme that was simply "Students grew in comprehension strategies" was broken down into two themes: "Students learned comprehension strategies" and "Students retained and transferred strategy learning to other texts and contexts."

Evidence for Reading Comprehension Development

Analysis of our first research question—What is the nature of fifth-graders' reading comprehension development as a result of our literature and

Table 1
Excerpts From Comprehension Strategy Data Index Summary

Teacher-research journal	From *Man From the Sky*: **Kids not particularly skillful w/ prediction at onset of instruction (October 11).** Some kids not vocal, but that doesn't mean they're not "with" me (October 13). How to move to more of a potpourri of strategies? (October 14). Good responses (October 15). **Excellent predictions (October 18).**
	From *The Not-Just-Anybody Family*: Discussion of persona/voice—who's telling the story; lots of work on summarizing; return to character point of view activity on note cards (see dialogue between Desmond and Sarah); reviewing known before moving on to new; kids asked to write an emotional response on their author cards (January 6). **Kids spontaneously make predictions (about Junior's health);** pairs asked to tell/record story ideas/events; talk about "look backs" as a viable/useful strategy; interesting tangent about what happens when they phone their moms at work (January 12).
Student reading journals	From *Yellow Bird and Me* (November 1-29): Strategies demonstrated in journals: Desmond **(prediction, p. 3 and several following)**; Joseph (summary, p. 1 and following), (journal dialogue, p. 2) **(prediction, p. 5)**; Lakesha (questioning, p. 1), **(prediction/questioning, pp. 3, 4, 5)**; Kendra (very thoughtful personal response/reaction, p. 2), **(prediction, pp. 4, 7)**; Patricia (personal reaction to characters, pp. 1, 3) (poetry, p. 2); Dario (summary, throughout), **(prediction, p. 6)**; Rontasha **(prediction, p. 1)**, (summary, pp. 1-2, 6); Jarvis **(prediction, "story didn't end like I thought it would," last p.)**; Emily **(predictions, p. 2)**, (character analysis, p. 3); Jonnita **(sort of a list of predictions, pp. 1-2)**; Latoya (character analysis, p. 1), **(prediction, pp. 2, 5)**, (summary, last p.); Kenneth (asking/answering his own questions, pp. 1-2), **(making own predictions, p. 3)** (author missing info. about Bird, last p.); Samantha **(prediction, pp. 1, 6)** ("creative writing"—poems for JB, pp. 4-5); Sarah (summary/retell, pp. 1, 5-7), **(predictions, p. 4)**, (story map, 2nd last p.).
	Interesting how some kids focus on different strategies (e.g., Joseph on summarizing; Lakesha on prediction; Rebecca always using a "Part I like Best...") followed by asking questions or putting themselves in the story; Jonnita's prediction listing; Sarah's artwork to accompany her text. **Also, evidence of prior strategy instruction showing in subsequent work, (e.g., Lakesha and Kendra making predictions in *Yellow Bird*, probably from work in *Man From Sky* group).**
Student interviews	From *April 22 interview With Quentin, Sarah, and Jarvis*: S says I was "teaching us how to comprehend"; also talked about retelling as a strategy. Q says "You've been trying to research how our minds work and are different, how you could teach them [us?]." **S comments that *Not Just Anybody* "just ends and you don't know what's going to happen next" [a form of unfulfilled prediction?]**
	Strategies demonstrated: J says that *YB & Me* is real, real, realistic [evidence of genre lessons?], and he retells *YB & Me* and interprets it when he talks about making friends etc. J/Q have a discussion of biographies—like and dislike [more genre?]. J talks about "rising action" etc. [evidence of work on narrative structure from Pat and Helene?]. J does a nice job explaining rising action, using evidence/examples from *The 18th Emergency*.

(continued)

Table 1
Excerpts From Comprehension Strategy Data Index Summary (*Continued*)

	Predicting: S, J, & Q have a detailed discussion of what predicting is, how it helps them, all drawing from examples in books they've read. S talks about reading w/ her older brother and how she used predicting.
	S and Q talk about retelling, the latter commenting that it helped him remember the book and **it also led to predicting [a kind of interstrategic phenomenon?]**. Later, Q also says that retelling helped him in his journal writing [another interstrategic example?]. J does an excellent job defining/ discriminating retelling from summarizing.
	J also does a nice job explaining what journal writing, including the dialogic aspects of it, is—uses diary as a descriptor. **S says** that **predicting** and retelling were better than journal writing as **useful strategies**. S also says that journals helped her "express my feelings on paper." Q says that character maps were "exciting, real exciting." S says that character maps helped them learn about characters more. J liked the character maps but wasn't so sure about the story maps. S says she likes asking questions and that "genres are fun."
Artifacts	Pat had the kids write summaries periodically as they were reading this story [*Not-Just-Anybody Family*]. This set of cards includes kids' summaries for the first 110 pages of the story and were done/turned in January 29. Nice job by the kids. Interesting variation of strategies, such as some more detailed than others, some have dialogue in them (Joseph); see Lakesha's for a "classic" summary of the main points (really good).
	Helene and Pat had the kids do story boards for *Not-Just-Anybody* and *Meet Addy*. We have some good copies/examples of the kids' boards. For example, Joseph and Kizzie did a nice *Meet Addy* story board that shows lots of detail of setting, character, situation, conflict, resolution, etc. We have copies of many and originals—showing very nice artwork—of a number of kids. A potential point from these is how P & H extended our strategy work to other books (*Meet Addy* series) and extrapolated/extended the skills we were dealing with, such as story mapping to story boarding.

Note. The preceding were color coded by comprehension strategy (e.g., yellow for prediction/verifying, pink for retelling, green for story/ character mapping). To illustrate this, we've used **boldface text** here to represent evidence of prediction and verification, which is yellow on the original summary.

comprehension strategies program?—revealed two main themes: (a) students learned the comprehension strategies we had taught them, and (b) they retained and transferred their strategic learning to other reading situations.

Students Learned Comprehension Strategies

There was evidence that students learned comprehension strategies as a result of the Elaborated, Brief, and Impromptu strategy lessons. For instance, regarding predicting and verifying, Jim saw limited initial knowledge of this skill (see Table 2). But one week later following an Elaborated lesson and several Brief lessons, he wrote, "The kids performed all right. I got some good, new predictions." The students also demonstrated growth through their journals. Quentin wrote, "I predict that Jamie will learn how to read," and Kendra wrote, "I predict that in chapter six, that Gillian will want to

Table 2
Evidence for Students' Ability to Employ a Predict and Verify Strategy

Data Source	Data Index Summary Entry	Raw Data Excerpt
Teacher research journal	"Kids not particularly skillful w/ prediction at onset of instruction" (October 11)	"I'll continue with the predicting scheme on Wednesday, since it's clear to me that these kids are not particularly facile with this strategy. However … doing an entire book on prediction is not sensible, and I need to think about how to integrate various aesthetic elements with the efferent ones…."
Teacher research journal	"Kids spontaneously make predictions (about Junior's health)" [*Not-Just-Anybody Family*]	"Interesting: Kids spontaneously make predictions about Junior's subsequent health—whether he'll recover from his injuries; whether he'll walk with a limp or not. They do this on their own … kind of a private conversation…."
Student journal	"Jarvis (prediction, 'story didn't end like I thought it would,' last p.)" [*Yellow Bird and Me*]	"Dear Mr. B: The story didn't end like I thought it would. I thought Amir would come back. I had a feeling inside of me that bird would get back in class. I think Mrs. Barker was guilty of treating bird crulty. I'm glad that Doris got her job back…."
Student journal	"Samantha (prediction, pp. 1, 6)" [*Yellow Bird and Me*]	"I think Doris might get grounded, and never go out of the house again for a job. I feel bad. I wouldn't like to be grounded anyway. I think Doris will never get to see Amir."
Student interview	"Strategies reported using: Kenneth & Kendra (prediction)"	Kenneth: "When I'm at home and reading … this is sometimes … I'll put my book down and think for about 5 minutes. Then I write down the things that have been happening in the story. And I think, well, like this guy's going to run down a terminal in an airport, and it happens. When the chapter's over, I make predictions…. I do these once in a while…." Kendra: "If I go somewhere and take my book with me, and if I have my journal, I try to make predictions. And when I get back I can write them in my journal."
Student interview	"Predicting: S, J, & Q have a detailed discussion of what predicting is, how it helps them, all drawing from examples in books they've read."	S: "I think that predicting probably helps you because you want to know if you are right or wrong, and you don't know, so when you get at the end you can go back and see if you predict right or wrong and you just want to keep on reading." Q: "Predicting helped me guessing and stuff. Making really good guesses…. Guesses that make sense!" J: "Every time that I predict, like I thought the book was going to be good, I get the prediction right. For example, I think that in this book [holds up *18th Emergency*] I think that Marv Hammerman and Benjie are going to get in a fight."

know why Jamie is always looking at the sky." Students also learned to evaluate predictions and modify them when necessary, as when Lakesha initially wrote *CT* for "Can't Tell" in front of her prediction, "I think that he is trying to get on the plane so he can get the money," and then later crossed it out and wrote *T* for "True" after she read on in the book and was able to verify the accuracy of her prediction.

Pat taught retelling and summarization as her students read *The Not-Just-Anybody Family*. Following an Elaborated lesson, Pat reviewed this in a Brief lesson. While observing this lesson, Jim wrote, "They [Desmond and Jarvis] then retell the 'More Mud' chapter.... The kids continue to retell the following chapters they have read.... Jarvis does an excellent job retelling 'Maggie Alone.' Desmond picks up where Jarvis left off." Pat then went on to review the distinction between retelling and summarizing, assigning the students another section to read for homework and having them write a summary of what they read.

Impromptu lessons also involved comprehension strategy instruction. For example, an informal discussion on characters from *The 18th Emergency* led to an Impromptu lesson on character traits. As a group of students was discussing a section of the story and sharing their reading journal responses, Kendra read from her journal, "It seems like Mouse keeps having visions, like what he would do in a jungle to defend himself." Kenneth responded by saying, "This is my observation about him: I just think he's weird." Quentin said, "Yes, he's weird.... He's a psychic." Emily chimed in, "I think he's crazy.... He's got a big imagination." Jarvis commented, "I think this story is life-like. I also think Mouse is a coward," to which Emily responded, "I think he's kind of like a dare person, a dare-devil." The group then created a character map for Mouse on the chalkboard, wrote a set of steps for constructing a character map, and drew character maps in their journals.

Students Retained and Transferred Strategy Learning to Other Texts and Contexts

It was nice to see that students acquired reading strategies as a result of the lessons we taught, but we were also interested in evaluating the persistence of the strategies and students' ability to apply them independently. Reading journal responses provided evidence of students' retention and adaptation of reading strategies. For example, although most of the instruction in prediction and verification occurred while reading *Man From the Sky*, students demonstrated the ability to make hypotheses as they read subsequent stories. We saw considerable evidence of this as students read and responded to *Yellow Bird and Me*, as when Lakesha wrote a series of predictive statements: "I'm happy that Bird is back in class. I think he will catch up with them. I think that Amir will come back. Doris might keep her job this time. She might keep helping Bird. Mr. Washington might come back and do another play." Likewise, Sarah wrote, "I think she [Doris] will make enough money to go see Amir because when you really want something you go after it," and Patricia wrote, "I predict that Doris and Yellow Bird will become best friends." Joseph commented, "I like this book because it makes me wonder what will happen next. How suspenseful it is!" And Dario demonstrated knowledge of prediction when he turned the tables on us one day in a note he wrote to Jim in his journal:

> Dear Mr. B.
>
> Do you have any predictions about the story? What do you think will happen next in the story? Do you think that Doris will become good friends [with] Bird? Do you think that the poem will come up again? I do. Have you read the book yet? Have you ever taught a class better than us?

We saw evidence of students applying other strategies through their journal entries:

- *Retelling*: "Chapter 1 is about Doris trying to write a poem but Yellow Bird is distracting her. She helps Yellow Bird with social studies and goes on. Then on Chapter 2 she continues to write the poem. Then when Micky bothers her Doris gets in trouble" (Joseph) (Baumann, Hooten, & White, 1996, p. 68).

- *Putting oneself in the place of characters*: "I think that Doris is feeling mad because Yellow Bird took her poem and said, 'It's mine.' I would feel very mad" (Desmond). "I would feel mad that mom wouldn't let me work and that my best friend was moved away" (Dario). "I am happy that Doris and Yellow Bird grow a happy friendship. I had a happy friendship to but I had to move. I was mad, and she was mad" (Jonnita).

- *Self-questioning*: "Doris should have quit, or told her mother and dad why she wanted a job. I wonder if she will keep the job, or not? I wonder if Bird will still get to be in the Drama Club?" (Lakesha).

Comments from the student interviews also documented retention and transfer of strategy usage. Kendra indicated that because of the program, reading "is more exciting. We like know something's going to happen and then we read for it to happen in the books … predicting." Kenneth supported Kendra's opinion: "I learned new strategies … predicting." Sarah reported using prediction in other contexts, "like when I was reading a social studies book with my big brother, I was predicting what was going to happen next."

Retelling and summarizing were also mentioned as useful strategies. Emily commented, "It's just like making a summary of the story.… If someone wants to know what a story is about, you can tell it." Jarvis concurred: "Retelling is like giving a quick summary without writing it on paper. Retelling is like telling the story to someone who read some but not all of it." Quentin offered, "Retelling what the story is about helped me write in my journal," and Sarah noted, "It [journal writing] helped me because I can express my feelings on paper. And when I write a summary about something for the teacher, I can express myself even more."

In summary, we found evidence that students learned the strategies we taught them. And perhaps more important, we also learned that the students applied the comprehension strategies they learned independently as they read, talked about, and wrote about the books.

Evidence for Growth in Attitudes Toward Reading and Literature

We uncovered two main themes in response to our second research question, What is the nature of fifth-graders' attitudes toward reading and literature as a result of our literature and comprehension strategies program? (a) students valued reading more and reported reading more, and (b) students demonstrated enhanced appreciation for books and literature.

Students Valued Reading More and Reported Reading More

Students' responses to the informal survey of reading habits and interests demonstrated modest growth over the course of the school year. For example, when asked how much time the students spent daily reading out of school, the average fall response corresponded to "10–30 minutes" per day whereas the average spring response corresponded to "30 minutes to 1 hour" daily. There were also small fall-to-spring increases in response to the question "How often do you go to the county public library?" (movement from "about once a month" toward "about once a week"), and in response to the question "How many books do you read each month?" (movement from "3 to 5 books" toward "more than 5 books"). When asked to write down titles of the most recent books the students had read, we found that in the fall, students wrote an average of 2.8 titles, as opposed to an average of 3.8 titles in the spring.

Other data indicated that students valued reading more and did indeed read more as the program progressed. For example, several students commented during the interviews that the program enhanced their reading interests and habits. Kendra said that due to the program "It's [reading] more exciting. I like it more. I guess it's because of the more books we read." Emily reported that because of the program, "Now I read bigger books," and Kenneth stated matter-of-factly, "I just didn't like reading before we started this program. Now I like it." Pat and Helene's day-to-day observations also documented growth in reading interest. For instance, in our final spring research meeting, Pat commented:

> He [Jarvis] came up to me this afternoon, "Mr. Jim is coming today, isn't he?" I said yes, and he said, "I'm going to read that book, *Man From the Sky*," that he didn't get to read before. He said he's going to borrow it. He seemed excited about that. I think it [the program] helped them a lot. I know two or three who weren't reading before. Sarah reads all the time now. She just doesn't put her books down.

Students' oral and written comments also supported this theme. For instance, immediately following spring break a group of six students engaged in a spontaneous discussion of their free-time reading habits. As the group convened, Quentin announced that read two books during the whole spring break." Sarah interjected, "I read three." Jarvis responded, "I read about football." We pursued this discussion, having the students share the titles they had read, learning in the process that Kenneth had read two books over spring break, Emily read one, Kendra read two, and Jarvis had read a variety of sports magazines. Several days later while reading *The 18th Emergency*, Kendra affirmed her developing reading habits by writing the following in her journal: "It's 10:37 at night. In the book it said, 'While Mouse was waiting to think of Emergency Fifteen, he fell asleep.' So did I, right after I read that. Weird, huh?"

Students Demonstrated Enhanced Appreciation for Books and Literature

One of our objectives for the literature and comprehension strategies program was to find the right balance between explicit instruction in comprehension strategies and enjoyment and appreciation of books and literature. Students' comments in class discussions and interviews, and through their open-ended statements in their reading journals, indicated that the skill instruction did not inhibit their enjoyment of and response to literature.

Students made a number of general expressions of how much they enjoyed the books they were reading. For example, *Yellow Bird and Me* seemed to foster an appreciation for literature among a number of students. At the end of an entry relating to *Yellow Bird*, Joseph added, "P.S. Reading and writing can be a lot of fun!" and a couple of days later, he wrote, "I love the book. I will check out 'The Gift Giver' [prequel to *Yellow Bird*]. I want to got to the library." Emily wrote, "This was an interesting story. I hope Joyce Hansen write another book that ties up the ends. I would read it if she did." Kendra also enjoyed *Yellow Bird*, writing, "I really love the book *Yellow Bird and Me*.... Do you know where I can find this book? I would like to have a copy of my own" (Baumann, Hooten, & White, 1996, p. 69). (We later bequeathed a copy of *Yellow Bird* to Kendra.)

One factor that seemed to be linked to the students' growing appreciation for books and literature involved the opportunity to express their opinions about what they were reading. Sarah commented, "I like the books that we read.... I like being in the group because we had fun and because we learned how to tell each other our feelings." Kenneth concurred: "Maybe it's because of the books. We had different opinions of the books." Quentin said that "My favorite part [of the program] is when we talked about stuff ... like now, like how we feel and stuff like that, or what the chapter meant."

The instructional environment that fostered students' ability to express themselves was reflected in how they became involved with the characters in the stories they read. For example, Patricia took serious exception with the actions of the teacher in *Yellow Bird*, Mrs. Barker:

> I think that Mrs. Barker is amazing. Not amazing cool, but amazing how mean she can be. I think she should close her mouth and listen to Bird. She

doesn't understand him, but she should. I feel sorry for Bird. Doris should keep her job. Mrs. Barker shouldn't yell so much, it is bad for her health. Well, that is all I would like to write.

Sincerely,
Patricia

P.S. Oh yes. If Mrs. Barker had her way, no one would be living. She nags too much! I am glad she is not my teacher!

But Patricia couldn't leave it alone. Mrs. Barker continued to trouble her, for in her very next entry, she wrote, "That woman is impossible!" And the following day she added this P.S. to her entry: "I won't forget Barker! I'll hunt her down like a dog after a fox, if she doesn't leave Bird alone. You may get tired of me talking/writing about Barker." Clearly, Patricia was able to achieve a powerful, emotive stance with one of the antagonists in this book.

Students also developed tastes and preferences for specific books. Sarah commented on the different emotions a book can evoke: "I like *The Not-Just-Anybody Family*. It was funny. It was sad. It was weird." Quentin indicated that he enjoyed humorous books: "I only like interesting books, like books that's funny, books with funny names like *Skinnybones*." Jarvis found that reading books can teach lessons about life: "It [reading books] teaches you how to make friends. *Yellow Bird and Me* teaches you how to make friends." Jarvis also learned the old adage about not judging a book by its cover: "I though *Yellow Bird and Me* was going to be pretty boring from the cover, but it turned out to be really good."

Students also had preferences for certain genres. Although most students liked the humorous books they read (e.g., *The Not-Just-Anybody Family*, *The 18th Emergency*) as well as the more serious realistic fiction titles (e.g., *Yellow Bird and Me*), students differed in their reaction to the book of biographies, *One More River to Cross*. Some students really enjoyed the collection. Kenneth wrote, "I liked the Matthew Henson biography. He made about 4 to 5 expeditions to try to reach the North Pole with Robert Peary. I am going to do [read the biography of] Marian Anderson next." On the other hand, Jarvis said,

"*One More River to Cross*, it just didn't interest me." Sarah concurred: "I don't really like reading biographies."

Interestingly, one of the most engaging discussions we had all year occurred following the reading of the Malcolm X biography in *One More River to Cross*, suggesting that students could distinguish between content and genre. To illustrate, during a discussion of genre one day, Quentin interpreted a comment by a fellow student as an expression that he did not like biographical content: "He [other student] just said that I don't like Black history." But when Jim, asked, "Is that true?", Quentin responded emphatically, "NO, that isn't true. I just don't like biographies. They're hard to understand. I like to see things, like looking at old movies about Martin Luther King and stuff."

In conclusion, we learned that as the program progressed the fifth graders came to value reading more and engaged in more free-choice reading both in and out of school. We also found that the students developed greater appreciation for books and literature and established preferences for styles, authors, and genres.

Reflections

We were pleased with the students' learning as a result of the program. We saw development in the sophistication of their reading comprehension skills, and they showed us that they could use them independently and generalize them across texts and tasks. We also were excited to see their growing interest in books and literature and their ability to react and respond to literary works. In short, we sensed a kind of synergy between the reading strategies and literature appreciation. We saw the students becoming more strategic readers, which enhanced their aesthetic understanding, while their growing aesthetic appreciation facilitated their growth in reading ability.

We also found that the 20%–80% Rule we postulated at the end of Phase I worked well in the next two phases. We learned that, on average, dedicating about one fifth of each period to explicit strategy instruction was sufficient to provide students insight into comprehension skills, which they then applied and extended in the remaining four fifths of the period. In reflecting on our ratio, we thought of Pearson's (1986) response in a debate on the merits of direct instruction. When asked how much direct instruction in comprehension is necessary, he responded tersely but insightfully, "as little as possible."

We also felt that we grew as teachers and researchers. Our inquiry was hard work, but our cooperation enabled us to see things about our teaching and the students' learning that we would have never uncovered had we not systematically reflected on our teaching. As we debriefed one day in April near the end of the program, we talked about the advantages and limitations of engaging in classroom research. Helene admitted that she initially was a bit intimidated by the process of engaging in classroom inquiry but that "I like the idea of being a teacher researcher now." Pat concurred. Helene also acknowledged that engaging in teacher research adds an additional dimension to a teachers' already busy work day. "The thing that frustrates me [is] we have so many things to do … juggling the act of the whole day's program and all of the other things we have to teach in addition to reading." In spite of the frustrations, the commitment was there— to the students, to the inquiry, to collaboration among colleagues. Helene said to Pat, "Maybe we could do it [the comprehension program] with another teacher next year? And whether we are doing a research project or not, I'd still like to do it again."

After finishing *Yellow Bird and Me*, Rontasha concluded her final journal entry by writing, "I just love that story. I want to read *The Gift-Giver* and *Home Boy*" [other titles by Hansen]. Thank you very much." Our unwritten, but most sincere, response to Rontasha would be as follows:

> You're welcome, Rontasha, but we think the "thank you" ought to go the other way. We wish to thank you and your classmates for working so hard and for being patient with us as we tried to figure out how to teach comprehension strategies. We thank you for sharing with us your fabulous insights into stories, characters, and literature. And thank you for allowing us to explore our own teaching and how

we might engage in it more effectively. You have no idea how much *you* taught *us*.

And that's what teacher research is all about: students and teachers working, learning, and growing together.

Authors' Note

This research was supported in part by the National Reading Research Center of the University of Georgia and the University of Maryland under the Educational Research and Development Centers Program (PR/Award no. 117A20007) as administered by the Office of Educational Research and Improvement, U.S. Department of Education. The findings and opinions expressed here do not necessarily reflect the position or policies of the National Reading Research Center, the Office of Educational Research and Improvement, or the U.S. Department of Education.

References

Baumann, J.F., & Duffy-Hester, A.M. (in press). Making sense of classroom worlds: Methodology in teacher research. In M.L. Kamil, P.B. Mosenthal, P.D. Pearson, & R. Barr (Eds.), *Handbook of reading research, Vol. III*. Mahwah, NJ: Erlbaum.

Baumann, J.F., Hooten, H., & White, P. (1996). Teaching skills and strategies with literature. In J. Baltas & S. Shafer (Eds.), *A staff development guide to balanced reading 3–6* (pp. 60–72). New York: Scholastic.

Baumann, J.F., Jones, L.A., & Seifert-Kessell, N. (1993). Using think alouds to enhance children's comprehension monitoring abilities. *The Reading Teacher, 47*, 184–193.

Campbell, J.R., Voelkl, K.E., & Donahue, P.L. (1997, September). *NAEP 1996 trends in academic progress* (U.S. Department of Education/Office of Educational Research and Improvement Publication No. NCES 97-985). Washington, DC: U.S. Government Printing Office.

Cochran-Smith, M., & Lytle, S.L. (Eds.). (1993). *Inside/outside: Teacher research and knowledge*. New York: Teachers College Press.

Cox, C., & Zarillo, J. (1993). *Teaching reading with children's literature*. New York: Macmillan.

Cullinan, B.E. (Ed.). (1987). *Children's literature in the reading program*. Newark, DE: International Reading Association.

Cullinan, B.E. (Ed.). (1992). *Invitation to read: More children's literature in the reading program*. Newark, DE: International Reading Association.

Delpit, L.D. (1988). The silenced dialogue: Power and pedagogy in educating other people's children. *Harvard Educational Review, 58*, 280–298.

Delpit, L.D. (1995). *Other people's children: Cultural conflict in the classroom*. New York: New Press.

Durkin, D.D. (1990). Dolores Durkin speaks on instruction. *The Reading Teacher, 43,* 472–476.

Hancock, J., & Hill, S. (1988). *Literature-based reading programs at work.* Portsmouth, NH: Heinemann.

Heald-Taylor, B.G. (1996). Three paradigms for literature instruction in grades 3 to 6. *The Reading Teacher, 49,* 456–466.

Hiebert, E.H., & Colt, J. (1989). Patterns of literature-based reading instruction. *The Reading Teacher, 43,* 14–20.

Hubbard, R.S., & Power, B.M. (1993). *The art of classroom inquiry: A handbook for teacher-researchers.* Portsmouth, NH: Heinemann.

Ladson-Billings, G. (1994). *The dreamkeepers: Successful teachers of African American children.* San Francisco, CA: Jossey-Bass.

Lincoln, Y.S., & Guba, E.G. (1985). *Naturalistic inquiry.* Newbury Park, CA: Sage.

McMahon, S.I., Raphael, T.E., Goatley, V.J., & Pardo, L.S. (1997). *The book club connection: Literacy learning and classroom talk.* New York: Teachers College Press.

Patterson, L., Santa, C.M., Short, K.G., & Smith, K. (Eds.). (1993). *Teachers are researchers: Reflection and action.* Newark, DE: International Reading Association.

Pearson, P.D. (1986, December). *Affirmative response to "Resolved: That there should be direct instruction in comprehension."* Paper presented at the annual debate of the National Reading Conference, Austin, TX.

Routman, R. (1988). *Transitions from literature to literacy.* Portsmouth, NH: Heinemann.

Routman, R. (1991). *Invitations: Changing as teachers and learners.* Portsmouth, NH: Heinemann.

Spiegel, D.L. (1998). Silver bullets, babies, and bath water: Literature response groups in a balanced literacy program. *The Reading Teacher, 52,* 114–124.

Strickland, D.S. (1994). Educating African American learners: Finding a better way. *Language Arts, 71,* 328–336.

Tompkins, G.E., & McGee, L.M. (1993). *Teaching reading with literature: Case studies to action plans.* New York: Macmillan.

Weisman, D.D. (1992). *Learning to read with literature.* Needham Heights, MA: Allyn & Bacon.

Wood, K.D., & Moss, A. (Eds.). (1992). *Exploring literature in the classroom: Contents and methods.* Norwood, MA: Christopher-Gordon.

Yopp, R.H., & Yopp, H.K. (1992). *Literature-based reading activities.* Needham Heights, MA: Allyn & Bacon.

Zarillo, J. (1989). Teachers' interpretations of literature-based reading. *The Reading Teacher, 43,* 22–28.

Children's Books Cited

Avi. (1980). *Man from the sky.* New York: Morrow.

Byars, B. (1973). *The 18th emergency.* Puffin.

Byars, B. (1985). *The Blossoms meet the vulture lady.* New York: Yearling.

Byars, B. (1986). *The not-just-anybody family.* New York: Yearling.

Greene, B. (1974). *Philip Hall likes me, I reckon, maybe.* New York: Yearling.

Hansen, J. (1986). *Yellow Bird and me.* New York: Clarion.

Haskins, J. (1992). *One more river to cross: The stories of twelve Black Americans.* New York: Scholastic.

Myers, W.D. (1988), *Me, Mop, and the Moondance Kid.* New York: Yearling.

Park, B. (1982). *Skinnybones.* New York: Random House.

Engagement Activities

In Your Classroom
Research indicates that to be strategic and motivated comprehenders, students need to be given a great deal of time to practice reading. These authors suggest the 20/80 rule whereby approximately 20% of reading time is spent in explicit instruction and 80% is spent reading, discussing, analyzing, and responding to books. Considering your reading block, how close are you to the 20/80 rule? How could you achieve it?

With Your Colleagues
Discuss the 20/80 rule with your colleagues. In particular, focus on factors that make it difficult to achieve this time allocation. What ideas do you and your colleagues have for increasing the time spent reading, discussing, analyzing, and responding to books?

Further Reading
Wigfield, A., & Guthrie, J. (1997). Relations of children's motivation for reading to the amount and breadth of their reading. *Journal of Education Psychology*, *89*(3), 420–432.

This study explored how reading motivation is related to children's reading habits. The findings indicate that motivation predicted the amount and breadth of reading. More important, children who were intrinsically motivated (as opposed to extrinsically) spent more time reading and read more broadly.

Growth of Literacy Engagement: Changes in Motivations and Strategies During Concept-Oriented Reading Instruction

John T. Guthrie, Peggy Van Meter, Ann Dacey McCann, Allan Wigfield,
Lois Bennett, Carol C. Poundstone, Mary Ellen Rice, Frances M. Faibisch,
Brian Hunt, and Ann M. Mitchell

Theoretical Framework for Reading Engagement

Motivations for Reading

Central to our investigation is the construct of reading engagement, which refers to the joint functioning of motivations and strategies during reading (Newman, Wehlage, & Lamborn, 1992). Engaged readers choose to read for a variety of purposes and comprehend the materials within the context of the situation. Engaged readers are self-determining (Deci, Vallerand, Pelletier, & Ryan, 1991) in the sense that they elect a wide range of literacy activities for aesthetic enjoyment, gaining knowledge, and interacting with friends. They are motivated to read for its own sake, and these motivations activate the self-regulation of higher order strategies for learning through literacy (Dole, Duffy, Roehler, & Pearson, 1991).

In our engagement perspective, motivations for reading are seen as internalized goals that lead to literacy choices and comprehension strategies (Pintrich & Schrauben, 1992). In this goal-oriented view, motivations may be regarded as reasons for reading. Students' goals can be classified as intrinsic or extrinsic. Intrinsic motivation refers to the activities in which pleasure is inherent in the activity itself (Gottfried, 1985). Extrinsic motivation refers to motivation that comes from outside the learner. Students who are more extrinsically motivated prefer to please the teacher, do easier reading tasks, and are dependent on the guidance of others. Some researchers (e.g., Harter, Whitesell, & Kowalski, 1992) proposed that motivations fall on a continuum from intrinsic to extrinsic implying that they are negatively correlated. Other investigators such as Wentzel (1991) reported that students may possess multiple motivational goals simultaneously—some of which are intrinsic and some extrinsic. We believe students have multiple motivations for reading.

Motivations for Strategy Use in Reading

Relationships between motivations and strategies have been explicated by Corno and Kanfer (1993), Covington (1992), and Ford (1992).

Abridged by J.A. Malloy, B.A. Marinak, & L.B. Gambrell with permission of J.T. Guthrie from Guthrie, J.T., Van Meter, P., McCann, A.D., Wigfield, A., Bennett, L., Poundstone, C.C., Rice, M.E., Faibisch, F.M., Hunt, B., & Mitchell, A.M. (1996). Growth of literacy engagement: Changes in motivations and strategies during Concept-Oriented Reading Instruction. *Reading Research Quarterly, 31*(3), 306-332.

Corno and Kanfer (1993) asserted that motivations consist of goals and intentions; however, they also emphasized the importance of volitional strategies that enable individuals to fulfill their motivational goals. They argued that without volition, individuals' intentions may not be realized in action.

Corno and Kanfer (1993) discussed many volitional processes. These included, first, action control processes, which empower the individual to manage cognitive and metacognitive resources for goal attainment. Second, goal-related cognitions form the basis for adaptive use of learning strategies, well-timed application of deep processing, self-monitoring, and self-evaluation. Finally, volitional styles such as conscientiousness, independence, and responsibility influence how strategies are used and regulated.

Corno (1993) asserted that volitional strategies are not merely energized by motivations, but more important, these strategies are contingent on different kinds of motivations. For example, when motivations possess personal significance, they are intrinsic and will be associated with higher level strategies. In contrast, a student who wishes to receive recognition for reading may not necessarily be concerned with understanding or enjoying the content of a book or story. This student will attempt to be perceived as competent and to comply with the demands of the teacher conscientiously. Yet the student may not read on his or her own, share books with friends, or pursue difficult tasks that are not assigned.

Some motivations, such as fear of failure, may lead to strategies of low goal setting, avoidance of risk, and minimal effort. These strategies may help a student fulfill the intention of avoiding failure but will not foster deep comprehension or extended reading for personal initiative. We expect that students who possess intrinsic motivations for reading will work independently, show responsibility, and conscientiously translate their intentions into actions. Thus, motivational and volitional systems work in close association, and exploring their joint functioning during reading was one purpose of this study.

Motivations for Conceptual Learning From Text

When motivations for reading are viewed as goals and commitments toward learning through literacy activities, the relationship of motivation to conceptual learning becomes apparent. Students who have a commitment to understand the content of an instructional unit are likely to get a deeper understanding of the content than students who possess different kinds of commitments.

Students whose motivations are more extrinsic, such as working just to complete an assignment or gain recognition for good performance, are likely to engage in rote learning and gain verbatim knowledge rather than a fully integrated conceptual understanding (Pintrich, Marx, & Boyle, 1993). Thus, it can be expected that intrinsic motivations will yield higher levels of conceptual learning than more extrinsic motivations.

Contextual Influences on Motivations for Reading

Although students come to school with motivational orientations developed during the preschool years (Deci, 1980), the different contexts of instruction also greatly influence student motivations as they go through school (Ames, 1992). Previous research suggests that contexts that increase intrinsic motivation will be socially interactive, with freedom for the learner (Blumenfeld, 1992; Turner, 1995), providing strategic tools for learning (Guthrie, McGough, Bennett, & Rice, 1996), and real-world literacy tasks (Newby, 1991).

The Study

We sought to answer the following:

1. Which aspects of literacy engagement increase during Concept-Oriented Reading Instruction (CORI)?

2. Were the increases in literacy engagement educationally significant?

3. How highly correlated were intrinsic motivation and engagement within and across time?

4. How do changes in intrinsic motivation, amount and breadth of reading, and volitional strategies relate to each other?

Method

To address these questions, we implemented an instructional program designed to enhance literacy engagement, charting the growth of students from fall to spring as they participated. Our description of growth was both quantitative and qualitative. The qualitative cases were selected for typicality (Erickson, 1986) to exemplify group trends. The quantitative analyses were done to assure that the conclusions about the growth of literacy engagement were warranted for the population of students and individuals within the populations (see a fuller rationale for this approach in Brown, 1992).

Participants and Setting

One Grade 3 and one Grade 5 teacher in one elementary school and one Grade 3 and one Grade 5 teacher in another elementary school in a diverse suburban school district in the mid-Atlantic region of the USA volunteered to embark on this venture, accompanied by one reading specialist in each school. Both schools were Chapter 1, K–6 schools with approximately 35 students in each of 15 classes. The schools had low (bottom quartile) reading and math achievement, and students were grouped heterogeneously in classes.

Concept-Oriented Reading Instruction: An Overview

The CORI program (see www.cori.umd.edu) was a year-long instructional design implemented in four classrooms in two elementary schools. A major purpose of the program was to increase students' engagement in literacy and science. The program was designed in collaboration with teachers and reading specialists in two elementary schools. The instructional framework contained four phases: (a) observe and personalize, (b) search and retrieve, (c) comprehend and integrate, and (d) communicate to others.

Observe and Personalize. Our first step in engaging students in literacy was to provide opportunities to observe concrete objects and events in their natural world. Observing natural objects such as a tree, flower, cricket, caterpillar, bird nest, or feather was intriguing. After experiencing an initial fascination with tangible, concrete objects, students began to wonder and to ask questions that led to conceptual interests. Students brainstormed and explicitly stated the questions they wanted to explore with additional observations, data collecting, reading, writing, and discussion. Observing the real world was a point of departure for extended literacy, and it provided a frame of reference that enabled students to select reading and writing activities and to self-monitor their pursuits.

Search and Retrieve. Teaching students how to search was fundamental to enabling them to pursue their interests and answer the questions they generated from observational activities. Students were encouraged to choose subtopics for learning and to search for books, resources, references, pictures, and explanations of the topics they chose. Students were taught how to search for books in the school library and to find books in the classroom. They learned to use the table of contents, index, headings, and pictures as guides.

Strategies for searching were taught explicitly through teacher modeling, peer modeling, teacher scaffolding, guided practice, and teamwork. Typically, teachers presented a directed lesson using a class set of one book for all students. Teachers emphasized book organization, relevance of information, appropriateness of detail, and the differences between facts, explanations, and opinions. Teams of students then explored their group sets of information books and exchanged ideas about how to search for ideas in them.

For 3–4 weeks in the middle of each unit, teachers addressed at least one aspect of the search daily for 15–30 minutes. Teachers modeled each of these stages, and students discussed them in groups and recorded progress toward each of them in their journals.

Comprehend and Integrate. As students followed the interests they had generated from their observational activities, they identified a wide range of texts and resources that were relevant. The phase of search and retrieve yielded a rich reserve of interesting material, but the students faced the challenge of comprehending and integrating. To help students in fully comprehending and integrating the texts with their own previous knowledge, teachers emphasized (a) determining the topic of a text selection, (b) detecting critical details, (c) summarizing the text, (d) making comparisons between texts, (e) relating illustrations to text, (f) developing criteria for evaluating a book, and (g) critically reflecting on the organization of information and the author's point of view. Students also learned that a novel or short story may address the same topic as an informational book and will provide a different experience of the theme.

Trade books were used exclusively. Basal readers were not used for any purpose, and science textbooks were used rarely for reference. To help students comprehend books, teachers provided explicit instruction in identifying topic, details, and writing summaries. Through teacher modeling, peer modeling, and small-group discussion, students were provided instruction in fix-up strategies, enabling students to (a) use pictures, illustrations, diagrams, and graphs; (b) refer to their own questions; (c) look up vocabulary in an index, glossary, or dictionary; (d) break text into parts and put it back together; (e) ask peers and teams; (f) form images about what they know; (g) reread the text in a new way; (h) slow down or speed up; and (i) consult their own background knowledge.

Besides comprehension strategies, students were taught note-taking and critical reflection on information from expository books. Using their own questions, interests, and topical knowledge as criteria for judgment, students learned to critique books.

Communicate to Others. Through CORI, students became experts on the topic about which they chose to learn. As they gained knowledge, students wanted to express their understandings to others. To foster this self-expression, teachers provided instruction that enabled students to present their understanding in many forms, including a written report, a class-authored book, dioramas, charts, and informational stories. Teachers coached students in identifying an audience, adapting their message to the audience, identifying critical details, and elaborating their writing. Students were encouraged to express their understandings in a variety of coherent, persuasive, and accurate communications to classmates or other audiences of their choosing.

Materials

Performance Assessment of Engaged Reading. We conducted an assessment designed to reflect a wide spectrum of motivational and strategic literacy processes that appeared in CORI. The assessment was intended to generate data for addressing research questions 1–3.

Our performance assessment was designed to enable students to do seven distinct, but connected tasks: (a) stating prior knowledge (writing what they know about the topic); (b) searching (finding resources and ideas about the topic); (c) drawing (expressing what they have learned through drawing); (d) writing (communicating their learning through composition); (e) conceptual transfer (addressing a related problem using conceptual knowledge learned during the unit); (f) informational text comprehension (understanding an expository text related to the theme); and (g) narrative interpretation (understanding and responding to a literary text on the theme of the unit).

Appraisal of Motivations for Literacy. To determine the nature of the students' motivations for literacy, we identified 24 students, 6 students from each classroom in the fall of 1993. Each teacher selected students to represent two highly engaged, two moderately engaged, and two less engaged readers. The interviewer followed a semi-structured, student-responsive questionnaire and tape-recorded the exchange. These appraisals were intended to generate data for addressing research questions 3 and 4.

Procedures. The performance assessments were conducted in Grade 3 and Grade 5 classrooms as teacher-led instructional units lasting 4 to 6 days. Half the students took one topic (owls for Grade 3; trees for Grade 5), and half took a different topic (ponds for Grade 3; tides for Grade 5) in September 1993; and the topics were reversed in the March 1994 administration. The program of CORI was provided for the students from the beginning of September 1993 through the end of May 1994. All reading/language arts and science were taught through this instructional framework for all students in these classrooms.

Findings and Discussion

This investigation was intended to initiate our study of how classroom contexts can be designed to enhance the development of literacy engagement.

Growth of Literacy Engagement. Our basic conclusion from this investigation is that literacy engagement of third and fifth graders increased during their year-long experience in CORI. Not only did teachers observe these increases in literacy engagement through students' portfolios and classroom participation, but our performance assessment also documented statistically significant increases.

Students' enhanced literacy engagement was evident in their work on tasks that reflected the merger of cognitive strategies and intrinsic motivations. We documented the growth of literacy engagement related to (a) searching for information in multiple texts, (b) representing ideas

through drawing and writing, and (c) transferring conceptual knowledge to new situations.

Success in these authentic literacy activities permits us to infer the successful use of strategies. Although many investigators use self-report as a measure of strategies (Collins-Block, 1992; Pintrich & De Groot, 1990), we believe that successful performance on authentic literacy activities in the classroom is a more secure ground for inferring the learning and use of literacy strategies.

These results confirm that literacy engagement increased during the year for these groups of students. Although the amount of increase was not compared to the changes in a control group because this was not a comparative, experimental study, the magnitude of the increase was noteworthy. Across time during elementary school, intrinsic motivation usually declines (Harter, 1981; Wigfield & Guthrie, 1995), leading us to suppose that literacy engagement might decline during the year. However, in this study, literacy engagement, which combines cognitive strategies with intrinsic motivation, increased during a year of schooling. In fact, in the case studies, one typical Grade 3 student in the spring, after participating in CORI for 6 months, surpassed the level of literacy engagement observed in one typical Grade 5 student in the fall before receiving any CORI. After documenting these increases in literacy engagement for the groups, we next described the nature of the growth.

Intrinsic Motivation and Literacy Engagement Increased Concurrently. The second finding was that increases in literacy engagement during the year were tied to increases in intrinsic motivation. Despite the previously cited trend for intrinsic motivations to decrease during the elementary school years, we observed that 68% of the students in our CORI classrooms increased in their overall levels of intrinsic motivation for literacy. Among the students who increased in intrinsic motivation, 100% increased markedly in literacy engagement.

Among students who did not increase in intrinsic motivation (e.g., who stayed the same or who decreased) 50% increased in literacy

Table 1
Changes in Frequency and Breadth of Reading and Intrinsic Motivation

	Frequency and Breadth of Reading	
	Increase	Decrease
Increase Intrinsic motivation	11	2
Decrease	2	5

engagement, and 50% decreased. These findings suggest that instruction that increases intrinsic motivations for literacy may improve the higher order cognitive competence of an extremely large proportion of learners. Of course, strategies may also increase for some learners who do not become more intrinsically motivated due to the power of extrinsic incentives such as recognition and rewards or general cognitive maturation.

Intrinsic Motivations Enhanced Amount and Breadth of Reading Activity. The third finding of this investigation was that increases in intrinsic motivation were tied to frequency and breadth of reading (See Table 1). Students who became more involved, curious, and social in their literacy activities read a broader range of topics and reported higher frequencies of reading activities than less motivated students. This linkage was particularly important because being an active reader is vital for many aspects of development.

Classroom Contexts That Enhance Literacy Engagement

Literacy engagement in Grades 3 and 5 was associated with distinctive qualities of the classroom context. Consistent with the motivational literature, our observations of CORI suggested that engaging classroom contexts were (a) observational, encouraging students to initiate learning by generating their own questions

from real-world observation (Lepper, 1988; Newby, 1991); (b) conceptual, with a focus on substantive topics rather than reading skills (Maehr & Fyans, 1989); (c) self-directing, supporting student autonomy and choice of topics, books, and peers (Skinner & Belmont, 1993); (d) metacognitive, with explicit teaching of reading strategies, problem solving, and composing (Collins-Block, 1992); (e) collaborative, emphasizing social construction of meaning and communities of learners (Almasi & Gambrell, 1994); (f) expressive, creating opportunities for self-expression through writing, debating, and group interaction (Oldfather & Dahl, 1994) and; (g) coherent, containing connections between classroom activities and tasks across the day, week, and month (Gamoran & Nystrand, 1992). Our theoretical perspective is that these classroom qualities accelerate the development of literacy engagement.

References

Almasi, J.F., & Gambrell, L.B. (1994). *Sociocognitive conflict in peer-led and teacher-led discussions of literature* (Reading Research Report #12). Athens, GA: National Reading Research Center.

Ames, C. (1992). Achievement goals and the classroom motivational climate. In D.H. Schunk & J. Meece (Eds.), *Student perceptions in the classroom* (pp. 327–349). Hillsdale, NJ: Erlbaum.

Blumenfeld, P.C. (1992). Classroom learning and motivation: Clarifying and expanding goal theory. *Journal of Educational Psychology, 84*, 272–281.

Brown, A. (1992). Design experiments: Theoretical and methodological challenges in creating complex interventions in classroom settings. *The Journal of the Learning Sciences, 2*, 141–178.

Collins-Block, C. (1992). Strategy instruction in a literature-based reading program. *The Elementary School Journal, 94*(2), 139–151.

Corno, L. (1993). The best-laid plans: Modern conceptions of volition and educational research. *Educational Researcher, 22*(2), 14–22.

Corno, L., & Kanfer, R. (1993). The role of volition in learning and performance. In L. Darling-Hammond (Ed.), *Review of research in education* (pp. 301–341). Washington, DC: American Educational Research Association.

Covington, M.V. (1992). *Making the grade: A self-worth perspective on motivation and school reform.* Cambridge, England: Cambridge University Press.

Deci, E.L. (1980). *The psychology of self-determination.* Lexington, MA: Lexington Books.

Deci, E.L., Vallerand, R.J., Pelletier, L.G., & Ryan, R.M. (1991). Motivation and education: The self-determination perspective. *Educational Psychologist, 26,* 325–346.

Dole, J.A., Duffy, G.G., Roehler, L.R., & Pearson, P.D. (1991). Moving from the old to the new: Research on reading comprehension instruction. *Review of Educational Research, 61*(2), 239–264.

Erickson, F. (1986). Qualitative methods in research on teaching. In M. Wittrock (Ed.), *Handbook of research on teaching* (pp. 119–161). New York: Macmillan.

Ford, M.E. (1992). *Motivating humans: Goals, emotions, and personal agency beliefs.* Newbury Park, CA: Sage.

Gamoran, A., & Nystrand, M. (1992). Taking students seriously. In F.M. Newmann (Ed.), *Student engagement and achievement in American secondary schools* (pp. 40–61). New York: Teachers College Press.

Gottfried, A.E. (1985). Academic intrinsic motivation in elementary and junior high school students. *Journal of Educational Psychology, 77,* 631–645.

Guthrie, J.T., McGough, K., Bennett, L., & Rice, M.E. (1996). Concept-oriented reading instruction: An integrated curriculum to -develop motivations and strategies for reading. In L. Baker, P. Afflerbach, & D. Reinking (Eds.), *Developing engaged readers in school and home communities* (pp. 165–190). Hillsdale, NJ: Erlbaum.

Harter, S. (1981). A new self-report scale of intrinsic versus extrinsic orientation in the classroom: Motivational and informational components. *Developmental Psychology, 17,* 300–312.

Harter, S., Whitesell, N.R., & Kowalski, P. (1992). Individual differences in the effects of educational transitions on young adolescents' perceptions of competence and motivational orientation. *American Educational Research Journal, 29,* 777–808.

Lepper, M.R. (1988). Motivational considerations in the study of instruction. *Cognition & Instruction, 5,* 289–309.

Maehr, M.L., & Fyans, L.J. (1989). School culture, motivation and achievement. In M.L. Maehr & C. Ames (Eds.), *Advances in motivation and achievements: Motivation enhancing environments* (Vol. 6, pp. 215–247). Greenwich, CT: JAI Press.

Newby, T.J. (1991). Classroom motivation: Strategies of first-year teachers. *Journal of Educational Psychology, 83,* 187–194.

Newman, F.M., Wehlage, G.G., & Lamborn, S.D. (1992). The significance and sources of student engagement. In F.M. Newman (Ed.), *Student engagement and achievement in American secondary schools* (pp. 11–39). New York: Teachers College Press.

Oldfather, P., & Dahl, K. (1994). Toward a social constructivist reconceptualization of intrinsic motivation for literacy learning. *Journal of Reading Behavior, 26,* 139–158.

Pintrich, P.R., & De Groot, E.V. (1990). Motivational and self-regulated learning components of classroom academic performance. *Journal of Educational Psychology, 82*(1), 33–40.

Pintrich, P.R., Marx, R.W., & Boyle R.A. (1993). Beyond cold conceptual change: The role of motivational beliefs and classroom contextual factors in the process of conceptual change. *Review of Educational Research, 63*(2), 167–199.

Pintrich, P.R., & Schrauben, B. (1992). Students' motivational beliefs and their cognitive engagement in classroom academic tasks. In D.H. Schunk & J.L. Meese (Eds.), *Student perceptions in the classroom* (pp. 149–184). Hillsdale, NJ: Erlbaum.

Skinner, E.A., & Belmont, M.J. (1993). Motivation in the classroom: Reciprocal effects of teacher behavior and student engagement across the school year. *Journal of Educational Psychology, 85,* 571–581.

Turner, J. (1995). The influence of classroom contexts on young children's motivation for literacy. *Reading Research Quarterly, 30,* 410–441.

Wentzel, K. (1991). Social and academic goals at school: Motivation and achievement in context. In M. Maehr & P.R. Pintrich (Eds.), *Advances in motivation and achievement: Goals and self-regulatory processes* (Vol. 7, pp. 185–212). Greenwich, CT: JAI Press.

Wigfield, A., & Guthrie, J. (1995). *Dimensions of children's motivations for reading: An initial study* (Reading Research Report #34). Athens, GA: National Reading Research Center.

Engagement Activities

In Your Classroom

In keeping with literacy tasks used in CORI, what problem-solving and writing opportunities could you plan to nurture motivation and self-regulation in your students? How could these activities reflect authentic learning and integrate material from two or more content areas (e.g., reading and science, reading and social studies)?

With Your Colleagues

Partner with a colleague and visit each other's classrooms to observe the literacy tasks presented to students. Discuss ways you and your colleague could increase opportunities for choice, authentic reading activities, problem solving, and collaboration.

Further Reading

Brozo, W.G., & Flynt, E.S. (2008). Motivating students to read in the content classroom: Six evidence-based principles. *The Reading Teacher, 62*(2), 172–174.

Included in this commentary are suggestions for elevating self-efficacy, planning interesting activities, connecting with the outside world, making an abundance of texts available, expanding choices, and structuring collaboration.

Creating Contexts for Motivation and Engagement

Motivating and engaging classroom contexts are created when students are allowed to develop personal agency with regard to their reading and are acknowledged for their unique strengths and goals. With an eye for pulling struggling readers in from the margins of the classroom, "Factors That Influence the Book Selection Process of Students With Special Needs" by Mary Katherine (Swartz) Rettig and Cindy Gillespie Hendricks guides teachers in helping these students choose books that will bolster their success and engagement with texts. "What Motivates Students to Read? Four Literacy Personalities," by Jill E. Cole is included to address the importance of making a place for all of the literacy personalities in your classroom. We conclude this section with Jacquelynn A. Malloy and Linda B. Gambrell's "New Insights on Motivation in the Literacy Classroom." This article offers ideas for creating a community of literate souls in your classroom by considering ways to make literacy instruction personally relevant and satisfying for today's students while preparing them to become tomorrow's successful and fulfilled citizens.

Recommended readings and engagement questions follow each article to support you in learning more about how to develop engaging classroom communities through reflection and interaction with your colleagues.

Factors That Influence the Book Selection Process of Students With Special Needs

Mary Katherine (Swartz) Rettig and Cindy Gillespie Hendricks

Choice is a motivator and a powerful force that, if given to students, allows them to take ownership and responsibility for their learning. Using the familiar tale of Goldilocks, Ohlhausen and Jepsen (1992) claimed that, as Goldilocks decided what to do in the story, she was "taking advantage of the opportunity to make choices, to learn from them, and to take a step toward self-discovery" (p. 32).

Self-selection and choice have a positive impact on learning, which leads to the conclusion that schools should foster environments that promote learning through self-selection, particularly when it comes to learning to read and becoming lifelong readers. Students who are given the opportunity to choose their own books are motivated to read and enjoy reading (Harmes & Lettow, 1986; Jenkins, 1959; Kragler & Nolley, 1996). Worthy, Moorman, and Turner (1999, p. 12) add, "One promising avenue for improving students' attitudes and reading competence, then, is to provide an array of materials from which students can choose." According to Veatch (1959, p. 33), "Children love to read when they choose their own books."

Because no two students are alike, it is important that students are given a choice in reading materials. "Seldom are two children ready to be taught reading from the same material at the same time" (Heilman, 1972, p. 389). "Individual children have unique needs, interests,

and backgrounds that affect choice" (Carter, 1988, p. 20). In their recent article, Worthy et al. (1999) stated "when students are both interested in what is being taught and have access to materials that interest them learning, motivation, effort, and attitudes improve" (1999, p. 12). They added, "Interest is an important resource for learning that is related to cognition and intrinsic motivation" (1999, p. 15).

Researchers (Chall, 1953; Howes, 1963; Norvell, 1946; Ohlhausen & Jepsen, 1992; Samuels, 1989) investigating the choices and interests of children's trade book selections have concluded that (a) males' and females' interests are similar through the primary grades; (b) primary students prefer stories about that which is familiar; (c) fiction is preferred; and (d) as children age, females choose more books dealing with love, home, or romance while males prefer adventure, mystery, and sports.

While the aforementioned investigators, as well as others, have focused on children's choices and interests, much of the research has not taken into consideration a unique group of students: those students with special needs, defined as students who are physically or mentally handicapped, learning or behaviorally disabled, or who have multiple handicaps (Harris & Hodges, 1981). Little research exists that examines the process used by special needs children when choosing a book for reading (see Huber, 1928;

Reprinted from Swartz, M.K., & Hendricks, C.G. (2000). Factors that influence the book selection process of students with special needs. *Journal of Adolescent & Adult Literacy, 43*(7), 608-618.

Lazar, 1937). Therefore, the purpose of this study was to investigate factors that influence the book selection process of middle school students with special needs.

Factors Known to Influence Book Selection

The importance of knowing why children choose the books they do is clearly explained by Wendelin and Zinck (1983):

> For students to become independent readers they need to choose and respond to literature. For teachers to develop situations in which students can respond to books and analyze their choices, they need to know what factors influence students' selection of books. (p. 85)

Factors known to influence the book selections of typically developing children include topic/subject matter, author, writing style, cover/illustrations, characters, and back-of-the-book summaries.

Topic/Subject Matter

In 1944 Rankin concluded, "the theme or specific topic of a book was the most important single factor influencing choice" (p. 136). Samuels (1989, p. 715), drew the same conclusion 45 years later: "Subject matter accounted for the largest number of students' positive responses to books." Past investigators (Ashley, 1963; Carter & Harris, 1982; Diaz-Rubin, 1996; Greenlaw, 1983; Huus, 1979; Norvell, 1946) have concluded that males and females react the same to adventure, mystery, suspense, ghost stories, horror stories, sports stories, and humor. Males seemed to favor war stories, wild animal stories, and science, while females tended to favor love stories or stories about home and family life (Norvell, 1946; Wolfson, Manning, & Manning, 1984). More recently, Worthy, et al. (1999) found that middle school students preferred scary stories, comics and cartoons, popular culture, sports, cars and trucks, and animals. Funny

books and series books were also mentioned as favorites.

Author

Wendelin and Zinck (1983) concluded that while reading one particular author may not give a student exposure to different reading material, it allows the reader to be confident in his or her ability because she or he is comfortable with the author's work. An earlier study by Carter (1988) yielded similar results: "children had chosen their present book by the author because they were familiar and wanted to read another book written by that same author" (p. 18).

Writing Style

An author's writing style is also an important factor in book selection. Samuels (1989, p. 719) concluded, "Students selected books because they liked the writer's style, especially the ability to create an exciting, fast paced story and to make them feel involved in the action through development of character or description of a place." Soares's (1963) analysis led to the conclusion that books chosen by students in his study were "written in clear style and concrete language, rather than abstract, figurative language" (p. 844).

Cover/Illustrations

Carter (1988) and Kragler and Nolley (1996) reported that illustrations on the cover or in the book were two of the top factors in book selections. Additionally, Vandergrift (1980, p. 81) stated that the cover of a book attracts people's attention, "Most children (and adults) are more likely to select an attractive looking book than one that is dull in appearance and gives no clue to its contents." In contrast, Wendelin and Zinck (1983) found that only a small number (8%) of their subjects said that the picture on the cover was important when selecting a book, and an even smaller number (5%) mentioned pictures in the book as important in trade book selection.

Characters

Kragler and Nolley (1996) found that students chose and enjoyed books that were part of a series because the characters recur in different situations and allow the reader to become acquainted with them, which makes the reader more comfortable. Reed (1994) stated, "young readers become hooked, wanting to know what happens to the characters who have become their friends" (p. 52). Altenbernd and Lewis (1969) stated that "there is considerable agreement among literary scholars that the greater the degree of similarity between the reader and the character, the greater the degree of identification that will result" (p. 19). Samuels's (1989) results indicated that character development, feelings of characters, and the way the reader could relate to the characters' feelings were important factors of book selection.

Back-of-the-Book Summaries

Gerlach, Rinehart, and Wisell (1994) investigated back-of-the-book (BOB) summaries. Their research was conducted using 37 BOB summaries for book selection. They concluded, "BOB summaries were helpful because students could gain an accurate sense of what the book would be about and thus use that information to make decisions about whether to read it or not" (p. 145).

Parameters of the Study

While each of the aforementioned factors influence the book selection process, it is far more likely that these factors are not considered individually, but rather are used simultaneously. The purpose of this investigation was to determine which factors influenced special needs students' book selections.

Participants

The population of this study included middle school students enrolled in northwestern Ohio schools. Professional contacts in the public schools were used to identify students for this investiga-tion. Race, ethnic background, and socioeconomic status were not considered for student selection.

Middle school students (Grades 6, 7, or 8) were considered for participation if they had either an Individual Education Plan ("a written statement for a disabled child to insure that to the maximum extent appropriate, disabled children, including children in public or private institutions, are educated with children who are not disabled," Ohio Department of Education, 1989, p. 31) or a 504 Plan ("No otherwise qualified individual with a disability in the United States shall, solely by reason of his or her disability, be excluded from the participation in, be denied the benefits of, or be subjected to discrimination under any program or any activity receiving Federal financial assistance," Heward, 1992, p. 33).

The present investigation did not focus on the contrasting aspects among sixth-, seventh-, and eighth-grade students in regard to selection of books; however, a balance of students across the middle school grades was desired. Therefore, the students who were chosen included 11 sixth graders, 9 seventh graders, and 11 eighth graders.

Of the 31 students, 19 (13 male and 6 female) had a specific learning disability (SLD). Specific Learning Disability refers to a disorder in one of the more basic psychological processes involved in understanding or using language, spoken or written, which may manifest itself in an imperfect ability to listen, think, speak, read, write, spell, or to do mathematical calculations. The term includes such conditions as perceptual handicaps, brain injury, minimal brain dysfunction, dyslexia, and developmental aphasia. The term does not include children who have learning problems that are primarily the result of visual, hearing, or motor handicaps; of mental retardation; or of environmental, cultural, or economic disadvantages (U.S. Office of Education, 1977).

Ten students (6 males and 4 females) were developmentally delayed (DD), a category that includes all children with significant delays or atypical patterns of development (Heward, 1992). One female was multihandicapped (MH), which is a severe impairment that makes it impossible to accommodate the needs of the child in any program but one designed specifically for multihandicapped children (Ohio Department of Education, 1989). One male had a severe behavior disorder (SBD), which is characterized by behavior that differs markedly and chronically from current social or cultural norms and adversely affects educational performance (Heward, 1992).

Methods

Worthy et al. (1999) stated that reading preference investigations have traditionally employed open-ended or closed-ended surveys, reading logs, and analysis of bestseller lists. Surveys usually require participants to rank or rate their preferences from a list of authors, books, stories, topics, excerpts, or descriptions. The validity of such survey instruments is often suspect. These authors suggest that one way to eliminate the limitations of survey research is to interview students or have them list materials they have read or would like to read.

To address the validity questions related to survey research, the present study employed informal book chats (discussions about books between the researcher and one to six students) to discuss various factors that might influence the book selection process of students with special needs. These chats were used to identify what the students had read or that they may want to read. Discussion also involved identifying reasons why students selected certain books. The researcher acted as facilitator for the group and directed the students through discussions.

All book chats were recorded to facilitate data analysis; however, students were told they could stop the tape player at any time if they did not want their remarks audiotaped and that they could ask questions if they did not understand something. The book chats took place in a space designated by the special education teacher of each school. One book chat (15–45 minutes in duration) was held with each group of students.

Procedures

To begin this investigation, we conducted a pilot study. After introductions and an informal discussion about books that the students had read put the students at ease, students were asked to name some books they had read and factors they considered when selecting books. Then, to facilitate discussion, we asked questions about authors, length, titles, covers, illustrations, and characters. Students were permitted to add unsolicited comments about books and reading.

To elicit more in-depth responses about the reasons why students selected books, five books (*Freak the Mighty*, Philbrick, 1993; *Howie Helps Himself*, Frassler, 1975; *Nick's Mission*, Blatchford, 1995; *Probably Still Nick Swansen*, Wolff, 1988; and *The Flunking of Joshua T. Bates*, Shreve, 1984) were shown to the pilot group as a collection, and then individually. After the title and author were read to the students, they were asked to look at the book and then indicate whether they would read the book by looking at the cover, title, illustrations, or the number of pages. Next, a general summary of the book was given to elicit more in-depth responses regarding reasons why students would or would not chose the book to read.

Following the pilot study, the same procedure for collecting data was followed during the book chats. During the pilot study, there was not enough time to adequately discuss all the books shown; therefore two books, *Freak the Mighty* and *The Flunking of Joshua T. Bates*, that had elicited the most response from the students in the pilot study were used for the present study because of the depth and breadth of the responses. *The Flunking of Joshua T. Bates* was used with 8 out of the 11 groups, and *Freak the Mighty* was used in 7 out of 11 groups. Due to time constraints, not all 11 groups were exposed to both of the books. Because some of the discussions were not as effective as they might have been in the pilot study, and to ensure all groups were treated similarly, a set of questions (based on responses in the pilot study) were developed:

1. Do you have a favorite author to read?

2. Is there any type of book you like to read? (Examples: science fiction, romance)

3. Are there any covers of books or illustrations in books that you find interesting?

4. Have you ever read a book because you thought the title was interesting?

5. Would you rather read a book that was shorter or longer?

6. Have you ever read the summary of a book?

7. Do you read a book because you like a particular character?

8. Do you choose to read books that allow you to see yourself as one of the characters in the story?

9. Do you select a book based on a friend's recommendation?

Data Analysis

Once the informal book chats were completed, all of the audiotaped discussions were transcribed for analysis. To ensure anonymity, students were given individual letter and number codes so they could be directly quoted. For example, in the letter number code MkMSLD, Mk refers to the student's full name, the second M refers to the gender of the student, and SLD refers to the disability of the student.

To transcribe the data from each of the 11 book chats, we devised a coding system to extract the factors known to affect book selection (topic/subject matter, author, writing style, cover/illustrations, characters, and back-of-the-book summaries). First, all book chats were coded for topic/subject matter. Then all book chats were coded for author. This was repeated for each of the factors. Once completed, all color-coded comments in each category were grouped to examine the comments for generalities and frequency counts. Additional categories were formed for comments that did not fit into the previously identified factors.

What We Learned About Selection of Books

Each book chat began with a discussion of the books that students had read. The students (see Table 1) mentioned a total of 80 book titles. Almost all 31 students in the study read at least

---

Table 1
Alphabetical List of Books Read by Participants

Alex Naps
Alice in Wonderland
All Star Team
Anne of Green Gables
Arthur
The Babysitters Club series
Biggest Planet
Black Beauty
The Box Car Children
Casper
Cat in the Hat
The Cat Ate My Gymsuit
Charlotte's Web
Congo
Devil's Court
Don't Forget the Bacon
Encyclopedia Brown series
Face Off
First Kiss
Frankenstein
Garfield
General Patton
Goosebumps series
Green Eggs and Ham
Hardy Boys series
Harriet Tubman
Hatchet
Haunted Mask
History of Flying
Howling
How the Universe Works
How to Eat Fried Worms
The Indian in the Cupboard
Jackson Five
Jurassic Park
The Magic School Bus series
The Man in the Iron Mask
Matilda
Michael Jordan's Career
Miss Piggle Wiggle
The Mouse and the Motorcycle
Night of the Living Dead
One Last Wish
The Outsiders
The Phantom Toll Booth
The Pinballs
Prom Queen
Run Away Ralph
Rosie O'Donnell

(continued)

**Table 1
Alphabetical List of Books
Read by Participants (Continued)**

Say Cheese & Die!
Scary Stories 3
Shane
Shiloh
The Shining
Sign of the Beaver
Snowman
Star Wars series
The Strange Case of Dr. Jekyll and Mr. Hyde
Sub
Summer of My German Soldier
Tex
Titanic
Tom Sawyer
Tough to Tackle
Treasure Island
Trumpet of the Swan
20,000 Leagues Under the Sea
Wayne Gretzky
Wednesday Witch
Welcome to the Dead House
When Mars Attacks
Wishbone series

**Table 2
Books Selected According to Topic/
Subject Matter**

Topic/Subject Matter	Number of Students
Horror	10
Mystery	7
Action	6
Biography	5
Information	5
Humorous	4
Science fiction	3
Adventure	3
Sports	2
Romance	1
Thrillers	1
Sad	1

one book in the Goosebumps series, except one who said, "I tried to read Goosebumps, but they're too hard" (ToMDD).

Topic/Subject Matter

Twenty-four of the 31 students who were involved in the book discussions made reference to different topics or subject matter of books they selected to read. A least one student (see Table 2) mentioned a total of 13 different topics/subjects. Horror books topped the list as being a favorite type of book to read. Mysteries were next, with 7 of the 24 students selecting this type of book; 6 of 24 students preferred action books. The list continued with students identifying the following types of books as preferable: topic books (including informational books and biographies), humorous, science fiction, adventure, sports, romance novels, thrillers, and sad books.

One student (JlMSLD) described his views on different types of books:

> Well, it's, I don't really read much books unless someone gives it to me and says read this book. If it's like a romance book I'll fall asleep … in the Harriet Tubman book … they tell about people but they don't have any excitement.

Some students elaborated on their responses, "I like action books because you can feel like you can shoot with the guy" (MkMSLD) or "I like to read mysteries that are hard to figure out, that are puzzling" (JbMSLD).

Author

The name of a particular author was also a reason why students selected books. R.L. Stine, the author of the Goosebumps series, was the favorite author of 5 of the students, while Stephen King was the favorite of 4 others. Other favorite authors, each with at least one student saying they were liked, were Marc Brown, Matt Christopher, and L.M. Montgomery. The other 9 students who mentioned the author did not say anything specific, but made references that they looked at the author's name but had no favorites, and liked to read books by all different authors.

For example, one student (StFDD) remarked, "I look at the back of the book where it has some writing on it and check to see about the author."

Writing Style

Few students made any mention of the author's writing style. One student stated he read a "paragraph on the inside of the book because the summary doesn't really tell how the author is going to write" (JbMSLD). ChMSLD commented, "I usually just go to the first page and read a little bit of the first paragraph and stuff and I find out if I like it or not and if I do I usually stick with it until I get done reading it." JbMSLD also stated that he read the first paragraph, "Because I want to see how it starts and what kind of book it is because the summary doesn't really tell how the author is going to write."

Characters

Eleven out of the 31 students said that they would select a book because of a particular character (see Table 3). Three students interjected that they liked reading books in a series because they were familiar with a specific character. One student explained, "I like stories about the same character, the next book you know what he's going to be all about and if you like him, you know it is a good book" (MkMSLD). Another student disagreed, "I don't really like books that have the same characters because then you sorta know everything that's going to happen and you can figure it out" (BrMSLD).

Another reason for selecting books based on characters was a desire to be like a particular character; one student stated, "I like the character [Anne] in *Anne of Green Gables*, because she's a poet and I want to be a poet someday" (StFDD). MkMSLD added, "if I like the person, like I read one on Michael Jordan and I play basketball a lot like him." Other reasons for selecting books based on characters were because the student thought a character was funny ("I read Garfield books because…he's funny and he sleeps a lot" AyMDH) or because the students had personal experiences similar to the characters ("I read

Table 3
Book Selections Based on Character

Student Responses	Number of Students
Familiar with a character	11
Want to be like a character	2
Funny character	1
Experiences similar to character	8
Identified with a character	9

Charlotte's Web, because I like the pig, I live on a farm and we have a couple hundred pigs" SvMSLD).

Nine of the 31 students also explained the ability to relate to a particular character when reading a book as important to them. Students emphasized the fact that they could see themselves as certain characters, wanted to be like a character, or did not want to be like a particular character. One student described an experience that came to her when reading a Babysitters Club book "one of the girls' parents were fighting and I feel so bad for her because a couple of years ago my parents got divorced" (BrFMH). One student talked about acting out parts of the book: "There was a Goosebumps book that had a mask, mask 1 and mask 2, and sometimes I realize me in there as the mask and I'll make my own mask out of tin foil and put it on my face" (ChMSLD).

One female explained that she read about people with problems because she is overweight and people make fun of her. A male said that he read about sports problems, "like basketball and soccer because I'm not that fast and I can't really handle a ball that good." BrMSLD added, "I think more people should read those books because it's sorta trying to give a message that it's not really nice to make fun of people."

Cover/Illustrations

Fifteen of the 31 students said they picked a book because of the pictures on the cover or illustrations in the book. While not all students elaborated on what they looked for, some students had these further comments: "I liked *Congo* because I saw a monkey on the cover" (MkMSLD); "I would see if there's any pictures and then I'll turn back and see what the story's about" (PmFDD). Of the 15 students who picked books because of the illustrations, 3 students said that before they picked a book, they checked through the book for pictures, but made no mention of looking at the cover of the book. One student (DnFSLD) responded, "I like the thing on the cover like the prom thing one, where there is half her face in the mirror."

Back-of-the-Book Summaries

Eighteen students said they read back-of-the-book summaries when selecting a book to read. Four students were much more elaborate in their responses about the summaries of books. One student explained that he picked the book *Say Cheese & Die!* "Because it said how the boy found the camera and he took a picture and then it just stopped, I wanted to find out what happened" (TjMSLD). Another student (JeFSLD) responded, "I'd probably read the back of the book to see if it's good. That way if I read it I wouldn't get it again. I glance through it to see if it is interesting or boring."

Title

Of the 31 students interviewed, 14 mentioned the titles of books as a reason for selecting books. These 14 students made general comments about the titles sounding interesting or the fact that the titles were based on a movie they had seen. One student indicated that, "*Say Cheese & Die!*, I thought the title was cool" (TjMSLD). Another student said that he liked the title of *The Indian in the Cupboard*, so he read the book.

Length

Two thirds of the students (21 of 31) made some comment about the length of the book as a factor in the book selection process. The comment most heard was that students first wanted to see how long the book was. Sixteen students said they like to read shorter books that averaged about 100 pages. Shorter books tended to be more popular among these students because they did not lose interest or become bored with the stories. Students also made suggestions that they did not become tired because the books were too long. One male student clarified his position, stating that he "liked to pick books that were between 50–80 pages because anything longer than that the words are a little too big and it gets too hard" (DjMSLD). Several students indicated they would be more inclined to read a longer book if it was something that they found interesting. For example, "I'd read a book about 160 pages if it has to do with excitement or the Civil War. If it has to do with battles and if it has to deal with learning whatever I'm interested in" (JlMSLD). Another student who liked to read longer books explained, "I like long books because if it's too short, like 150 pages, there isn't enough drama and it seems like [the author] is trying to cut the story" (JbMSLD).

Recommendations

Sixteen of 31 students interviewed discussed a friend's recommendation of a book as a possible reason to read or not read a book. Three of those 16 students said that they would not read a book based on a friend's recommendation. They stated that they did not trust their friends' judgment about a book. DjMSLD remarked that if someone suggested a book, he "probably would not read it 'cause mostly I have a different view of what kinds of books, like I am very picky and I'll read certain books." Another student claimed he would read a book based on a friend's recommendation "if they explain it and the book is interesting" (TjMSLD).

Movies/Television Shows

Eleven of the students selected books because there was a movie or television show either about a particular book or that somehow related to a book. Three students, who indicated movies or television shows were a factor in book selection, stated that they would rather read the book before watching the movie or television show. One student said:

> I like to read the book and then watch the movie. Usually I notice that the books are different than the movies and if I know what the book is before I see the movie, I can picture what it is going to be about. (JbMSLD)

Two students read books to find out more information about certain topics after watching a movie or seeing a television show. Another student commented, "I'd rather read the book because in my mind I get a totally different picture than the movie. I like my picture better" (TjMSLD).

Other students commented that they compare the book with the movie. DnFSLD said, "like on the Goosebumps books it's not always the same as is the [show]," while ChMSLD commented, "They have *Night of the Living Dead*. I read that and then seen the movie. Most [scary] books are exactly like the movie." Another student (BrMSLD) had a more practical reason to read the book before seeing the movie, "Well, I like reading books first because if you start to read a book and you don't really think it's interesting, why would you go and rent the movie and watch it?"

Combined Strategies

Many of the students' responses indicated that they used a variety of strategies in selecting books. For example, AoFSLD added:

> At the mall, I read this one book, *Alex Naps*, and what I do is read the title and then sometimes read the back cover of it and see what's going on in it and if I read the back of it and I like it then I'll sometimes pick that book and start reading it.

MkMSLD reported that the process he followed when choosing books was, "First I go to the computer and I go to title or author or illustrator and then I type in what it is and it shows where it is and I go to it and see if I like it or not and

if I don't I just do the process over." JbMSLD described his book selection process as follows:

> Like usually when I go to the library I have in mind what kind of book I like to read and then I type it into the computer like the author or something and then I go get the book and look inside to see how it is typed and read the summary in the back, look at the cover and read a paragraph inside the book to see if I like it.

LyFSLD said she would, "open the book and make sure it's not torn or ripped and if it's okay I look at the title and the pictures, who wrote it and if I decided I liked it I would read it."

Children With Special Needs Are Children First

Generally, the process by which students with special needs select books is not altogether different from the "typically" developing child. Although general factors previously identified (topic/subject matter, writing style, cover/illustrations, characters, and back-of-the-book summaries) were used by students with special needs, the students who participated in this investigation used additional strategies. In addition to the factors identified earlier, students with special needs also identified title, length of book, movie/TV adaptations, and a friend's recommendation as important factors in book selection. Additionally, students also used a combination of strategies simultaneously when selecting a book to read.

Clearly, students with special needs want to read the same books as typically developing children. It seems evident from this research that while students may have a special need, they selected the same types of books for the same reasons that typically developing students select books.

Topic/subject matter of books seems to be an important factor in the book selection process of students with special needs. The participants in this investigation selected what would seem to be the same types of books that typically developing students select. Students with special needs were more likely to pick books that contained themes of horror, mystery, or action and less likely to select books that dealt with romance.

The results of this study are very much in line with the results of the Worthy et al. (1999) investigation. The author of a book and the author's writing style seemed to play insignificant roles in the book selection process of special needs students. Although only 5 students mentioned R.L. Stine as their favorite author, most students had read at least one of the Goosebumps books. Writing style received little or no mention by most students in terms of book selection. Again, these results are similar to those of Worthy et al. (1999) whose participants were typically developing middle school children.

Character was important to students as they selected books. The majority of the students selected books for four major reasons: (a) students were familiar with and liked a particular character, (b) students believed they could relate to a character, (c) students wanted to be like a particular character, and (d) students believed they had an experience similar to a particular character. The characters in a story seemed to be a very important factor in the book selection process.

Students with special needs, like typically developing students, seem to make a connection with characters in stories and select books because of the personal connection they have made. The majority of students with special needs selected books because of the picture on the cover rather than pictures in the story. It could be said that these students are literally judging a book by its cover. Although this may be a great way to gain a student's attention, it may leave some very good books on the shelf.

Back-of-the-book summaries had a significant impact on students' selecting books. Many students selected books because they had read the summary, whether on the inside cover or on the back of the book. It seems that this category was one of the most influential reasons why students selected certain books over others.

Title, length, recommendations, and movies/television shows all seemed to have some impact on the selection of books by students with special needs. Of the four factors, length seemed to be the most important. Most students who mentioned length were adamant that they preferred to read short books (under 100 pages) rather than long books. The other three factors were discussed briefly.

Many recommendations can be made about book selection for students with special needs. First and foremost, it is vital that teachers, whether special education or regular education, try not to "dumb down" reading lists for students with special needs. This research demonstrates that students with special needs want to read the same books as typically developing students.

Teachers do not need to have a lot of books about different disabilities; however, what they do need is a number of books representing a variety of topics and subject matter such as horror, mystery, action, and adventure books. The more books in a classroom library, the more choices students will have.

To make all students acquainted with different types of books, teachers could implement lessons on how to select a book that fits the need of the individual student in the classroom. Students with special needs would then have the skills, if not already present, to find a book that they not only liked (based on character or length), but that they could read without becoming frustrated.

Another option for teachers is that they could start being more aware of what their students are reading in the classroom during recreational reading or silent reading time. This would allow teachers to become more acquainted with what their pupils actually want to read. Teachers could then read the books that a majority of their students are reading (e.g., Goosebumps), and develop lessons to go along with those specific books.

Teachers could develop and implement lessons for one different book per quarter focusing on specific skills needed by individual students or a book that was a favorite among the students. This would be likely to increase the students' interest and, in turn, allow for more reading time because the students would like what they were reading.

Because students become better readers by reading, it is important that the teachers are not the only ones teaching reading and, more important, trying to help students enjoy reading. Parents also need to stress the importance of reading and could follow some of the same recommendations as were given for the teacher. For example, parents, like teachers, could have a wide array of books from which their child could select. Parents could also read aloud to their children, take trips to the library with children, have book discussions, or purchase books.

Libraries and librarians should be aware that whether a child is typically developing or has special needs, a large collection of favorite book genres like horror, mystery, action, and humorous books is vital. Worthy et al. (1999) concluded that students who have access to materials of interest are more likely to read and thus to improve their reading achievement and attitudes. Because character was also an important factor when students with special needs selected books, it would be beneficial to have many series books included in the library's collection.

The final recommendation from this research is that the education departments of universities should implement children's literature courses in their special education programs if they are not already in place. Through a children's literature course, preservice special education teachers will become aware of the literature that is popular among middle school readers. Preservice teachers may be asked to design specific lessons focused on popular books. The preservice teachers can adapt those lessons for use with individuals, small groups, or whole-class instruction.

Above all, educators should remember that students with special needs are not so different. They enjoy reading the same books as typically developing children. Perhaps the reason why the results of this investigation are similar to those conducted in the past with typically developing children is that simple: Children with special needs are children first.

References

Altenbernd, L., & Lewis, L. (1969). *Introduction to literature: Stories* (2nd ed.). New York: Macmillan.

Ashley, L. (1963). Children's reading interests and individualized reading. *Elementary English, 47,* 486–490.

Blatchford, C. (1995). *Nick's mission.* Minneapolis, MN: Lerner Publications.

Carter, M. (1988). How children choose books: Implications for helping develop readers. *Ohio Reading Teacher, 22,* 15–21.

Carter, B., & Harris, K. (1982). What junior high students like in books. *Journal of Reading, 26,* 42–46.

Chall, J. (1953). Ask him to try on the book for fit. *The Reading Teacher, 7,* 83–88.

Diaz-Rubin, C. (1996). Reading interests of high school students. *Reading Improvement, 33,* 169–175.

Frassler, J. (1975). *Howie helps himself.* Chicago: Whitman.

Gerlach, J., Rinehart, S., & Wisell, D. (1994). Choosing a book: Are BOB summaries helpful? *Reading Psychology, 15,* 139–153.

Greenlaw, J. (1983). Reading interest research and children's choices. In M. Firth & N. Roser (Eds.), *Children's choices: Teaching with books children like* (pp. 90–92). Newark, DE: International Reading Association.

Harmes, J., & Lettow, L. (1986). Fostering ownership of the reading experience. *The Reading Teacher, 40,* 324–333.

Harris, T.L., & Hodges, R.E. (1981). *A dictionary of reading and related terms.* Newark, DE: International Reading Association.

Heilman, A. (1972). *Principles and practices of teaching reading.* Columbus, OH: Merrill.

Heward, W. (1992). *Exceptional children.* Columbus, OH: Merrill.

Howes, V.M. (1963). Children's interest: A keynote for teaching reading. *Education, 83,* 495–498.

Huber, M. (1928). *The influence of intelligence upon children's reading interests.* New York: Teachers College Press.

Huus, H. (1979). A new look at children's interests. In J. Shapiro (Ed.), *Using literature and poetry affectively* (pp. 37–45). Newark, DE: International Reading Association.

Jenkins, M. (1959). Self-selection in reading. In J. Veatch (Ed.), *Individualizing your reading program* (pp. 181–191). New York: G.P. Putnam's Sons.

Kragler, S., & Nolley, C. (1996). Student choices: Book selection strategies of fourth graders. *Reading Horizons, 36,* 354–365.

Lazar, M. (1937). *Reading interests, activities, and opportunities of bright, average, and dull children.* New York: Teachers College Press.

Norvell, G.W. (1946). Some results of a 12-year study of children's reading interest. *The English Journal, 35,* 531–536.

Ohlhausen, M., & Jepsen, M. (1992). Lessons from Goldilocks: Somebody's been choosing my books but I can make my own choices now! *The New Advocate, 5,* 31–46.

Ohio Department of Education. (1989). *Rules for the education of handicapped children*. Columbus, OH: Author.

Philbrick, W.R. (1993). *Freak the mighty*. New York: Scholastic.

Rankin, M. (1944). *Children's interest in library books of fiction*. New York: Teachers College Press.

Reed, A. (1994). *Reading adolescents: The young adult book and the school*. New York: Macmillan College.

Samuels, B. (1989). Young adults' choices: Why do students really like particular books. *Journal of Reading, 32*, 714–719.

Shreve, S. (1984). *The flunking of Joshua T. Bates*. New York: Random House.

Soares, A. (1963). Salient elements of recreational reading of junior high school students. *Elementary English, 40*, 843–845.

U.S. Office of Education. (1977). Procedures for evaluating specific learning disabilities. *Federal Register, 42*, 65082–65085.

Vandergrift, K. (1980). *Child and story: The literary connection*. New York: Neal-Schuman.

Veatch, J. (1959). *Individualizing your reading program*. New York: G.P. Putnam's Sons.

Wendelin, K., & Zinck, R. (1983). How students make book choices. *Reading Horizons, 23*, 84–88.

Wolff, V. (1988). *Probably still Nick Swansen*. New York: Holt.

Wolfson, B., Manning, G., & Manning, M. (1984). Revisiting what children say their reading interests are. *Reading World, 24*, 4–10.

Worthy, J., Moorman, M., & Turner, M. (1999). What Johnny likes to read is hard to find in school. *Reading Research Quarterly, 34*, 12–29.

Engagement Activities

In Your Classroom

According to the authors, students with special needs should be offered access to the same books as typically developing children. In addition, teachers should be aware that students with special needs often attend to book title and length, movie adaptations, and the recommendations of friends. How can you use these strategies to support students in their book selections?

With Your Colleagues

How can you and your colleagues increase your awareness of what your special needs students are reading? How can you support the interests of these students during your read-alouds and book talks? Consider the value of meeting regularly with students to discuss their interests and reading preferences. How can you make this happen?

Further Reading

Ivey, G., & Broaddus, K. (2001). "Just plain reading": A survey of what makes students want to read in middle school classrooms. *Reading Research Quarterly, 36*(4), 350–377.

This study identified several factors that caused middle school students to engage with books. According to the findings, adolescents valued independent reading time and teacher read-alouds. Reading for purpose and pleasure were also important. When asked what motivated them to read, these middle schoolers said that the quality and diversity of reading material was more important than classroom setting or the influence of other people.

What Motivates Students to Read?
Four Literacy Personalities

Jill E. Cole

Amy (all student names are pseudonyms) was a cheerful, motivated reader in my second-grade class. She had a strong self-efficacy—she believed she would succeed—and an excellent attitude toward reading and school. Amy valued books and read often at school and at home. She also liked to share books with her classmates and was a positive role model for them.

Mark was another good reader with a healthy self-concept. However, while he was an excellent student who received superior grades, he was just beginning to truly value books and reading. Mark worked hard and always completed his assignments correctly, but he was often uninterested in his work and rarely took risks in his literacy. He read and wrote only when he was required to do so.

Of course, not all the students in the class were as positive and motivated as Amy and Mark. Trae worked hard to acquire competence in literacy, but it wasn't easy for him. His attitude toward reading had suffered because of his older brother's difficulty in learning to read. Trae had witnessed his brother's frustration along with his mother's discouragement. Nevertheless, Trae was amazingly determined and persistent. He wanted to learn to read, but he wanted it to be instantly easy for him. It wasn't, and Trae's attitude toward school was poor. His distrust of school-like activities clashed with his desire to become a good reader.

A fourth student, Brooke, loved books, and she had an exceptionally positive attitude toward reading, preferring it to many other activities. However, Brooke lacked a strong self-efficacy. She was often unsure of her capabilities and did not know how to express herself confidently. Even when classroom activities showed that Brooke had proficient reading skills, she still seemed to think she was a poor reader. As a result, she was self-conscious, and her participation in literacy activities in the classroom was inadequate.

These four students took part in my classroom study of intrinsic motivation to read. As this topic was explored throughout the school year, one thing became clear—the students were motivated by very different books, activities, and other classroom components. They had their own beliefs, purposes, and reactions. In short, each one had a unique "literacy personality."

The Study

What motivated the students in my classroom to read? That was the question I set out to explore at the beginning of the 1998–1999 school year. When I decided to use a qualitative research approach, I knew I would be unable to generalize my results to other classrooms, or even to my own classroom, during subsequent school terms. However, I still felt that children have so much to tell us about their education. Along with their teachers, they are the experts (Oldfather & Dahl, 1994). I decided that students' opinions, feelings, and choices were crucial to my understanding of their intrinsic motivation to read and that this information would enable me to be a more effective reading teacher. To further strengthen the research design, I chose a case study approach

Reprinted from Cole, J.E. (2002). What motivates students to read? Four literacy personalities. *The Reading Teacher, 56*(4), 326-336.

with Amy, Mark, Trae, and Brooke selected as the target students.

A significant aspect of this research project was my role of teacher-researcher. During the study, I was the classroom teacher as well as the researcher. The advantages of this dual role seemed to outweigh any disadvantages. Although at times I had to focus my attention on the other 13 students in the classroom, I felt that the insights gained from being teacher *and* researcher were more valuable than those an observer with less knowledge of the four subjects might have gleaned. Intrinsic motivation seemed to be enhanced simply by the students acting as researcher-helpers (Thomas & Oldfather, 1995) and working with me to discover what enticed them to read. In a compelling study, Baumann and Ivey (1997) entered a second-grade classroom (Baumann as full-time teacher, Ivey as participant observer) where they did qualitative research on the effects of strategy instruction embedded within a literature-based reading and writing curriculum. Their discussion was enlightening because of the study's immersion in the real life of the classroom, with the classroom's principal players combining their teaching and researching roles. As in the Baumann and Ivey research, personal experiences and theoretical perspectives as teacher-researcher influenced my study. Accordingly, the conclusions reported relate only to a specific context; for generalizations to be made, further qualitative and quantitative studies would have to be performed.

Criterion-based sampling was used to select the case study students. I was looking for two boys and two girls—two students of average to below average reading ability and two students of average to above average reading ability—as well as students who were verbal and could discuss their choices, feelings, and opinions. Using our district's standardized test scores, report cards from the previous year, and the recommendations of the students' first-grade teachers, I selected Trae and Brooke as students of average to below average reading ability and Amy and Mark as students of average to above average reading ability. I received parental permission for all the students to participate in the project.

During the period of the study (the seven months from the end of August 1998 to the end of March 1999) data were collected from six sources: extensive observations recorded as field notes; one hour per week of videotape of the case study students working within the context of the classroom; reading logs written by the students; artifacts of the case study students' reading and writing collected during the study (including lists of books read, writing notebooks, and audio samples of their oral reading); three semistructured interviews with each case study student conducted at the beginning, middle, and end of the study; and two semistructured interviews with the four students' parents in September and March. The information presented in the vignettes later in the article comes from these sources.

This was a qualitative, interpretive case study (Merriam, 1988), and content analysis was used to define categories, detect patterns and trends, and describe student behaviors. I specifically looked for evidence of intrinsic motivation to read in the written work, actions, and voices of Amy, Mark, Trae, and Brooke. The information that was gathered from the process of collecting, organizing, and analyzing the data enabled me to better understand these four students as readers and learners and led to a greater appreciation of their abilities, interests, voices, and ultimately of their total literacy personalities.

Conceptual Framework

Wigfield and Guthrie (1997) concluded from their research that reading motivation is "multifaceted." Being aware of at least some of the facets involved in developing intrinsic motivation in students can help educators come closer to the goal of instilling in all students a love of reading and learning. Pintrich and DeGroot's (1990) three categories of general motivation constructs were used to organize and present the facets of intrinsic motivation explored in this study: readers' beliefs, readers' reasons and purposes for participation and engagement, and readers' affective reactions. Figure 1 provides an illustration of these categories and how they led to one another, worked together, and overlapped

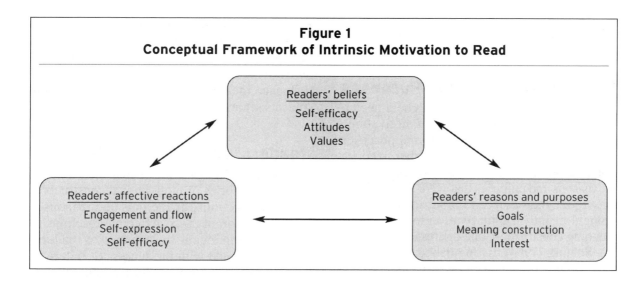

**Figure 1
Conceptual Framework of Intrinsic Motivation to Read**

Readers' beliefs

Self-efficacy
Attitudes
Values

Readers' affective reactions

Engagement and flow
Self-expression
Self-efficacy

Readers' reasons and purposes

Goals
Meaning construction
Interest

in a cycle of motivation as they guided the research study.

Readers' Beliefs

All students bring their own sets of beliefs into the classroom. Classroom activities do not directly cause beliefs, but students' beliefs may affect their participation in the learning process (Pintrich, Marx, & Boyle, 1993). Beliefs may be formed by environmental factors or past learning experiences (McKenna, 1994), and students may not even be aware of their existence. While positive beliefs may foster learning, negative beliefs often block learning. However, if the educator is aware of these beliefs, then they can be used to help students learn. The beliefs that affected the four case study students' reading and motivation involved self-efficacy, attitude, and values.

Self-efficacy incorporates a student's beliefs about his or her capabilities to participate in and succeed in a learning situation (Bandura, 1986). Students with positive self-efficacies feel in control of their learning and believe they have the power to succeed. Students with poor self-efficacies do not feel in control and think they will not succeed. It is important for educators to evaluate students' self-efficacies and then provide meaningful, motivational activities that will

improve and enhance students' confidence in their abilites.

Attitude is defined as "a learned predisposition to respond in a consistently favorable or unfavorable manner with respect to a given object" (Fishbein & Ajzen, 1975, p. 6). The Mathewson Model (Mathewson, 1994) of attitude influence upon reading is one example of a structure used to describe attitude development. The model represents three components of attitude: prevailing feelings about reading, action readiness for reading, and evaluative beliefs about reading. These components can be a causal factor during reading and can especially affect the intention to read. While students often arrive in our classrooms with attitudes firmly in place, it is our goal to help them enhance positive attitudes and modify negative ones.

Although research in the area of values is limited, it is becoming clearer that a student's values are important, especially in relation to goal adoption and cognition (Pintrich et al., 1993). Mathewson (1994) argued that the values students hold affect their attitude toward reading, which in turn affects their intrinsic motivation to read. While the main source of the values students bring to school is the home context (Spiegel, 1994), values can be shaped by classroom experiences, and this process is an important one for teachers to be aware of and to monitor (Mathewson, 1994).

Readers' Reasons and Purposes

Pintrich (1991) stated that researchers need to explore how the three families of motivational constructs (i.e., beliefs, reasons and purposes, and affective reactions) work together in educational settings. The constructs described here are the reasons and purposes that were applied in my classroom and observed for subsequent development of intrinsic motivation to read: goals, meaning construction, and interest.

Schunk (1994) distinguished two types of goals used in the classroom—performance goals and learning goals. Performance goals specify a task to be completed or a product to be created. Learning goals refer to knowledge and strategies that need to be acquired. Progress feedback is also crucial. Both types of goals were used with Amy, Mark, Trae, and Brooke, and then progress feedback was provided so they would be aware of their improvements and successes. Progress feedback also encourages students to move ahead and set new goals for themselves (Schunk & Swartz, 1993).

According to the social constructivist view, learning involves the active construction of meaning (Piaget, 1971) in a supportive social context (Vygotsky, 1978). Oldfather and Dahl (1994) extended these concepts by asserting that literacy learning and intrinsic motivation are embedded in social construction of meaning. In order for students to construct meaning and become learners their social interactions need to be taken into account.

Dewey (1913) said that to educate our children successfully we must find out what interests them. When a book or story interests a child, an emotional response occurs (Anderson, Shirey, Wilson, & Fielding, 1987). This emotional reaction can induce students to read and contributes in developing their intrinsic motivation. Schiefele (1991) differentiated between two types of interest. Individual interest is a disposition for certain topics or activities, while situational interest is brought about by proceedings in the environment.

Both types of interest can be found and nurtured in the classroom. Respecting students' interests can have a profound effect on their learning and motivation. An interesting curriculum can also influence meaning construction and the goals students set and accomplish.

Readers' Affective Reactions

The third of Pintrich and DeGroot's (1990) general categories of motivational constructs is affective reactions, or feelings and responses to participation in tasks. Affective reactions to reading events occur in response to readers' beliefs combined with the success or failure of their reasons and purposes for reading. Pintrich (1991) stated that researchers need to investigate whether there is an influence on reading motivation when beliefs about reading, reasons and purposes for reading, and affective reactions to reading are noted, honored, and encouraged. The affective reactions demonstrated by the four case study students are engagement, flow, and self-expression.

Gambrell (1994) characterized engaged readers as those who choose to read, read widely for enjoyment and information, use strategies when needed, and read in order to understand themselves and others better. When students are engaged, they are participating in activities that are not too easy and not too difficult, that promote student ownership and self-expression, and that encourage social collaboration and support.

Reading engagement is closely related to the affective reaction of flow. Nell (1988) said that when reading is done for pleasure only, it becomes "play." Csikszentmihalyi (1991) also recognized pleasure reading, or reading done for intrinsic purposes, and originated the term *flow*. When students become so involved in a reading event that they lose track of time and can only think about finishing the task, they are experiencing flow (see also Gambrell, 1994). I want all students to experience such pleasure in reading, and so I promote it in the classroom by advocating positive beliefs and clear reasons and purposes for reading.

Self-expression also plays a key role in supporting learner motivation (Oldfather & Dahl, 1994). Guthrie and McCann (1997) distinguished two types of expression. When students display their knowledge by way of an artifact according to preset, external requirements, they make a standards-based expression. Self-expression is when students relate personal experiences to their responses and allow their own viewpoints to be heard. Guthrie and McCann advised a balance of both kinds of expression because both meet various students' needs in a motivating classroom.

Self-Efficacy Revisited

Self-efficacy is important at the beginning of a literacy event because it incorporates a belief that a student holds about his or her chance of successfully completing the task. But it is important at the end as well, because each reading event affects a student's beliefs, values, and attitudes about learning. This cycle of motivation was in motion as I watched the efforts of Amy, Mark, Trae, and Brooke to become successful, fluent readers. Teachers who incorporate into the classroom their knowledge of the readers' beliefs, reasons and purposes for reading, and affective reactions can improve students' self-efficacies and their intrinsic motivations to read (Schunk & Zimmerman, 1997).

The Classroom Context

Because I was both the classroom teacher and the researcher for this study, my personal philosophy of education is important to discuss. My teaching was based on a constructivist theory of learning that embraces the idea that all children can learn. In a classroom of this nature, the teacher's role is to focus on students' strengths (Routman, 1991); create a rich, literate environment (Butler & Turbill, 1984); and become a colearner along with the students. The processes children go through to learn are treated as being just as important as the products they create (Routman, 1996), and assessment is authentic, varied, and fair. My students were allowed to choose what books to read and what written work to produce, and

their opinions were encouraged and respected (Atwell, 1987). I labored to establish the main goal of my classroom: to provide a joyful journey toward lifelong literacy and learning.

My literacy curriculum included a variety of components. Each day began with 20 minutes of sustained silent reading (SSR) and was followed by reading workshop, which included a guided reading lesson, response activities, and flexible small-group meetings to practice strategy use and fluency. A language-arts block later in the morning comprised writing, spelling, and grammar workshops. After lunch, the students would gather for 30 minutes of storytime that included various picture books—fiction and nonfiction. Some books were related to themes and projects taking place in the classroom, while others were read simply to enjoy wonderful literature. The last 15 minutes of the school day were reserved for a read-aloud from a novel so that students could leave for home with another chapter to ponder and discuss with family and friends.

I found that the mood permeating the second-grade classroom could be influenced by the content and continuity of the literacy curriculum. The weaving of literature choices and methods of response with all the curricular areas was meant to create a classroom environment that captured students' imaginations, encouraged self-expression, allowed connections, met individual needs, and promoted success. In this classroom, I endeavored to cultivate positive self-efficacies and intrinsic motivation to read and learn among all the class members.

Literacy Personalities

The main question of this study was complex: What motivated the four case study students to read? As my research progressed, I discovered that Amy, Mark, Trae, and Brooke were each motivated by different beliefs, reasons and purposes for reading, and affective reactions to reading. I found that they each had a unique literacy personality.

Table 1 shows the various factors that contributed to the literacy personalities of Amy, Mark, Trae, and Brooke. During the course of the study,

Table 1
Summary of the Motivators of the Four Case Study Students

Motivators	Amy	Mark	Trae	Brooke
Reading goals set by the teacher	Yes			
Reading goals set by the student	Yes	Yes		
Reading goals set by peers			Yes	
Reading materials related to classroom activities	Yes			Yes
Social component—whole-class discussions	Yes			
Social component—peers		Yes	Yes	
Making connections between reading and real life	Yes			Yes
Chapter books	Yes	Yes	Yes	
Connecting reading and writing	Yes	Yes		Yes
Vocal participation (e.g., Big Books, choral readings)	Yes			
Physical participation (e.g., Readers Theatre, acting)		Yes		
The format of books				Yes
Allowing adjustment time before reading or writing				Yes
Allowing space in which to think, read, and write				Yes
Allowing frequent breaks during reading and writing			Yes	
Specific topics or books (e.g., nonfiction, dinosaurs)		Yes	Yes	Yes
Oral self-expression	Yes			
Self-expression through writing	Yes	Yes		Yes
Self-expression through actions and behaviors				Yes

I documented 19 motivators that were demonstrated by the four case study students. Eleven of the motivators were exhibited by one student, while four were demonstrated by two students, and four were demonstrated by three students. Perhaps the most significant finding of the study was that none of the motivators were common to all four case study students.

Being aware of the differences between students and honoring their literacy personalities enabled me to build this information into the curriculum and provide a learning environment that endeavored to meet each student's needs and capitalize on his or her interests. The students were then able to participate in a classroom context that encouraged them to develop positive beliefs, establish reasons and purposes for reading and learning, and gain trust that their affective reactions to literacy events would be respected. Through this process, intrinsic motivation to read could be nurtured and advanced. The following sections present each of the case study students as their literacy personalities were revealed, acknowledged, and supported.

Amy

Amy was an intrinsically motivated reader and seemed to have a natural desire to read and share her reading with others. The following vignette illustrates Amy's influence on the other children in class.

> During a session of DEAR (Drop Everything And Read), Amy went around the room and invited several girls and boys to join her in the story area. They obliged and surrounded her in small student chairs while she sat on the larger teacher chair. She read Clifford the Small Red Puppy (Bridwell, 1972) in the same manner the teacher would read aloud to the class. The students seemed to enjoy the story.

Amy was kind to others, so her peers respected her and wanted to spend time with her. They knew she was a good reader and that they would have a good time in her group.

Amy also set goals. She was motivated to read by the reading goals I set for her and enjoyed completing assignments and demonstrating her academic skills. Soon, Amy began setting goals for herself. She always kept track of the pages and chapters she had completed in a book as well as how many pages and chapters she had yet to go. She said it felt good to complete a chapter book and then set a new goal for herself to begin another book. Progress feedback also motivated Amy. It was necessary for her to show me how far she had read in her current book at least once daily. She wanted approval and encouragement from the teacher to help motivate her to continue reading. The following vignette shows how this worked for Amy.

The students were involved in a partner-reading activity with the book The Three Wishes (Perrault, 1979). Amy and her partner started taking turns reading pages and were so involved that they hardly looked up from the book. Suddenly, Amy happened to look at the pair of boys reading next to her and noticed that they had finished the book. She stopped reading and checked how many pages she and her partner had left to read. Then she asked me how much time was left to read the book. I assured her that there was plenty of time left and that they could take their time to read. Amy and her partner continued reading at a comfortable pace, discussing the illustrations, and enjoying the humorous parts of the story.

Most of the books Amy was motivated to read during the school year were related to the thematic units and author studies that were used in the classroom. Her favorite book was often by the current author of the month, and the books she chose to read and check out were almost always connected with a past or present thematic unit. Amy developed an interest in chapter books early in the school year. She often had a flow experience while reading a chapter book and was motivated by longer books throughout the months of the study. Amy also used her reading to motivate her writing. Many of the stories in her writing notebook and the pieces she published were based on books she had read, such as her story "Amelia Bedelia's Got the Chicken Pox."

The social component of the classroom also motivated Amy to read. Participation in class discussions was important to her, and it motivated Amy to read the book or story about to be discussed. She enjoyed talking about books so much that discussion seemed necessary for her to feel she had successfully completed a book or story. Amy also liked to participate in buddy and small-group reading, as well as in whole-class discussions. She was engaged in the learning process when she was interacting socially and often felt flow when discussing a book or story with others in the class, as the following vignette demonstrates.

Amy was at the bookshelves choosing books for SSR before the bell rang to start the school day. She chose several books but stayed at the shelves to chat and look at the books others had chosen. She compared her books with those of other classmates, changed her mind about some books, and browsed some more. She sat down when the bell rang. Browsing and choosing at the bookshelves was very much a social event.

Amy was motivated by being able to engage in self-expression. When she had finished a book or a written piece, it was important for her to express her feelings about the literacy event and to announce what she would be reading or writing next. She thoroughly enjoyed sharing her reading and writing with others. In fact, I discovered it was a necessity for her, as illustrated by the next vignette.

One day, the class was working in groups to read and illustrate a parody of "The Three Little Pigs" called "The Three Little Teeth." One person from the group was to read the story aloud, while the others in the group were to share their illustrations. Amy was very upset that she was not chosen to read the story aloud. She almost refused to share her illustrations because she was so frustrated. Expressing herself aloud through sharing was so important to Amy that she did not seem to feel her work was complete without it.

Amy's literacy personality was formed by her beliefs, strengthened by her reasons and purposes for reading, and confirmed by the affective reactions to reading she experienced. She became a strong, capable, outgoing reader, which enabled her to be a good literacy role model for other students as well.

Mark

Mark was a serious student. It was important to his parents that he do well in school, and Mark reflected their values in the classroom. Mark wanted to be successful in the classroom, yet he showed only reserved enthusiasm about his tasks, as the following vignette demonstrates.

> During a partner-reading session, Mark and Gary alternated reading pages, giggling often. They pointed to pictures and smiled, but when Gary got distracted, Mark said, "Come on, Gary," and they continued reading. Mark followed directions and completed the partner activity correctly, but when I discussed the book *Doctor DeSoto Goes to Africa* (Steig, 1992) with the two boys, only Gary spoke excitedly about the book. Gary was an average ability reader who would not have completely comprehended the challenging book without Mark's input. Mark said he liked the book but would not elaborate.

Although Mark took the literacy goals that I set for him seriously, they did not intrinsically motivate him to read. It wasn't until he began to set his own goals later in the school year that his reading really advanced. That's when he found genres he particularly enjoyed like nonfiction and humorous books. He also discovered the Goosebumps series by R.L. Stine and the Wayside School series by Louis Sachar. When Mark could read the books *he* chose, he read voraciously and stuck with the books until finished, as demonstrated in the following vignette.

> Mark cheered each time I began to read aloud a chapter from *Sideways Stories From Wayside School* (Sachar, 1978). He laughed at the black-and-white sketches of the students from Wayside School and smiled through the entire reading. When the book was finished, I introduced another book in the series, *Wayside School Gets a Little Stranger* (Sachar, 1995). Mark grabbed the book first and spent the next week reading it on his own. When he finished, he went on to another book in the series and read it whenever he had a free moment. He read it to his reading buddy, even though his reading buddy was not interested and was reading a different book aloud at the same time.

Mark was also motivated by social interaction with his friends. He enjoyed participating physically in Readers Theatre or making up skits. Mark didn't like to share his opinions of books aloud or discuss books with the whole class, but when he was with a small group of friends or a partner he was motivated to share and discuss, and he easily became the leader of the group. It seemed important to Mark that his peers approve of the books he was reading. He showed off the chapter books and humorous books he had and encouraged others to read them. This was also true for writing workshop. The next vignette demonstrates Mark's creativity and the importance of social interaction in his work.

> The last activity in the dinosaur thematic unit was to make up a dinosaur name and write a story about it. Most students used their own name for their dinosaur, but Mark created a "killingosaurus." The other boys in the class loved this name, and several copied from Mark. Mark did not mind; he seemed proud and helped the boys with their stories as well. When they shared their stories out loud with one another, they acted them out and especially enjoyed making the sound effects.

Mark was a competent, hard-working student, but he was not always intrinsically motivated to read and learn. Mark's literacy personality required that his interests and choices be honored in the classroom as much as possible so that he would become engaged in reading and choose to continue his literacy progress.

Trae

Trae was a struggling reader. His literacy personality required me to consider what discouraged him from reading as well as what motivated him. The next vignette shows the struggles Trae faced.

> Trae was working on his second basal reading test of the school year. The comprehension section comprised four three-paragraph stories with three or four questions after each story. Trae strained to complete the section. He grimaced, erased hard, and rewrote often. He was the last one done. He scored below average but had tried his best.

I seldom seemed to motivate Trae to read, but as the year progressed I watched him become motivated by his peers. While my reading goals for Trae were frequently viewed with disinterest, reading goals supplied by his friend gained Trae's attention. I discovered he needed excellent student role models to enhance his literacy development. When Trae sat by Mark and other high-ability readers, he became motivated to read riddles and other humorous literature, study meat-eating dinosaurs, and read chapter books. The next vignette shows how Trae was able to experience interest, engagement, flow, and intrinsic motivation.

> Trae wanted to read a chapter book. His friends Mark and Justin were reading chapter books and seemed to enjoy them. Trae had told me at one point that he knew reading chapter books was a "grown-up" thing to do, and he did not want to read any more "baby" books. However, Trae could not read all the words in the chapter books he chose. I suggested some easier chapter books for him, but he was not interested in those. He tried some of the more difficult books. He read them for a few days but then put them back. He told me he had finished the books, but I knew he had not. I had just finished reading aloud Sideways Stories From Wayside School (Sachar, 1978), and it had been put on the shelf for free reading. Mark was reading the sequel to the book and told Trae how much he liked it, so Trae set a goal for himself. He decided to read Sideways Stories From Wayside School. The vocabulary was easier because he had heard me read the book aloud. The chapters were short and interesting. Trae had found a book he could read and enjoy, and he doggedly read it over the next two weeks until he finished it.

Trae was not motivated by sustained reading and writing. He needed frequent breaks to complete an activity, and the breaks often included discussing the project with peers as well as enlisting their help. Trae did not copy their work but needed their suggestions to help him form ideas of his own. The following vignette demonstrates Trae's habits as he worked on a dinosaur report.

> Trae was at work on his report even before directions were given. He was engaged with his topic, taking a break every few minutes. On one break, he roared like a dinosaur—and being noisy was unusual for Trae. I closely observed Trae as he continued to work on his report. He worked in spurts, as many students do. However, while most second graders finished a couple of sentences in each spurt, Trae completed one or two words. He would work for three minutes and then walk around the room. He would work again and then chat with some friends. Trae finally finished his report, using the maximum time available to produce a short but competent report.

Trae was a struggling reader who was willing to work diligently to become successfully literate. Acknowledging his literacy personality and encouraging his intrinsic motivation to read helped me assist and support him in reaching that goal.

Brooke

Of all the case study students, Brooke probably valued books the most and loved to be surrounded by them. She kept books on and in her desk at all times. She read books avidly; however, she also liked to look at their physical properties. She noticed a book's size, color, thickness, and texture. Her desk usually looked messy, but she treated her books with care and was unhappy if anyone moved any of them without her permission. This vignette shows an example of Brooke's behavior around books.

> Brooke always kept a large pile of books in her desk. She told me she just liked having them close by. She would share them if another student asked for a specific book, but she made sure it was returned to her. If I "cracked down" and asked Brooke to put

the books back on the shelf for everyone to read, it was only a few hours before she had accumulated a new pile of books.

Although Brooke was a motivated reader, her behavior often concealed it. She seemed off-task at times and looked as if she were daydreaming much of the school day. Through this study, however, I discovered that this was not the case. Brooke was often engaged when she seemed off-task, and she was sometimes experiencing flow when it seemed she was daydreaming. The following vignette about Brooke shows both her shaky self-efficacy and her love of books.

The students streamed into the classroom after lunch and settled into the story area for storytime. It did not take them long to quiet down and listen to the first story. I was reading *Alexander and the Terrible, Horrible, No Good, Very Bad Day* (Viorst, 1972). Brooke chose a seat in the back, as usual. She hid behind some students for a while, but finally stood up to see the book. Her expression was blank, and she spent a lot of time looking around the room instead of focusing on the book. Most students started reading along with me at the repetitive parts, but Brooke never did. She showed no reaction to the humorous parts. As the discussion of the book began, Brooke sat down again to hide in the back. Later that afternoon, when the book was put back on the shelf, Brooke was the first one to notice and slipped it into her desk to read later.

As the school year progressed, two characteristics of Brooke's literacy personality became apparent. First, she needed adjustment time to begin and to continue working on assignments and projects. She often took longer to complete literacy activities, but if she was allowed time to think, plan, and revise her work her project was often the most detailed and best in the class. Second, Brooke needed space. She enjoyed working with peers at times, but when she had a choice she almost always preferred to read and write alone. Even when she was listening to a book during storytime, she liked to put space around her in order to concentrate and experience the book. The next vignette illustrates these characteristics.

Brooke was working on a poster about one of her favorite books. Most of the other students had theirs completed, but Brooke was still writing and drawing. Indoor recess had begun, but Brooke was unconcerned. She kept working at a leisurely, yet steady pace. Some girls came over to admire her poster and to ask her to play, but she continued working. Brooke was still not finished by 2:30 p.m. that day, so she worked during Show and Tell. When it was her turn for Show and Tell, she calmly went up to the front of the room to share and then went back to her seat to resume working. She finished right before the dismissal bell. Her poster was well done and included one of the longest reports in the class. She beamed with pride as she turned it in.

Brooke's literacy personality was easy to misunderstand. The distance she put between herself and the rest of the class could have been misconstrued as an attempt to escape from literacy activities, but it was Brooke's way of becoming more involved. The time she needed to complete assignments could have been seen as a lack of skill or ability, but Brooke was a talented reader. I saw growth in Brooke's self-efficacy and intrinsic motivation as her literacy personality was honored, and I tried to allow her to experience literacy in ways that were meaningful to her.

Classroom Implications

At the end of this study, I returned to my original question: What motivated the four case study students to read? The answer was as multi-faceted and complex as the question. Each reader held his or her own beliefs about reading; applied specific and unique reasons and purposes for reading; and participated in varied, personal affective reactions to reading and literature. My exploration revealed that the students were motivated to read by totally different factors and exhibited their own distinctive literacy personalities. My desire as a classroom teacher, then, was to become more responsive to the literacy personalities of my students and provide a classroom culture that fostered their strengths, honored their voices, and met their needs.

Perhaps my study can also provide some practical ideas for classroom teachers who are motivated to discover and value their own students' literacy personalities and promote an intrinsic motivation to read in their classrooms.

- It is crucial to offer students a rich, literate environment in the classroom. An array of books that represents a variety of topics, levels, and genres of literature is necessary to capture students' interests.

- A wide variety of reading experiences can foster engaged reading—SSR, buddy reading, choral reading, teacher-led small groups, storytimes, read-alouds, and so on. You never know what style of reading practice might motivate a child to read more and comprehend better.

- Students' voices are so important; many opportunities for them to express their opinions should be part of the fabric of the classroom culture. Response sheets to fill out after reading, class opinion graphs, and free choice of books are just a sampling of the activities that can be used to honor students' voices and choices.

- Thematic units and author studies allow students to experience literature and reading beyond basic comprehension and reading skills. Units such as these also make it easy for the teacher to incorporate choice into the curriculum and promote students' interests and motivation.

- Arranging opportunities for students to engage in social interactions is essential. While some students learn efficiently on their own, many children need the support of peers and talk to learn and achieve.

It is a teacher's greatest challenge to motivate and meet the needs of each literacy personality in the classroom. While it can be overwhelming at times, flexible literacy activities such as those featured in this article can ease the stress of trying to teach 20 or more unique individuals. All students may learn in different ways, and all teachers may teach in different ways, but we can celebrate that diversity. Perhaps an awareness of literacy personalities can help lift the burden of trying to teach all children the same way, and we can focus instead on intrinsically motivating students to become independent, successful readers and learners.

References

Anderson, R.C., Shirey, L.L., Wilson, P.T., & Fielding, L.G. (1987). Interestingness of children's reading material. In R.E. Snow & M.J. Farr (Eds.), *Aptitude, learning, and instruction: Vol. 3. Cognitive and affective process analysis* (pp. 287–299). Hillsdale, NJ: Erlbaum.

Atwell, N. (1987). *In the middle: Writing, reading, and learning with adolescents.* Portsmouth, NH: Heinemann.

Bandura, A. (1986). *Social foundations of thought and action: A social cognitive theory.* Englewood Cliffs, NJ: Prentice Hall.

Baumann, J.F., & Ivey, G. (1997). Delicate balances: Striving for curricular and instructional equilibrium in a second-grade literature/strategy-based classroom. *Reading Research Quarterly, 32*, 244–275.

Bridwell, N. (1972). *Clifford the small red puppy.* New York: Scholastic.

Butler, A., & Turbill, J. (1984). *Towards a reading-writing classroom.* Portsmouth, NH: Heinemann.

Csikszentmihalyi, M. (1991). Literacy and intrinsic motivation. In S.R. Graubard (Ed.), *Literacy: An overview by fourteen experts* (pp. 115–140). New York: Hill & Wang.

Dewey, J. (1913). *Interest and effort in education.* Boston: Riverside.

Fishbein, M., & Ajzen, I. (1975). *Belief, attitude, intention, and behavior: An introduction to theory and research.* Reading, MA: Addison-Wesley Higher Education.

Gambrell, L.B. (1994). *What motivates children to read?* (Scholastic Literacy Research Paper, Vol. 1). New York: Scholastic.

Guthrie, J.T., & McCann, A.D. (1997). Characteristics of classrooms that promote motivations and strategies for learning. In J.T. Guthrie & A. Wigfield (Eds.), *Reading engagement: Motivating readers through integrated instruction* (pp. 128–148). Newark, DE: International Reading Association.

Mathewson, G.C. (1994). Model of attitude influence upon reading and learning to read. In R.B. Ruddell, M.R. Ruddell, & H. Singer (Eds.), *Theoretical models and processes of reading* (4th ed., pp. 1131–1161). Newark, DE: International Reading Association.

McKenna, M.C. (1994). Toward a model of reading attitude acquisition. In E.H. Cramer & M. Castle (Eds.), *Fostering the love of reading: The affective domain in reading education* (pp. 18–40). Newark, DE: International Reading Association.

Merriam, S.B. (1988). *Case study research in education: A qualitative approach.* San Francisco: Jossey-Bass.

Nell, V. (1988). The psychology of reading for pleasure: Needs and gratifications. *Reading Research Quarterly, 23*, 6–50.

Oldfather, P., & Dahl, K. (1994). Toward a social constructivist reconceptualization of intrinsic motivation for literacy learning. *Journal of Reading Behavior, 26*, 139–158.

Perrault, C. (1979). *The three wishes.* Mahwah, NJ: Troll.

Piaget, J. (1971). *Psychology and epistemology.* New York: Grossman.

Pintrich, P.R. (1991). Editor's comment. *Educational Psychologist, 26*, 199–205.

Pintrich, P.R., & DeGroot, E.V. (1990). Motivational and self-regulated learning components of classroom academic performance. *Journal of Educational Psychology, 82*, 33–40.

Pintrich, P.R., Marx, R.W., & Boyle, R.A. (1993). Beyond cold conceptual change: The role of motivational beliefs and classroom contextual factors in the process of conceptual change. *Review of Educational Research, 63*, 167–199.

Routman, R. (1991). *Invitations: Changing as teachers and learners K–12.* Portsmouth, NH: Heinemann.

Routman, R. (1996). *Literacy at the crossroads.* Portsmouth, NH: Heinemann.

Sachar, L. (1978). *Sideways stories from Wayside School.* New York: Avon.

Sachar, L. (1995). *Wayside School gets a little stranger.* New York: Avon.

Schiefele, U. (1991). Interest, learning, and motivation. *Educational Psychologist, 26*, 299–323.

Schunk, D.H. (1994, April). *Student motivation for literacy learning: The role of self-regulatory processes.* Paper presented at the annual meeting of the American Educational Research Association, New Orleans, LA.

Schunk, D.H., & Swartz, C.W. (1993, April). *Goals and progress feedback: Effects on self-efficacy and writing achievement.* Paper presented at the annual meeting of the American Educational Research Association, Atlanta, GA.

Schunk, D.H., & Zimmerman, B.J. (1997). Developing self-efficacious readers and writers: The role of social and self-regulatory processes. In J.T. Guthrie & A. Wigfield (Eds.), *Reading engagement: Motivating readers through integrated instruction* (pp. 34–50). Newark, DE: International Reading Association.

Spiegel, D.L. (1994). A portrait of parents of successful readers. In E.H. Cramer & M. Castle (Eds.), *Fostering the love of reading: The affective domain in reading education* (pp. 74–87). Newark, DE: International Reading Association.

Steig, W. (1992). *Doctor DeSoto goes to Africa.* New York: HarperCollins.

Thomas, S., & Oldfather, P. (1995). Enhancing student and teacher engagement in literacy learning: A shared inquiry approach. *The Reading Teacher, 49*, 192–202.

Viorst, J. (1972). *Alexander and the terrible, horrible, no good, very bad day.* Hartford, CT: Aladdin Books.

Vygotsky, L. (1978). *Mind in society.* Cambridge, MA: Harvard University Press.

Wigfield, A., & Guthrie, J.T. (1997). Relations of children's motivation for reading to the amount and breadth of their reading. *Journal of Educational Psychology, 89*, 420–432.

Engagement Activities

In Your Classroom

How can you learn about the literacy personalities of your students? What discussions can you hold with your students that might reveal their personalities? What tasks can you devise to learn more about their literacy personalities?

With Your Colleagues

What is the literacy personality of your school? What cross-classroom or cross-grade-level experiences can you plan to nurture positive literacy personalities?

Further Reading

Casey, S., & Chamberlin, R. (2006). Bringing reading alive through Readers' Theater. *Illinois Reading Council Journal, 34*(4), 17–25.

This article describes the use of Readers Theatre as an authentic method to support fluency and motivation. A five-day plan that affords readers the time to practice and perform is described. Included in the plan are suggestions for minilessons and coaching.

New Insights on Motivation in the Literacy Classroom

Jacquelynn A. Malloy and Linda B. Gambrell

Motivation does not reside solely in the child; rather it is in the interaction between students and their literacy environments.

—Turner and Paris (1995, p. 672)

It's Monday morning, and as Angie sits at her desk looking over her daily plan, students begin filing into the classroom.

"Good morning! How was your weekend?" She smiles, greeting students as they enter.

"Can we read a little since we're early?" asks Ben. "I found a book last Friday that might help me with my PowerPoint on meteorites. I think it would also be a great one for book sharing, if I finish it today!"

"Sure," Angie replies, glad to see Ben interested in reading. "Knock yourself out!" As Ben settles in with his book, a gaggle of girls approaches Angie's desk.

"Can we print out the information we gathered on dog breeds? We saved it on the computer last week and want to get started on our 'How to Choose the *Totally* Right Dog' brochure. We want to publish it and take it to the animal shelter before spring break."

"Absolutely," Angie replies. "I think your brochure will help a lot of people to choose the right pet. Go ahead and print it out—you can talk about how to synthesize the info a little later on."

After all of her students are seated and accounted for, and the announcements have been read, Angie begins the class with, "OK! What are *you* looking forward to working on today?"

Highly motivated students come into the classroom ready to work on projects they've started, books they've discovered, and projects they've left unfinished. Most teachers would agree that motivation is the Holy Grail of effective comprehension instruction. Creating a motivating instructional climate, where students are ready and willing to learn, to read, to comprehend, and to compose, requires a willingness on the teacher's part to get to know students' interests and needs. With this knowledge, teachers can assist students in setting goals, finding resources, developing strategies, and negotiating ways to engage with topics in personally relevant ways. When students are supported in cognitively and socially engaging ways with text, they make meaningful connections that have the potential to build their knowledge base—and by broadening and deepening their knowledge base, students are equipped to make connections with newly presented material. It is a wonderfully replenishing cycle that happens every day in classrooms where high motivation exists.

Clearly, teachers would prefer a room full of students who are engaged in the instruction provided, and who progress in their ability and willingness to read and write for school and for personal enjoyment. The most basic goal of any comprehension program is the development of highly motivated readers who *can* read, and who *choose* to read for pleasure and information. However, because motivation is not currently one of the "five pillars" of reading instruction

Reprinted with permission of the publisher from Malloy, J.A., & Gambrell, L.B. (2000). New insights on motivation in the literacy classroom. In C.C. Block & S.R. Parris (Eds.), *Comprehension instruction: Research-based best practices* (2nd ed., pp. 226–240). New York: Guilford.

identified by the National Reading Panel Report (2000)—that is, phonemic awareness, phonics, vocabulary, fluency, and comprehension—it does not receive the same focus or emphasis as the instructional goals. While all students deserve high-quality instruction in these areas, it is clear that if our students are not motivated to read, they will never reach their full literacy potential. We believe that motivation exerts a tremendous influence on comprehension development. In an attempt to place motivation at the heart of comprehension instruction, this chapter explores the following:

- The theories of achievement motivation and their influence on our developing understanding of literacy engagement.

- What research has to say about the factors that influence an individual student's motivation to engage in literacy tasks and the potential for this engagement to enhance comprehension.

- A theoretical framework for incorporating research findings in the literacy classroom.

Established Theories of Achievement Motivation

In the field of literacy research, a fair amount of activity has been aimed toward understanding the construct of literacy motivation and the components of that construct. In so doing, a number of factors that seem to be related to an individual student's motivation have been delineated. "Motivation for literacy," defined for the purposes of this discussion as the likelihood of engaging in a literacy task, and persisting in the activity despite challenges, grew out of decades of research by behavioral, humanistic, cognitive, and social-cognitive psychologists. Therefore, to ground the current state of our understanding of literacy motivation, we begin at the beginning with pertinent theories of achievement motivation.

In the early part of the 20th century, *behaviorists* maintained that our motivations grow from interactions with our environment—meaning that we are driven by things we want to attain (e.g., a reward or incentive) or avoid (e.g., an unpleasant consequence; Skinner, 1953; Thorndike, 1910; Watson, 1913). In today's classroom, whenever you see students reading *solely* for the purpose of receiving points, pizzas, or parties, they are responding to an environment that treats literacy as something that is externally controlled and quantifiable, as in the number of books read or tests taken. Of course, there are some who question the quality of the student's interaction with text when using these methods and the value of these extrinsic motivators in our attempts to encourage students to read intrinsically for information or for pleasure (Labbo, 1999; Lepper, Greene, & Nisbeit, 1973; Mallette, Henk, & Melnick, 2004). However, there are teachers (and parents) who argue that these extrinsic rewards are the only reason some students pick up a book.

Proposing that the source of human motivation is more internal than external, the view of *humanistic psychologists* is that we are driven by our internal needs and our quest to control our lives. For example, Maslow's hierarchy (1943) delineated four *deficiency* needs and three *growth* needs. The deficiency needs include *survival* (food, shelter, water), *safety* (free from emotional or physical threat or harm—such as bullies!), *belonging* (connections to others like oneself), and *self-esteem* (positive regard for oneself). If these deficiency needs are not met—and many of us can think of students for whom these needs are woefully unfulfilled—the growth needs of *intellectual achievement, aesthetic appreciation*, and *self-actualization* cannot be addressed.

Similarly, Deci and Ryan (1985) described in their *self-determination theory* that we have a need to experience control in our lives. Students who feel they have some control over their learning have been found to engage more meaningfully with learning tasks (Turner, 1995) and to be willing to accept greater challenges in learning (Csikszentmihalyi, 1990). In classrooms, for example, students may be offered a choice of three different assessments at the end of a unit, such as taking a multiple-choice test, writing a paper, or presenting a project. In this way, students can engage with and respond to the material in a manner that provides for them an internal locus of control and a choice in how they express their knowledge.

Cognitive psychologists (Atkinson, 1964; Festinger, 1957; Vroom, 1964) would agree that the source of our motivation is internal. In their view, we are motivated by what we think—our attitudes, beliefs, ideas and goals. One such subtheory of these cognitive views, *attribution theory*, was developed by Weiner (1979, 1985), who proposed that individuals explain events in their lives by assigning an attribution to the expected outcome of engaging in an activity. These attributions are described by three continua of causality: *internal to external locus of control*, or the degree to which a student perceives ownership or direction of a behavior, or cedes it to others; *stability to instability*, indicating the reliability of behavior to elicit similar results; and *controllability to uncontrollability*, which describes the perceived potential for influencing or changing the behavior. According to this theory, a student might explain a poor test grade with a remark such as "My teacher hates me!" (external, stable and uncontrollable) or "I didn't study enough!" (internal, unstable and controllable). This focus on student expectations for success heralded an interest in cognitive and affective factors of motivation.

A second cognitive subtheory, which involves an interest in how and why students set goals for achievement, stimulated research that has settled on two broad categories of goals that might be valued by students (Ames, 1992; Dweck & Leggett, 1988). These include *task* (or *mastery*) goals, described as a desire for personal improvement and mastery of a skill, and *ability* (or *performance*) goals that focus on one's performance in relation to others. Broadly related to the developing understanding of goal theory are the constructs of intrinsic and extrinsic motivation (Lepper et al., 1973). "Intrinsic motivation" can be described as self-generated interest in an activity that brings a pleasure that is inherent in engaging in the activity itself. Describing a heightened form of intrinsic involvement, Csikszentmihalyi (1978) cited the experience of being totally absorbed in an activity as "flow,"

such as when reading a book that is so interesting that one loses the perception of place or of time passing. This can be differentiated from "extrinsic motivation," which is more closely associated with other-oriented aspects of goal setting, such as rewards, recognition, and approval or obedience, as are the ability goals previously described.

A more contemporary view of motivation is expressed by the social-cognitive theorists, who believe that we are driven by what we think of ourselves (internal source) and the task presented (external source). In 1983, Eccles and her colleagues introduced a theory of motivation that has been highly influential in current literacy motivation research. The *expectancy–value* theory of motivation has its roots in the work of Atkinson (1957) and, broadly defined, poses that an individual's perception of potential success (*expectancy*) in performing a task and the perceived *value* attributed to the activity are determinants of the person's willingness to engage in achievement behaviors. Eccles and her colleagues (1983) posited three essential components of an individual's perceived value of engaging in a task: *importance* (attainment value), *intrinsic value* (personally generated), and *utility value* (usefulness). These aspects are described as *subjective task values* (Eccles & Wigfield, 2002) and refer to the individual's incentive or reason for engaging in the task. Perceptions of expectancy, thought to be influenced by the individual's sense of competence in completing a specific task successfully, are based on Bandura's (1977, 1982) work on self-efficacy, which he describes as a self-judgment of a domain-specific ability to perform a task successfully. The expectancy–value theory serves as a suitable initial framework for organizing the more specific research on literacy motivation.

Established Research on Literacy Motivation in the Classroom

Reading is an activity that is initially full of effort. In learning to read, children make a purposeful transition from a world of oral language to one of printed language. In so doing, the relationship of letters to sounds and the visual negotiation of symbols situated on pages that beg to be decoded into meaningful words seems a monumental task, but one they have seen others successfully accomplish. If children perceive a value in learning to read and write, and if the environment provides resources and opportunities to guide the endeavor, it is quite likely they will attain some level of comprehension. But what then? Once the code is broken and the mystery is solved, what maintains their interest and engagement in the process of developing into mature and discerning literate beings?

Perhaps the most concentrated and foundational effort to understand literacy motivation and instruction was the research conducted through the National Reading Research Center (NRRC), which received funding from the Office of Educational Research and Improvement of the U.S. Department of Education in the 5-year period from 1992 to 1997. During this time the *engagement perspective* of literacy motivation guided investigations into reading instruction that would develop "motivated and strategic readers who use literacy for pleasure and learning (National Reading Research Center, 1997, p. 5). Drawing on the body of research that led up to the 5-year research initiative, the engagement perspective assumes that the desire to read, strategies to improve reading ability, knowledge, and social interactions are key components to cultivating "highly engaged, self-determining readers who are architects of their own learning" (Alvermann & Guthrie, 1993, p. 2). Several studies explored home, school, and community contexts of literacy motivation for preschool-, elementary-, and secondary-age students. A sampling of this research across grade levels follows.

The 1997 NRRC report indicated that preschool children can become engaged readers when the following factors are present: Their homes contain an abundance and variety of print materials; they are given opportunities to read and to be read to; they see caregivers modeling reading behaviors; they have opportunities to play, to interact with environmental print, and to gain knowledge by exploring their world inside and outside of the home; they have caring interactions and discussions with adults and older siblings, and make connections with schools (p. 22).

NRRC researchers Gambrell, Codling, and Palmer (1996) explored the reading motivation of elementary students and found that access to books, choice of reading materials, and discussion of readings (e.g., through book clubs) were highly motivating factors in the school setting. Furthermore, students are motivated to engage in reading when teachers and students share books together. Palmer, Codling, and Gambrell (1994) found that when teachers read selections from high-quality literature aloud to the class and discuss what they like about the books, students are more motivated to read those selections than to read books not introduced by teachers. Research evidence also suggests that children benefit from opportunities to discuss books with others, and the social interactions have been found to have a positive effect on reading engagement (Almasi, 1995; Oldfather & McLaughlin, 1993).

At middle and high school levels, NRRC researchers investigated reading for pleasure through programs designed to encourage students to read for pleasure with their peers in Read and Talk clubs (Alvermann, Young, & Green, 1997). In each instance, students were permitted to choose materials that reflected their personal interests or preferences and social interactions with others—two personally relevant aspects of literacy involvement.

The importance of the NRRC initiative was that it incorporated motivation to read into a broader understanding of reading engagement as it affected social and instructional contexts for learning to read. NRRC research findings, especially with regard to classroom contexts and instructional methods, highlighted the interrelatedness of values, beliefs, and social factors for reading engagement and rich comprehension.

How Motivation Can Improve Comprehension Instruction

Research into the effects of instruction on reading engagement suggests that certain aspects of the classroom environment and the instructional practices used by teachers can encourage reading engagement and increase comprehension. Classroom environments that provide appropriate materials, strategic support, and instructional resources are more likely to nurture literacy engagement (Anderman & Midgley, 1992; Gambrell & Morrow, 1996). Several researchers (e.g., Morrow, 1992; Neuman & Celano, 2001) have suggested that classrooms with an abundance and variety of print materials positively affect the quality and frequency of literacy behaviors in the classroom.

In continuing research on the effects of Concept-Oriented Reading Instruction (CORI), Guthrie and his colleagues (Guthrie & Cox, 2001; Guthrie, McGough, Bennett, & Rice, 1996; Guthrie, Wigfield, & Von Secker, 2000) explored the features of classroom contexts that were related to long-term comprehension growth and reading engagement in fifth graders. The CORI program introduced by Guthrie et al. (1996) was designed to merge reading comprehension strategy instruction and content material, such as science or social studies, to produce a combined positive effect on both reading comprehension and motivation. Their results suggested that strategic instruction that utilizes text-to-self connections, including trade books, student choice in reading, and small-group collaborations result in significantly higher measures of motivation for fifth-grade students (based on the Motivation for Reading Questionnaire; Wigfield & Guthrie, 1997).

Designing Engaging Literacy Tasks

Brophy (2004) and Cunningham and Allington (1999) found that children are more motivated to engage in literacy activities that are authentic—based on real-world purposes—and that connect them to their home cultures. Students are also more engaged in tasks that permit them to choose materials for reading and to set their own goals (Cambourne, 1995; Schunk & Zimmerman, 1997; Turner, 1995), and children report a higher level of interest and enjoyment in books they personally have chosen (Schiefele, 1991; Spaulding,

1992). Supporting these findings, Turner and Paris (1995) stated: "The most reliable indicator of motivation for literacy learning is not the type of reading program that districts follow, but the actual daily tasks that teachers provided in their classrooms" (p. 662).

In her research with 84 6-year-olds, Turner (1995) utilized classroom observations and student interviews to understand the effects of classroom tasks on student engagement with literacy tasks. Based on a view that intrinsic motivation to learn is key to literacy engagement, Turner found that certain tasks increased students' internal locus of control and intrinsic motivation to participate. These *open tasks* were distinguished from *closed tasks*. Open tasks involved several of the factors found in previous research to be motivating, such as choice of topics, partners, or materials; personally relevant or authentic tasks that related to students' interests, goals, and abilities; enough challenge to make the outcome personally rewarding; and social collaboration, in which interactions expand students' knowledge and point of view. When tasks were "closed," students were forced to find the "one right answer" or to complete a task that was not relevant or connected to their lives, or that involved a product or outcome determined by the teacher. Turner found that open tasks predisposed students to associate literacy with cognitive involvement and provided a focus for the uses and purposes of literacy.

Literacy Engagement and Reading Comprehension

Reading comprehension can be thought of as a cognitive act; that is, without a cognitive investment on the part of the student, comprehension is not likely to occur. The strategies and self-regulation required to understand text—especially at an instructional reading level—necessitate a continued effort on the part of the student. Cognitive engagement occurs when the student voluntarily accesses higher-order skills, such as self-regulation and monitoring strategies (Blumenfeld & Meece, 1988). So the question becomes, how do we use what research has shown us regarding contexts, tasks, and literacy motivation to entice our students to *cognitively engage* in comprehension, and how do we encourage them to continue when the search for meaning becomes effortful?

To answer these important questions, we must recall the basic framework of expectancy–value theory. We are all more likely to involve ourselves in activities when we feel we can participate successfully and value the process or outcome. Teachers already know a great deal about how to assist students in experiencing success with literacy tasks: They provide students with strategies for decoding and comprehension, processes for writing, and metacognitive awareness to monitor their progress. Teachers model these strategies, present opportunities for practice, and provide feedback.

To increase the value of literacy activities, teachers should create classroom climates that encourage intrinsic motivations for learning, and a task or mastery orientation. They should surround students with books and other types of text, online computer access, and opportunities to share with each other in pairs, or in literacy groups or workshops. Teachers want their students to feel that they are literate souls within a *community* of literate souls. But even with this attention rightfully focused on value and expectancy factors, there may be an aspect of value that is left unattended; however, it is one that can be thoughtfully addressed, with hopes of rounding out a student's motivation to *cognitively* engage in literacy tasks and improve the quality of their learning.

Teasing Out the Utility Value of Tasks

In his 1999 theoretical piece, Brophy proposes that we mirror the progress we have made in matching content to cognitive strategies by creating optimal matches between content and motivational strategies. Here Brophy agrees with Turner (1995) and Turner and Paris (1995) that the source of a student's engagement with the content we present does not exist solely within the student, but in the interaction between the student and the material. Students might be predisposed to learn material in which they already are interested or for which they currently hold

some level of curiosity, but what about the things we feel students should learn that have no intrinsic value to them at all? Brophy proposes that we tease out the *utility value* of the material and scaffold the student toward some appreciation for the worth of the learning target. Here are some of Brophy's suggestions for increasing students' interest in and comprehension of content when they are not intrinsically predisposed to the topic:

1. *Create some situational interest in the learning domain by presenting enough information to make the topic familiar and relevant to the student.* The initial goal of many comprehension strategies is to assist the student in accessing some prior knowledge of the topic, but it's important to do so in a way that connects to students' lives or their sense of self. This has been done in the CORI research (Guthrie et al., 1996, 2001) on science topics by involving the students in natural observations or experiments that pique their interest and entice them to know more. When you have matched the topic or learning target to some aspect of the students' lives and made it relevant in some way, you move into what Brophy terms "the Motivational Zone of Proximal Development" (1999, p. 77).

2. *Encourage the development of curricula that tie learning outcomes to students' lives.* Although curricular development is often determined by school districts and administrators or coordinators, teachers are often asked to assist on curricular development committees. Consider how much easier it would be to motivate interest in a topic if the learning outcomes were tied to some aspect of students' lives outside of the classroom. For example, the learning target, "recognize and discriminate among a variety of informational texts" could be tied to the purposes and uses of the genre in school and home environments. [Examples of how this might be done are provided in the paragraph that follows.] Not every curricular standard is easily transposed into a relevant and authentic purpose, but if we take the time to know more about our students and their lives, their communities and their interests, we can make connections between learning and living. And if the learning target is *not* easily

tied to some aspect of living in society, perhaps we should question why we must teach it.

3. *Once curricular goals are set and the learning targets are established, it is incumbent upon the teacher to create an "optimally mediated learning experience."* Teachers can scaffold a student's appreciation of the material by stimulating interest and connecting the learning outcome to the student's life and to previous learning.

To continue the example of introducing the genre of informational text to your third graders: After defining the genre briefly and passing around a few examples of these types of reading materials, you might want to poll the students for the types of informational texts they've seen or used before—such as newspapers that carry information about what's going on in the world; directions for putting together a new bicycle; Web pages on the Internet where they might search topics of interest; and course books and trade books that provide specific information from which they might learn. Perhaps after discussing times when they needed to find specific information to answer a question or to know more about a subject of interest, students could survey various informational texts to determine features they have in common, such as headings, pictures, diagrams, and sidebars. By being entirely explicit in your comprehension instruction, you model for your students how you access these features to realize your goal of finding general or specific information, depending on your goal in using the text. In this way, you have begun to teach students comprehension strategies for accessing a particular genre in a manner that should lead to their successful interactions with text and ability to engage cognitively with the materials. This is done by modeling what you're thinking as you access new material ("Because I don't have to read expository text straight through like a story, I can just look at the headings and zero in on the information I want right now"), providing opportunities to practice ("Choose a book on a topic that you already know something about. Did they lay out the information in a way that makes sense to you? How would you do it?"), and feedback ("I think your idea of putting the map

on the first page would help a lot! Now, where would you put the text that describes what the map shows?"). Ultimately, students can choose projects that showcase the ways they might utilize their knowledge, such as creating a brochure on choosing a dog as a pet and donating it to the animal shelter, or creating a slide show presentation on sites where meteorites have landed on the earth.

When we move the utility value of a comprehension target out into the open, such as in the examples discussed previously, we create for the student a *clear path* from their existing knowledge and experiences to new knowledge and experiences. Clear paths are created when the content is made relevant to our students' present and future lives, and when they are given strategies to comprehend and to apply the knowledge gained from this new comprehension. It is in these connections and interactions between the content we present and the lives of our students that comprehension and understanding can flourish, and where we can allow our students to build some intrinsic interest and measure of competence in moving toward the motivated and strategies learners that we (and they!) hope to become.

Directions for Future Research

1. *How do literacy practices and teacher interactions influence student expectancies for literacy tasks—particularly for students with varying levels of ability?* Chapman and Tunmer (2003) reviewed studies that indicate the self-concepts and self-efficacy related to reading in young children develop in response to their initial successes or failures with learning to read. Students who experience early difficulties in learning to read may begin to label themselves as "poor readers" and, with this reduced self-efficacy, may be less willing to engage in or value reading comprehension tasks. As predicted by the Matthew effect (Stanovich, 1986), the poor indeed do become poorer. Research that documents the development and trajectory of these attitudes, such as through repeated interviews with students by gender and varying levels of ability across the

early grades, would help educators to visualize where the "clear path" to valuing and expecting literacy attainment is being obstructed, and to consider how best to intervene.

2. *What classroom contexts and instructional practices facilitate the growth of intrinsic motivation for students from various cultural and linguistic backgrounds and varying levels of ability?* Turner's (1995) work involving open versus closed tasks, and the work of Guthrie and his colleagues (1996, 2000; Guthrie & Cox, 2001) in developing CORI, presents evidence that literacy engagement is enhanced when comprehension instruction offers choice, relevance, explicit strategy instruction, and access to resources. Additional research that explores the efficacy of these promising instructional practices with an expanded array of grade levels, subject areas, and diversity of participants would provide much-needed information regarding the specific needs of certain individuals and particular sub-groups of the student population.

3. *What formative comprehension assessments or practices can be designed to help teachers stay attuned to students' changing interests, values, and self-concepts as readers?* At present, measures exist that are helpful in determining students' school and recreational reading interests, such as the Elementary Reading Attitude Scale (McKenna & Kear, 1990), and students' value and self-concept of reading, as with the Motivation to Read Profile (Gambrell, Palmer, Codling, & Mazzoni, 1996). Although these instruments help teachers to assess important elements of motivation, they do not assist in determining the effect of the interface between students' needs and the comprehension instruction offered—the utility value. Interestingly, Vroom (1964) posits a strikingly similar construct, using the term *instrumentality*, as being differentiated from value and expectancy. The addition of instrumentality to the existing constructs of value and expectancy may provide an avenue for exploring what we described earlier as utility value. His VIE theory of motivation (Motivation = Value × Instrumentality × Expectancy), sometimes used in business applications, may find its way into the field of educational research. For example, there

is a need to develop assessment measures that, when administered periodically throughout the school year, validly and reliably target a student's perceived value, instrumentality, and expectancy for reading comprehension activities and tasks. Such an instrument would assist teachers in fine-tuning instruction and providing suitable materials and resources to meet individual student needs and interests.

Projections and Possibilities for the Classroom of 2030

In the year 2030, motivation will be seen as a crucial component of teaching and learning in all areas of instruction, such as phonemic and phonological awareness, phonics, fluency, vocabulary, and comprehension. Teachers in highly motivating classrooms will create opportunities to become familiar with their students' interests and goals through cooperative projects and individualized tasks in which students use the knowledge they have to delve brain-first into the knowledge they crave. Teachers will view themselves as colearners with their students as they cognitively engage in learning tasks that are instrumental to their current lives as well as their perceived future lives.

Furthermore, research that investigates new instructional practices will be required to consider the possible motivational influences in addition to student mastery of comprehension targets. For a preview of what those classrooms might look like, please see the work of McCombs (2003) and her discussion of learner-centered psychological principles. These principles involve cognitive and metacognitive factors, such as strategic thinking and contexts for learning, motivational an affective factors that highlight intrinsic motivations to learn and the effects of motivation on effort, as well as developmental and individual factors that consider social factors and individual differences (p. 95). These hopeful predictions are based on the assumption that in the year 2030, educators and administrators will see the value of basing policy on well-researched and agreed-upon principles.

Summary

Our knowledge of literacy engagement has its roots in the study of general achievement motivation, and the research of numerous, past educational psychologists continues to inform our comprehension practices today. Reading comprehension instruction in classrooms is both a cognitive and a social enterprise that requires thoughtful intervention to suit a variety of student interests and needs. Comprehension necessitates a connection between what is already known and new content in a strategic and self-regulated manner. However, as one student's background knowledge, intrinsic involvement, ability, and efficacy for a particular comprehension task will likely be quite different than that of nearly every other student in the classroom, effective instruction should incorporate some manner of choice, collaboration, and situated interest with which students engage and persist in the specific meaning-making activity.

Although curricula are often set by district policies—sometimes with little teacher input—teachers can position themselves as change agents in connecting students' lives to the content presented, and their minds to the texts. The NRRC initiative provided the field of literacy research with a valuable standard: to evaluate our practices in terms of how they promote motivated, strategic, knowledgeable, and socially interactive learners. Although the NRRC has concluded its 5-year effort, we would do well as educators and researchers to continue striving to provide well-integrated and engaging reading comprehension instruction to all of our students.

References

Almasi, J.F. (1995). The nature of fourth graders' sociocognitive conflicts in peer-led and teacher-led discussions of literature. *Reading Research Quarterly, 30*(3), 314–351.

Alvermann, D.A., & Guthrie, J.T. (1993). *Themes and directions of the National Reading Research Center* (Project Report No. 1). Athens, GA: National Reading Research Center.

Alvermann, D.A., Young, J.P., & Green, C. (1997). *Adolescents' negotiations of out-of-school reading discussions* (Research Report No. 77). Athens, GA: National Reading Research Center.

Ames, C.A. (1992). Classrooms: Goals, structures, and student motivation. *Journal of Educational Psychology, 84*(3), 261–271.

Anderman, E.M., & Midgley, C. (1992). Changes in achievement goal orientations, perceived academic competence, and grades across the transition to middle-level schools. *Contemporary Educational Psychology, 22*(3), 269–298.

Atkinson, J.W. (1964). *An introduction to motivation.* Princeton, NJ: Van Nostrand.

Atkinson, J.W. (1957). Motivational determinants of risk-taking. *Psychological Review, 64*, 359–372.

Bandura, A. (1977). *Social learning theory.* New York: General Learning Press.

Bandura, A. (1982). Self-efficacy mechanism in human agency. *American Psychologist, 37*(2), 122–147.

Blumenfeld, P.C., & Meece, J.L. (1988). Task factors, teacher behavior, and students' involvement and use of learning strategies in science. *Elementary School Journal, 88*(3), 235–250.

Brophy, J. (1999). Toward a model of the value aspects of motivation in education: Developing appreciation for particular learning domains and activities. *Educational Psychologist, 34*(2), 75–85.

Brophy, J. (2004). *Motivating students to learn.* Mahwah, NJ: Erlbaum.

Cambourne, B. (1995). Towards and educationally relevant theory of literacy learning: Twenty years of inquiry. *Reading Teacher, 49*(3), 182–192.

Chapman, J.W., & Tunmer, W.E. (2003). Reading difficulties, reading-related self-perceptions, and strategies for overcoming negative self-beliefs. *Reading and Writing Quarterly, 19*(1), 5–24.

Csikszentmihalyi, M. (1978). Intrinsic rewards and emergent motivation. In M. Lepper & D. Greene (Eds.), *The hidden costs of reward: New perspectives on the psychology of human motivation* (pp. 205–216). Hillsdale, NJ: Erlbaum.

Cunningham, P.M., & Allington, R.L. (1999). *Classrooms that work: They call can read and write* (2nd ed.). Reading, MA: Addison-Wesley/Longman.

Deci, E.L., & Ryan, R.M. (1985). *Intrinsic motivation and self-determination in human behavior.* New York: Plenum Press.

Dweck, C.S., & Leggett, E.L. (1988). A social-cognitive approach to motivation and personality. *Psychological Review, 95*, 256–273.

Eccles, J., Adler, T., Futterman, R., Goff, S.B., Kaezala, C.M., Meece, J.L., et al. (1983). Expectancies, values, and academic behaviors. In J.T. Spence (Ed.), *Achievement and achievement motives: Psychological and sociological approaches* (pp. 75–146). San Francisco: Freeman.

Eccles, J.S., & Wigfield, A. (2002). Motivational beliefs, values, and goals. *Annual Review of Psychology, 53*, 109–132.

Festinger, L. (1957). *A theory of cognitive dissonance.* Evanston, IL: Row, Peterson & Company.

Gambrell, L.B., & Morrow, L.M. (1996). Motivating contexts for literacy learning. In L. Baker, P. Afflerbach, & D. Reinking (Eds.), *Developing engaged readers in school and home communities* (pp. 115–136). Mahwah, NJ: Erlbaum.

Gambrell, L.B., Codling, R.M., & Palmer, B.M. (1996). *Elementary students' motivation to read* (National Reading Research Center Report No. 52). Athens, GA: National Reading Research Center.

Gambrell, L.B., Palmer, B.M., Codling, R.M., & Mazzoni, S.A. (1996). Assessing motivation to read. *Reading Teacher, 49*(7), 518–533.

Guthrie, J.T., & Cox, K.E. (2001). Classroom conditions for motivation and engagement in reading. *Educational Psychology Review, 13*(3), 283–302.

Guthrie, J.T., McGough, K., Bennett, L., & Rice, M.E. (1996). Concept-oriented reading instruction: An integrated curriculum to develop motivations and strategies for reading. In L. Baker, P. Afflerbach, & D. Reinking (Eds.), *Developing engaged readers in school and home communities* (pp. 165–190). Hillsdale, NJ: Erlbaum.

Guthrie, J.T., Wigfield, A., & Von Secker, C. (2000). Effects of integrated instruction on motivation and strategy use in reading. *Journal of Educational Psychology, 92*(2), 331–341.

Labbo, L. (1999). Five more questions worth asking. In *Reading Online.* Retrieved October 20, 2006, through the International Reading Association at www.readingonline.org.

Lepper, M.R., Greene, D., Nisbeit, R.E. (1973). Undermining children's intrinsic interest with extrinsic reward: A test of the overjustification hypothesis. *Journal of Personality and Social Psychology, 28*(1), 129–137.

Mallette, M.H., Henk, W.A., & Melnick, S.A. (2004). The influence of Accelerated Reader on the affective literacy orientations of intermediate grade students. *Journal of Literacy Research, 36*(1), 73–84.

Maslow, A.H. (1943). *A theory of human motivation.* Psychological Review, 50, 370–396.

McCombs, B.L. (2003). A framework for the redesign of K–12 education in the context of current educational reform. *Theory Into Practice, 42*(2), 93–102.

McKenna, M.C., & Kear, D.J. (1990). Measuring attitudes toward reading: A new tool for teachers. *Reading Teacher, 43*(8), 626–639.

Morrow, L.M. (1992). The impact of a literature-based program on literacy achievement, use of literature and attitudes of children from minority backgrounds. *Reading Research Quarterly, 27*(3), 251–275.

National Reading Panel Report. (2000). *Teaching children to read: An evidence-based assessment of the scientific research literature on reading and its implications for reading instruction.* Washington, DC: National Institute of Child Health and Human Development.

National Reading Research Center. (1997). *Engaged reading for pleasure and learning: A report from the National Reading Research Center* (J.F. Baumann & A.M. Duffy, Eds.). Athens, GA: Author.

Neuman, S.B., & Celano, D. (2001). Access to print in low-income and middle-income communities: An ecological study of four neighborhoods. *Reading Research Quarterly, 36*(1), 8–26.

Oldfather, P., & McLaughlin, J. (1993). Gaining and losing voice: A longitudinal study of students' continuing impulse to learn across elementary and middle school contexts. *Research in Middle Level Education, 17*(1), 1–25.

Palmer, B.M., Codling, R.M., & Gambrell, L.B. (1994). In their own words: What elementary students have to say about motivation to read. *Reading Teacher, 48*(2), 176–178.

Schiefele, U. (1991). Interest, learning, and motivation. *Educational Psychologist, 26*(3–4), 299–323.

Schunk, D.H., & Zimmerman, B.J. (1997). Social origins of self-regulatory competence. *Educational Psychologist, 32*(4), 195–208.

Skinner, B.F. (1953). *Science and human behavior.* New York: Free Press.

Spaulding, C.L. (1992). *Motivation in the classroom.* New York: McGraw-Hill.

Stanovich, K.E. (1986). Matthew effects in reading: Some consequences of individual differences: I. The acquisition of literacy. *Reading Research Quarterly, 21*(4), 360–407.

Thorndike, E.A. (1910). The contribution of psychology to education. *Journal of Educational Psychology, 1,* 5–12.

Turner, J. (1995). The influence of classroom contexts on young children's motivation for literacy. *Reading Research Quarterly, 30*(3), 410–441.

Turner, J., & Paris, S.G. (1995). How literacy tasks influence children's motivation for literacy. *Reading Teacher, 48*(8), 662–673.

Vroom, V.H. (1964). *Work and motivation.* New York: Wiley.

Watson, J.B. (1913). Psychology as the behaviorist views it. *Psychological Review, 20,* 158–177.

Weiner, B. (1979). A theory of motivation for some classroom experiences. *Journal of Educational Psychology, 71*(1), 3–25.

Weiner, B. (1985). An attributional theory of achievement motivation and emotion. *Psychological Review, 92*(4), 548–573.

Wigfield, A., & Guthrie, J.T. (1997). Relations of children's motivation for reading to the amount and breadth of their reading. *Journal of Educational Psychology, 89*(3), 420–432.

Engagement Activities

In Your Classroom

Knowing that motivation is influenced by the interactions between students and their literacy environments (Turner & Paris, 1995), how can you create a classroom climate that is more engaging? What tasks can you offer that would provide authentic and challenging comprehension instruction for your students?

With Your Colleagues

How can you and your colleagues incorporate more "open tasks" (Turner, 1995) in your literacy instruction? How would these open tasks support the development of what the authors call "a community of literate souls"?

Further Reading

Nolen, S.B. (2007). Young children's motivation to read and write: Development in social context. *Cognition and Instruction*, 25(2), 219–270.

This longitudinal study investigated the development of reading and writing motivation in grades 1 to 3. The findings suggest that classroom context plays an important role in the development of literacy motivation. From a "kid's-eye" perspective, Nolen found that teachers should be deliberate in their efforts to nurture inertest in a wide variety of books and writing opportunities. In addition, children should be given the freedom to express their imagination and opinions when reading and writing.